Reinaldo Arenas was born in Holguín, Cuba, in 1943. His first novel, *Singing from the Well*, was awarded First Mention in Cuba's Cirilo Villaverde National Competition. It was to be his only book published in his native country. Both as a homosexual and a writer, he found himself persecuted by the Cuban government, and had to smuggle his work out of the country for publication in France. He left Cuba in 1980 and settled in New York, where he died of AIDS in 1990. He is the author of over twenty books, including novels, short stories and poems. *The Doorman*, *The Color of Summer: Or the New Garden of Earthly Delights* and *The Palace of the White Skunks* are all currently available in the UK.

"One of the most shattering testimonials ever written on the subject of oppression and defiance" Mario Vargas Llosa

"A document of a particular and disturbing honesty by one of the few truly great writers to come out of Latin America in this century" *Chicago Tribune*

"An extraordinary book" *New York Times Book Review*

BEFORE NIGHT FALLS

—

REINALDO ARENAS

A complete catalogue record for this book can
be obtained from the British Library on request

The right of Reinaldo Arenas to be identified as the author
of this work has been asserted in accordance with the
Copyright, Patents and Designs Act 1988

Originally published in Spain as *Antes que anochezca
(Autobiografía)* by Tusquets Editores, S.A.
© Estate of Reinaldo Arenas, 1992

English translation copyright © the Estate of Reinaldo Arenas
and Dolores M. Koch, 1993

Published in 2001 by Serpent's Tail,
4 Blackstock Mews, London N4 2BT
www.serpentstail.com

Printed by Mackays of Chatham, plc

10 9 8 7 6 5 4 3

CONTENTS

CONTENTS

INTRODUCTION

T H E   E N D I thought I was going to die in the winter of 1987. For months on end I had been having terrible fevers. I finally went to a doctor and he told me I had AIDS. Feeling worse every day, I bought a plane ticket [from New York] to Miami and decided to die close to the sea. Not exactly in Miami but at the beach. However, due to some diabolic bureaucracy, everything we desire seems to be slow in coming, even death.

I really cannot say that I want to die; yet I believe that when the alternative is suffering and pain without hope, death is a thousand times better. Besides, some months ago when I entered a public rest room I became painfully aware that my presence failed to arouse the old expectant feeling of complicity. Nobody paid any attention to me, and the erotic games going on proceeded undisturbed. I no longer existed. I was not young anymore. Right then and there I thought that the best thing for me was to die. I have always considered it despicable to grovel for your life as if life were a favor. If you cannot live the way you want, there is no point in living. In Cuba I endured a thousand adversities because the hope of escaping and the possibility of saving my manuscripts gave me strength. At this point, the only escape for me was death. I had been able to correct most of the manuscripts smuggled out of Cuba, and they either were in friendly hands or had been published. During six years of exile I had also written and published other works: a book of essays on what was really happening in Cuba, A Need for Freedom"*; five plays under the title "Persecution; A Trip to Havana" [three long stories] and I had just finished [a New York City novel,] *The Doorman*, although while writing it I was already beginning to feel ill. My main regret, however, was to die without having been able to finish my *"pentagonía,"* a cycle of five novels of which I had already published *Singing from the Well*, *The Palace of the White Skunks*, and *Farewell to the Sea*. I was also sorry about leaving some of my friends, such as Lázaro, Jorge, and Margarita. I felt sorry for the pain that my death would cause them, and my mother too. But death was knocking at my door and the only thing I could do was face it.

When my friend Lázaro found out how sick I was, he flew to Miami to bring me back, and delivered me unconscious to New York Hospital. Getting me admitted, as he told me later, was an ordeal because I had no medical insurance. My pockets were empty except for a copy of my will, which I had just sent to Jorge and Margarita in Paris. I was practically dying, but hospitals refused to admit me because I did not have the means to pay. Fortunately, there was a French doctor at the hospital who was acquainted with Jorge and Margarita, and he helped to get me in. In any event, another physician, Dr. Gilman, announced to me that I had only a ten percent chance of surviving.

In the emergency room all the patients were in the throes of death. I had tubes coming in and out everywhere—my nose, my mouth, my arms. I looked more like a being from

* He also published "The Will to Live Manifesting Itself" (poems, Madrid, 1989). For clarity, translations of some Spanish titles and additional explanatory notes have usually been incorporated in brackets into the text. References within the text to works not yet translated appear in English within quotes, and are not italicized.—D.M.K.

another planet than a patient. I will spare the reader all my vicissitudes at the hospital. The important fact is that I managed not to die that time as expected. The same French physician, Dr. Olivier Ameisen (also an excellent composer), suggested that I write the words for some songs and he would set them to music. With all those tubes and a mechanical respirator I managed, as best I could, to scribble two songs. Once in a while Olivier would come to the intensive care unit, where all of us were dying, and he would sing the songs that I had written, for which he had composed the music. He accompanied himself with an electronic synthesizer, a device that imitates any instrument and produces all kinds of notes. The sounds of the synthesizer and Olivier's voice filled the room. I thought he was more talented as a musician than as a doctor. I, of course, could not speak, having in my mouth a tube that went down to my lungs; in fact, I was alive only because that machine was breathing for me. But, with some effort, I had been able to jot down a few words for Olivier's compositions. I really liked the songs. One was called "Una flor en la memoria" [A Flower to Remember], and the other one, "Himno."

Lázaro came often. He would always bring with him an anthology of poetry, open it at random, and read to me. If I did not like the poem, I would move one of the tubes stuck in my body and he would change to a different poem. Jorge Camacho called me from Paris every week. *The Doorman* was then being translated into French and Jorge would ask my advice on this word and the other. At first I could only babble a reply. Then I improved a little and was transferred to a private room. Although I could not yet move, I was lucky to be in a room and have some peace. By that time the tube had been removed and I could speak. That is how the French translation of *The Doorman* was completed.

Three and a half months later, when I left the hospital, I could hardly walk. Lázaro helped me up the stairs to my apartment, which unfortunately is a sixth-floor walk-up, and it took a lot of effort. Lázaro left utterly dejected. Once at home, I started to dust here and there as best I could. On the night table I unexpectedly came upon an envelope that contained Troquemichel, a rat poison. That made me very angry, because obviously someone had left the poison there for me to take. Right then I decided that my suicide, which I had secretly planned, had to be postponed for the time being; I was not going to play into the hands of whoever had left that envelope in my room.

The pain was awful and the tiredness overwhelming. After a short while René Cifuentes arrived and helped me clean the apartment and get something to eat. Then I was alone. I did not have the strength to sit at my typewriter, so I started dictating the story of my life into a tape recorder. I would speak for a while, take a rest, and then continue. I had already started my autobiography in Cuba, which I had titled *Before Night Falls*. Being a fugitive living in the woods at the time, I had to write before it got dark. Now darkness was approaching again, only more insidiously. It was the dark night of death. I really had to finish my memoirs before nightfall. I took it as a challenge. And so I continued working on them. After filling a cassette, I would give it to a friend, Antonio Valle, for typing.

I recorded more than twenty cassettes, and night still had not fallen upon me.

In the spring of 1988 *The Doorman* was published in France. It was both a critical and a commercial success, and was chosen as one of three finalists for the International Medici Prize. The publisher sent me a plane ticket when I was invited to take part in *Apostrophe*, the highest-rated cultural program in France, telecast live throughout Europe. I accepted the invitation without knowing whether I could get down the five flights of stairs and make it to the airport. Perhaps the enthusiasm of my friends Jorge and Margarita helped me. When I arrived in Paris and showed up at the studio, few people knew that as I was speaking on that program for an hour or more, I was really close to death. After several days in Paris I came back to continue working on my autobiography. At the same time, I was also reviewing Liliane Hasson's excellent French translation of *La loma del Angel* [Angel Hill, published in English as *Graveyard of the Angels*], which I had written as a sarcastic but loving parody of Cirilo Villaverde's novel *Cecilia Valdés* [a Cuban literary classic].

My physical deterioration did not ease up; on the contrary, it advanced relentlessly. I came down once more with a type of pneumonia called PCP, and the probabilities of my surviving this time were diminished with my weaker body. I got over the pneumonia, but while at the hospital I developed other terrible diseases—cancer (Kaposi's sarcoma), phlebitis, and something horrible called toxoplasmosis, which is a kind of brain blood poisoning. The physician in charge of my case, Dr. Harman, seemed to be so grief-stricken that I sometimes tried to comfort him. However, I survived again, at least the worst attacks. I really had to finish my *pentagonía*. While in the hospital I had started working on the fourth, and for me essential, novel in the series, *El color del verano* [The Color of Summer]. I still had some IVs stuck in my hands, making writing somewhat difficult, but I was committed to continue. Instead of beginning with Chapter 1, I started with the chapter called "The Turtle-Buses." I finished my autobiography after leaving the hospital (except for this introduction, of course), and continued working on "The Color of Summer." At the same time, with the help of Roberto Valero and María Badías, I was also revising *The Assault*, the fifth novel of the *pentagonía*. The manuscript had been written in Cuba in great haste so it could be smuggled out of the country. Roberto and María had to transcribe it from my almost unintelligible scribblings into readable Spanish. The novel was finally typed and added to my other original manuscripts, in the Firestone Library at Princeton University, where all of them can be consulted.

Around that time my mother came from Cuba to visit, under one of those permits that Castro cunningly grants to old people in order to obtain U.S. dollars. I had no choice but to fly to Miami. My mother did not notice that I was dying, and I accompanied her while she did all of her shopping. I did not tell her about my illness, and I haven't told her yet, even as I write this, in mid-1990. In Miami I caught pneumonia again and returned directly to the hospital in New York. After my release I decided to go to Spain, to Jorge and Margarita's country house, where I could breathe clean air.

This was during the fall of 1988, and while we were at Jorge's retreat, a farmhouse called Los Pajares, the idea came to us to issue an open letter to Fidel Castro requesting him to hold a plebiscite similar to the one held by Pinochet [in Chile]. Jorge asked me to draft the letter, and we worked on it together and both of us signed it. Even if we were unable to get additional signatures, we would send that letter to Castro on our own. As it happened, thousands of signatures poured in from all over, including those of eight Nobel laureates. We worked furiously in that farmhouse without running water or electricity. The newspapers published the letter, and it turned out to be a terrible blow for Castro; it proved that his dictatorship was worse than Pinochet's, and that he would never allow free elections in Cuba. Those who still naively believe that a dialogue with Castro is possible should remember his reaction to that letter: first he called all who signed it agents of the CIA, and then, SOBs. Obviously, there is only one thing Castro can do now in order to remain in power: promote a dialogue and accommodation with the Cuban exile community in the United

States. It is unbelievable that many exiles, even many of those who consider themselves intellectuals, are in favor of establishing this dialogue. Such a view completely ignores Castro's personality and ambition. Of course, Castro himself has created pro-dialogue committees, and their members pass themselves off as presidents of human rights committees. On the one hand, there are agents of Castro, operating in and out of Cuba, busy on his behalf; on the other, ambitious people looking for any position of prominence; and there is yet another group, the scoundrels, who are into this business of dialogue strictly for personal gain.

One day, eventually, the people will overthrow Castro, and the least they will do is bring to justice those who collaborated with the tyrant with impunity. The ones who promote dialogue with Castro, well aware that Castro will never give up his power peacefully and that a truce and economic assistance are what he needs to strengthen his position, are as guilty as his own henchmen who torture and murder people. Those who are not living in Cuba are perhaps even more to blame, because inside Cuba you exist under absolute terror, but outside you can at least maintain a modicum of political integrity. All the pretentious people who dream of appearing on TV shaking Fidel Castro's hand and of becoming politically relevant should have more realistic dreams: they should envision the rope from which they will swing in Havana's Central Park, because the Cuban people, being generous, will hang them when the moment of truth comes. The only consolation left for them will be to have avoided bloodshed. Perhaps such an act of justice would be a good lesson for the future, because as a country Cuba has produced scoundrels, criminals, demagogues, and cowards in numbers disproportionate to its population.

—

Back to the plebiscite: A number of constitutionally elected presidents and many intellectuals of every political persuasion signed our petition.* This brought me additional problems of a practical nature; my small apartment was bustling with photographers and newspaper reporters. Speaking made me very uncomfortable because cancer was beginning to spread to my throat, but I even had to make an appearance on television. In the meantime, I had not been able to finish "The Color of Summer," which covers a good part of my life and especially my youth, all of course in a very imaginative, almost defiant manner. It is also the story of an aging and crazed dictator, and it deals openly with homosexuality, a forbidden subject for most Cubans and for almost the whole human race. The story develops during a carnival, when the people manage to dislodge Cuba from its island platform and sail off as if they were on a ship. Once on the high seas, no one can agree on where to land, or on what kind of government should be instituted. A frightful, Cuban-style free-for-all ensues and in the midst of all the stomping, the Island, having no supporting platform, finally sinks into the sea.

While still writing this novel, over six hundred pages long, I was also going over my poetic trilogy *Leprosorio* [Leper Colony], which is now in print, and the excellent translation into English, by Dolores M. Koch, of *The Doorman*, to be published shortly.

Now I see that I am almost coming to the end of this introduction, which is also my end, and I have not said much about AIDS. I cannot. I do not know what it is. Nobody really knows. I have spoken with dozens of doctors and it is a puzzle to all of them. Illnesses related to AIDS are treated, but the actual nature of AIDS seems to be a state

---

* Arenas also published "Plebiscite for Fidel Castro," a collection of documents and articles from all over the world (Madrid, 1989).—D.M.K.

secret. I can attest, though, that as a disease it is different from all others. Diseases are natural phenomena, and everything natural is imperfect and can somehow be fought and overcome. But AIDS is a perfect illness because it is so alien to human nature and has as its function to destroy life in the most cruel and systematic way. Never before has such a formidable calamity affected mankind. Such diabolic perfection makes one ponder the possibility that human beings may have had a hand in its creation.

Moreover, all the rulers of the world, that reactionary class always in power, and the powerful within any system, must feel grateful to AIDS because a good part of the marginal population, whose only aspiration is to live and who therefore oppose all dogma and political hypocrisy, will be wiped out.

And yet it seems that the human race, the long-suffering human race, cannot be destroyed so easily. Despite all my suffering, I am grateful that I was allowed to witness the fall of one of the most sinister empires that ever existed, the Stalinist empire.

Besides, I am fortunate to leave this world without having to endure the insults of old age.

On my return home from the hospital, I dragged myself toward a photograph I have on my wall of Virgilio Piñera (who died in 1979), and I spoke to him in this way:

"Listen to what I have to tell you: I need three more years of life to finish my work, which is my vengeance against most of the human race."

I think Virgilio's face darkened, as if I had asked for something outrageous. It is almost three years now since that desperate request. My end is near. I expect to keep myself calm and collected until the very end.

Thank you, Virgilio.

New York, August 1990

THE STONES I was two. I was standing there, naked. I bent down and licked the earth. The first taste I remember is the taste of the earth. I used to eat dirt with my cousin Dulce María, who was also two. I was a skinny kid with a distended belly full of worms from eating so much dirt. We ate dirt in the shed. The shed was the place next to the house where the animals slept, that is, the horses, the cows, the pigs, the chickens, the sheep.

Someone reprimanded us for eating dirt. Who was it? My mother? My grandmother? One of my aunts? Or maybe it was my grandfather? One day I had a terrible bellyache. I did not even have time to get to the outhouse, and I used the chamber pot that was under the bed I shared with my mother. The first thing that came out was a huge worm, a red creature with many legs like a centipede. It was jumping up and down in the pot, no doubt enraged at having been expelled from its home in such a violent way. I was deathly afraid of this worm, which now appeared in my dreams every night trying to get into my belly while I embraced my mother.

My mother was a very beautiful, very lonely woman. She had known only one man, my father, and had enjoyed love for only a few months. My father was an adventurer. He fell in love with my mother, became formally engaged to her by asking my grandfather for her hand, and three months later left her. My mother first lived with her prospective parents-in-law. There she waited for a year, but my father never returned. When I was three months old my mother returned to my grandparents' home with me, the proof of her failure. I do not remember where I was born and I never met my father's family, but I think it was in the country, in the northern part of Oriente province. My grandmother and everyone else at home always tried to instill in me a great hatred toward my father because he had deceived (that was the word) my mother. I remember they taught me a song about a son who kills his father to avenge his abandoned mother. I would sing that song to the whole family, who listened enraptured. The song, which was very popular in those days, relates the sufferings of a woman whose lover seduced her and vanished after getting her pregnant. The song ended as follows:

> The boy grew up and became a man,
> and to the wars he went to fight.
> In vengeance he killed his father:
> The sons who love will do what's right.

One day my mother and I were on our way to visit one of my aunts. As we walked down to the river, a man came toward us; he was good-looking, tall and dark. My mother fell into a sudden rage; she began picking up stones from the riverbank and throwing them at his head, while the man, in spite of the shower of rocks, kept coming toward us. When he was close to me, he put his hand into his pocket, pulled out two pesos, and gave them to me. He then patted me on the head and ran away to avoid being hit by one of the stones. My mother cried all the way to my aunt's house, where I found out that the man was my father. I never saw him again, nor the two pesos; my aunt asked my mother to lend them to her and I do not know if she ever paid them back.

My mother was a "fallen" woman, as they used to say. It would have been difficult for her to find another husband; marriage was for virgins and she had been seduced. If any man approached her it was, as common wisdom had it in those days, to "take advantage of her." My mother, therefore, had to be very mistrustful. We went to dances together;

she always took me along, although I was then only about four years old. If a man asked her to dance, I would wait on a bench; once the dance was over my mother would come and sit next to me again. If someone invited her to have a beer, she dragged me along; I did not drink beer, but my mother's suitor had to buy me many *rallados,* which is what we in the country called ice grated with a plane and flavored with colored fruit syrup. Perhaps my mother thought that at one of those dances she would find a dependable man who might marry her. She did not find him, or did not want to. I think my mother was always faithful to my father's infidelity—and chose chastity; a bitter chastity, unnatural and cruel, because she was then only twenty years old. My mother's chastity was worse than that of a virgin, because she had known the pleasures of love for a few months and then gave all of it up for the rest of her life. This created in her a great sense of frustration.

One night, when I was already in bed, my mother asked me a question that at the time disturbed me greatly. She wanted to know if I would feel really sad if she died. I hugged her and started to cry. I think she cried too, and told me to forget she had ever asked. I realized later, or perhaps even then, that my mother was contemplating suicide but had refrained because of me.

I was still an ugly boy, potbellied and with a very big head. I think that my mother did not have enough practical sense to be raising a child. She was young, had no experience, and was living in my grandmother's home. It was my grandmother who was in charge of the household; in her own words, she was "the captain in command." My mother was single and with a child, a sort of freeloader. She was not in a position to make any decisions, not even about me. I do not know whether my mother loved me then; I remember that if I cried she would pick me up, but always so violently that I would slide back down over her shoulders and hit the floor head-on. At other times, she would rock me in a hammock made from a flour sack, but she rocked me so hard that I would fall out. I think that was why my head was full of scabs and bumps. But I survived. As luck would have it, our house was a large, typical Cuban *bohío*, a hut with a thatched roof and a dirt floor.

That house was full of women. There were unmarried aunts as young as my mother, and others already considered old maids because they were over thirty. There was also a daughter-in-law, abandoned by one of my grandparents' sons, who was Dulce María's mother. The married aunts would also come and stay for long periods of time. They came with their children, who were older than I was, and I would envy them because they knew their fathers and this gave them a self-assured and confident manner that I never had. Most of these relatives lived close to my grandfather's home. Sometimes they just came for a visit and my grandmother would make a special dessert and turn the whole thing into a party. My great-grandmother also lived in the house; she was very old and could hardly move. Most of the time she sat on a stool near a crystal radio receiver that she would never listen to.

The heart of the house was my grandmother. She peed standing up, and spoke with God. She always called God and the Virgin Mary to account for all the misfortunes that threatened us or that had befallen us: the droughts, the thunderbolt that had scorched a palm tree or killed a horse, the cows that died of an incurable disease, and my grandfather's drinking sprees, after which he would come home and beat her up. My grandmother then had eleven unmarried daughters and three married sons. In time, the unmarried daughters would find temporary husbands who would take them away and, as with my mother, a few months later abandon them. They were attractive women who for some fatal reason could not hold any man. My grandparents' home was full of their very pregnant daughters or crying kids like me. The world of my childhood was filled with abandoned women; the only man in that house was my grandfather. My grandfather had been a Don Juan, but now he was a bald, old man. He did not talk with God as my grandmother did; he talked to himself. Sometimes he would look up to the heavens and swear. He had fathered several children with other women of the neighborhood, who in time also came to live in my grandmother's house. At that point, my grandmother decided not to sleep with my grandfather again, and so she also was celibate and as frustrated as her daughters.

My grandfather had his bouts of rage too; he would stop talking altogether, leave home and go into the woods, sleeping under the trees for weeks. He said he was an atheist, but he spent a lot of energy cursing the Mother of God. Perhaps he did all this to irritate my grandmother, who would always devotedly fall down on her knees, even in the middle of the fields, to ask the heavens for something or other, which, in general, she did not get.

T H E   G R O V E I think the splendor of my childhood was unique because it was absolute poverty but also absolute freedom; out in the open, surrounded by trees, animals, apparitions, and people who were indifferent toward me. My existence was not even justified, nobody cared. This gave me an incredible opportunity to escape it all without anyone worrying about where I was or when I would return. I used to climb trees, and everything seemed much more beautiful from up there. I could embrace the world in its completeness and feel a harmony that I could not experience down below, with the clamor of my aunts, the cursing of my grandfather, or the cackling of the hens. . . . Trees have a secret life that is only revealed to those willing to climb them. To climb a tree is to slowly discover a unique world, rhythmic, magical, and harmonious, with its worms, insects, birds, and other living things, all apparently insignificant creatures, telling us their secrets.

Once, walking among those trees, I discovered the fetus of a child, no doubt abandoned in the grass by one of my aunts who had miscarried or who simply did not want any more children. Now I have my doubts and I am not sure whether that little body covered with flies was a fetus or a dead newborn baby. In any case, I thought of it as my lost cousin, with whom I would never be able to play.

Sometimes my grandmother's house was full of cousins who came with their mothers so we could all celebrate New Year's together. At other times, one of my aunts would come running away from her husband because he had given her a vicious beating. When she later returned to her husband, she would leave one of her kids behind with my grandmother. There was usually a cousin about my age in the house. The household was in constant turmoil; my aunts would wash, sweep, dust, iron, in the midst of incessant clatter. My grandmother would reign in the kitchen. None of my aunts ever learned how to cook; my grandmother would not let them. The kitchen was sacred; she was the high priestess who ministered to the oven with dry firewood, which I helped her gather. Although the house was always full of people, I managed to escape alone to the hills, the grove, or the brook. I think my childhood was the most creative time of my life; it was a world of pure creativity. To relieve the deep loneliness I felt while surrounded by the constant household bustle, I peopled the fields, which were somewhat barren, with almost mythical and supernatural characters and apparitions. One of the characters I saw very clearly every night was an old man turning a hoop under the prodigiously huge fig tree growing in front of the house. Who was that old man? Why was he turning that hoop, which looked like a bicycle wheel? Did he represent the terror awaiting me? The terror awaiting every human life?

Was it death? Death has always been very close to me, it has always been my loyal companion. Sometimes I am sorry that I'll die, only because then death will perhaps abandon me.

At five I contracted a disease then considered fatal: meningitis. Almost no one who got it survived. I had swollen lymph nodes, could not move my neck, and suffered from bouts of terrible fever. How to cure, or at least fight, that disease in the country, without medical attention, with no sanitary facilities of any kind? My grandmother took me to the temple of a famous psychic healer from Guayacán; his name was Arcadio Reyes. He tried to rid me of evil spirits and gave me a bottle of water called "medicinal water" because he had blessed it, and prescribed some medicine that we had to get in town. While blessing me, he beat me on the back and all over my body with some herbs, then made an infusion with those same herbs, which I was to drink before breakfast. And I survived. I also survived when the highest branch of the plum tree on which I was sitting snapped, and I fell down while my mother screamed, sure that I was going to die. Nor did I get hurt when the wild colt I was trying to break threw me headfirst onto some rocks; and I suffered no harm when I tumbled through the opening of the well, which was covered by nothing more than a couple of crossbeams, and fell to the bottom, luckily full of water.

My world continued to be the world of trees and of the roofs, which I also climbed at the risk of breaking my neck. The river was a little farther away, and getting to it was not easy. I had to cross the fields and venture into places unknown to me then. I was always afraid, not of wild animals or of the real dangers that threatened me but of those phantoms that kept haunting me: that old man with the hoop under the fig tree, and the other apparitions, like the old woman with the big hat and giant teeth who kept approaching, I do not know how, from both sides at the same time, with me in the middle. It was also said that on one of the riverbanks a white dog used to appear and that whoever saw him would die.

T H E   R I V E R As time went on, the river became for me a place of deep mystery. Its waters followed the most intricate patterns through nooks and crannies, then plunged down, gathering in dark pools and flowing on to the sea, never to return. When it rained and the storms came, the river rumbled and its roar could be heard from our house; it was a raging, relentless river, leveling everything in its path. Eventually I was able to approach it and swim in its waters. It was called Río Lirio though I never saw any lilies growing on its banks. This was the river that gave me a gift: an image that I will never forget. It was June 24, Saint John's Day, when everyone around would come and bathe in the river. The ancient baptism ritual had turned into a festival for swimmers. I was walking along the riverbank with my grandmother and some cousins my own age when I saw over thirty men bathing in the nude. All the young men of the neighborhood were there, jumping from a rock into the water.

To see all those naked bodies, all those exposed genitals, was a revelation to me: I realized, without a doubt, that I liked men. I enjoyed seeing them come out of the water, run among the trees, climb the rocks, and jump. I loved to see their bodies dripping wet, their penises shining. The young men were carefree, cavorting in the water, coming out again, and jumping into the stream. I was only six years old, but I watched them spellbound, in ecstasy before the glorious mystery of beauty. The following day I discovered another "mystery": masturbation. Of course, at six I could not ejaculate but, thinking of those naked boys, I rubbed my penis until I had a spasm. The pleasure and surprise were so intense that I thought I was about to die: I knew nothing about masturbation and I felt sure this could not be normal. Though I feared I might die at any moment, I kept at it until I almost fainted.

At the time one of my solitary diversions was a game with jars: a number of empty glass containers of all sizes represented a family, that is, my mother, my aunts, my grandparents. Those jars suddenly turned into young swimmers who jumped into the river, while I masturbated. Then, one of the young men would find me, fall in love with me and take me into the bushes. This was paradise; my spasms became so frequent that I developed huge dark circles under my eyes, and became so pale that my aunt Mercedita was afraid I had again contracted meningitis.

S C H O O L At the age of six I started going to school. It was Rural School 91 in Perronales County, where we lived, an area of sparsely populated plains and hills. A main road, not much more than a dirt esplanade, crossed the whole district and led to the town of Holguín, about four or five miles away. Perronales lay between Holguín and Gibara, a seaport I had yet to visit. The school was far from home and I had to get there on horseback. The first time, my mother took me. The school was a large building, a structure of palm fronds with a thatched roof, just like the *bohío* where we lived. Our teacher lived in Holguín, and had to come by bus, or *guagua* as we say in Cuba, and then walk for several miles. At the nearest crossing of the Lirio River, one of the older students would be on his horse waiting for her and would bring her to school. She was a woman blessed with innate wisdom and sincerity. She had a gift (I don't know if teachers today still have it) that enabled her to communicate with all of her students, and teach them every subject from the first to the sixth grade. Classes lasted more than six hours, and on weekends there was a sort of literary evening that we called "*El Beso a la Patria*" [Kiss to the Homeland]. After pledging allegiance to the flag, each student had to recite a poem learned by heart for the occasion. I was very eager to recite my poem, though I always made mistakes. Once when I was reciting Jose Martí's poem "The Two Princes," instead of the line "In and out wanders a sad dog," I said, "In and out wanders a mangy mutt." The whole class exploded in laughter. Now, this is a solemn poem about the burial of two young princes, and to say such a thing as "a mangy mutt" was totally undignified. My subconscious no doubt played a trick on me, and I confused Martí's dog with Vigilante, the egg thief, our own mangy mutt.

Of course, I fell in love with some of my classmates. I remember one, Guillermo, who was violent, handsome, arrogant, and a little crazy. He sat behind me and used to poke me with his pencil. We were never involved erotically; it was only a matter of glances and horseplay, the typical preadolescent romps that mask desire, infatuation, and sometimes even love. But, in practice, it only got as far as a display of genitals, as if by chance, while urinating. The most daring boy, Darío, was already twelve. When riding home from school on his horse, he would expose his penis—which, by the way, was pretty amazing—and would show it off to anyone who wanted to behold such a wonder.

Although I had no sexual encounters with those boys, their friendship at least taught me that my solitary masturbation was not unique and would not kill me. All of the boys were constantly talking about their last "jerk-off," and they were in excellent health.

My sexual activity was all with animals. First there were the hens, then the goats and the sows, and after I had grown up some more, the mares. To fuck a mare was generally a collective operation. All of us boys would get up on a rock to be at the right height for the animal, and we would savor that pleasure: it was a warm hole and, to us, without end.

I don't know whether the main pleasure was having sex with the mare or the real excitement was watching the other boys. The fact is that, one by one, all the schoolboys, some of my cousins, and even some of those young men who bathed nude in the river copulated with the mare.

My first sexual intercourse (though incomplete) with a person was not with any of those boys but with Dulce María, my cousin, the one who also ate dirt like me. I should make it clear right away that to eat dirt is not a metaphor, or a sensational act. All the country kids did it. It has nothing to do with magic realism, or anything of the sort. One had to eat something, dirt was the only thing we had plenty of, and perhaps that was why we ate it. . . . My cousin and I played doctor behind the bed and, because of some strange medical procedure I can't remember, we always ended up naked and embracing each other. Though we played this game for months, there was never any penetration or consummation. We seemed to have our backward spots and were not consistently precocious.

The *consummated* act, in this case mutual penetration, was performed with my cousin Orlando. I was about eight years old, and he was twelve. Orlando's penis was a source of fascination for me, and he took pleasure in showing it to me whenever he had the chance. It was somewhat large and dark, and once erect, its foreskin would slide back and reveal a pink glans that demanded, with little jerks, to be caressed. One day, up on a plum tree, Orlando was showing me his beautiful glans, when his hat landed on the ground. (Out in the country we all wore hats.) I grabbed his hat and ran off to hide behind a bush in a secluded place. Right away he understood exactly what I wanted; we dropped our pants and began to masturbate. What happened then was that he stuck his penis into me and later, at his request, I stuck mine into him while flies and other insects kept buzzing around us, apparently wanting to participate in the feast.

When it was all over, I felt completely guilty but not entirely satisfied. I could not help but feel very much afraid. It seemed to me that we had done something terrible, that in some way I had condemned myself for the rest of my life. Orlando lay down on the grass to rest, and in a few minutes we were romping around again. "Now there is definitely no way out for me!" I thought, or believe I thought, when I crouched and felt Orlando grabbing me from behind. While he was sticking it into me, I was thinking of my mother, and of all the things that during all those years she never did with a man, which I was doing right there in the bushes within earshot of her voice, already calling me for dinner. In a rush I separated from Orlando and ran home. Of course, neither of us had ejaculated. I really think I only satisfied my curiosity.

THE TEMPLE
OF THE SPIRITS The following day my mother and I went to Arcadio Reyes's temple, and while the most powerful mediums in the séance, directed by Arcadio, were circling around us to deliver us from evil spirits, I felt terribly scared. I thought that one of those mediums, among whom was one of my eleven aunts, would fall to the ground, possessed by a spirit, and that right then and there before the whole town, this spirit would reveal all that Orlando and I had done in the bushes.

Then my aunt Mercedita became possessed by a spirit, and I felt sure that this was the end of me. In her fall, she banged her head several times against the temple wall, which fortunately was made of wood. But my aunt said nothing about what worried me, only that she was engulfed in flames, and that she desperately needed many prayers so that the fire that was consuming her, or rather was consuming us, would disappear. Perhaps it was a discreet spirit which did not want to refer too directly to my involvement with Orlando.

For my part, though still feeling guilty, I enjoyed some sense of relief. The spirits had not openly revealed my sin, a sin I was not, by the way, at all eager to give up. In time, Orlando grew into a handsome young man, and even acquired a bicycle of his own, something unusual in our neighborhood. He got married, and now has many children and grandchildren.

T H E   W E L L One afternoon I went to the well, a little far from our house, to fetch water. I never understood why houses in the country are not built close to wells. Anyway, one of my chores was to go continually to the well to get water: for watering the plants in the garden, for bathing, for the animals, for keeping the barrels and earthen jars full. Behind the well, I saw my grandfather; he was bathing naked, dumping buckets of water over his head. When all of a sudden my grandfather turned, I realized how huge his testicles were: I had never seen anything like it. He had a prominent penis but his testicles were exceptionally large and hairy. I went back home without the water; the sight of my naked grandfather had disturbed me. For a long time afterward I watched over my mother; in my imagination I saw her being possessed by him, and him raping her with his big penis and huge testicles. I wanted to do something to help her but could not. In all honesty, I didn't know whether I was jealous because of my mother or because of my grandfather. Perhaps it was a multiple jealousy. Later I found out that my grandfather had a hernia. I also became jealous of my aunts, and especially of my grandmother, who slept in her own bed, but had more rights than anyone else to enjoy those testicles. Although all this existed only in my imagination, for quite a long time I was obsessed with the vision of my naked grandfather.

CHRISTMAS EVE In the countryside there were other rituals that filled me with joy and made me forget my erotic obsessions. One of them was Christmas Eve. The whole family would get together at my grandfather's home. Pigs were roasted, Christmas nougat was made, bottles of wine were uncorked, tubs of orange compote were prepared, bright-colored wrappers filled with red apples were opened (apples that, for me, came from the other end of the world), walnuts and hazelnuts were cracked, and everybody got drunk. People would laugh, and dance. . . . Sometimes an orchestra was improvised, with a hand organ, a *guayo* [a homemade percussion instrument], and a couple of drums. The whole countryside became a magic place. It was one of the occasions I most enjoyed, up in a tree, watching people have a good time in their backyards and walk around in the grove. At home, Vidal, an uncle of mine who was a real inventor, made yellow ice cream by hand in a tub with a crank. In order to be able to produce this exotic concoction, my uncle would bring a huge chunk of ice from the ice factory in Holguín. That piece of ice, later transformed into delicious yellow snow, was the most glorious proof that it was really Christmas.

I would finally come down from the trees when several tables were joined and dinner was about to be served. The suckling pig was brought on huge palm fronds and placed on the table, together with boiled plantains and mountains of lettuce. My grandmother would host the ceremony, carving the meat, offering bottles of wine, taking care that no one lacked anything. Since dinner lasted for hours, kerosene and oil lamps were brought out; under those lights the party attained a legendary brilliance. Everybody was happy, and even when they argued, which they did often, it all ended in a friendly way.

In the midst of all the celebrations I would take Orlando's bicycle, ride up the hill in front of the house, and zoom down at full speed, finally braking or crashing right next to the party's merrymaking.

THE HARVEST Another ceremony, another memorable occasion that marked my childhood, was harvest time. My grandfather farmed mostly corn. Almost the entire community had to be summoned to harvest his cornfields. Of course, my grandmother, my aunts, my mother, and I also picked corn. The corn was then carted to the storeroom—or *prensa,* as we called it—which was a hut behind the house. One evening the neighbors were invited to husk the corn and remove the kernels from the cobs. This was another feast. Huge pieces of cloth were spread on the floor, and I would roll around on them as if at the beach, which, at the time, I had never seen. For those evenings my grandmother would prepare coconut sweetmeats with a wonderful, sweet smell I have never experienced since. They were made with brown sugar and grated coconut. This delicacy was served at midnight, while the cloths were still being filled with kernels and I was rolling around and around on them.

T H E D O W N P O U R Perhaps the most extraordinary event I enjoyed during my childhood was one provided by the heavens: the heavy downpour. It was no ordinary rainfall. It was a tropical drenching, heralded by violent thunder in cosmic, orchestral bursts that resounded across the fields, while lightning traced the wildest designs on the sky, striking palm trees that suddenly burst into flames and then shriveled like burnt matches. And in no time the rain would come down strong and seem like a massive army marching across the trees. It would reverberate on the zinc roof of the passageway like gunfire; on the palm-frond thatch above the living room, it sounded like a million footsteps overhead. Water rushed down the gutters with the rumble of overflowing brooks and cascaded thundering into the barrels. And on the trees in the patio, from the uppermost leaves to the ground, the rain became a concert of drums with different registers and amazing rhythms; it was a fragrant resonance. I would run from one end of the passageway to the other and into the living room, look out the window, go to the kitchen and watch the pines in the patio, drenched and whistling out of control in the wind. Finally I would run outside, naked, and let the rain soak me through. I hugged the trees, rolled around in the grass, built small mud dams, behind which water would collect, and in those miniature ponds I would swim, plunge, and splash. I would go over to the well and watch water falling on water. I would look up at the sky and watch flocks of green *querequetés* also celebrating the torrential rains. I was not satisfied with rolling in the grass, I wanted to fly, to fly like those birds, alone in the downpour. I would go as far as the river, a river that roared under the spell of violence let loose. The power of the overflowing current would sweep away almost everything in its path: trees, stones, animals, houses. It was the mystery of the law of destruction, but also of the law of life. I did not know then where that river was headed, where that frenzied race would end, but something was calling me to go with it, saying that I too had to throw myself into those raging waters and lose myself, that only in that torrent, always on the move, would I find some peace. But I did not dare jump, I was always a coward. I would go as far as the riverbank, where the currents were roaring my name; another step, and the whirling waters would swallow me. How much trouble could have been avoided if I had done just that! Those waters were turbid and restless, powerful and lonely. It was all I had; only in those waters, in that river, had nature accepted me and now summoned me in its moment of greatest glory. Why not throw myself into those waters? Why not lose myself, vanish in them, find peace in that clamor that I loved? What joy to have done just that! But I returned home soaked; it was already dark. My grandmother was cooking dinner. It had stopped raining. I was shivering while my aunts and my mother set the table without paying much attention to me. I always thought that my family, including my mother, saw me as a weird creature, useless, confused, or crazy; a being outside the framework of their lives. They were probably right.

THE SPECTACLE Perhaps because I was so lonely and confused, and yet yearned to play a brilliant role, I started all alone to provide myself with scenarios that differed radically from my everyday life. I created and performed a series of endless songs and staged them all across the fields. The words were corny and always impassioned, and I would perform them in those lonely fields as if they were theater pieces. The acting consisted of jumps, yells, chest beating, kicking up stones, shrieks, races through the trees, imprecations; sticks and dead leaves thrown together into the air. And all the while, I was singing those endless songs that would drive away anyone who ~~might hear them. Once I made such a commotion that my~~ own mother and my grandmother, who were weeding a corn-field, ran away in fear, not knowing where those ghostly howls were coming from.

Of course, I never wrote down the words of those songs. At the time, I hardly knew how to write. Instead, those operatic songs (or whatever they were) came to me spon-taneously as I enacted them in the fields. The words, the music, and my voice were probably horrendous, but after performing one of those outrageous "cantatas," I had a feel-ing of peace and could go back home. I was more in harmony with my world and would go to sleep early, next to my mother, in the smallest room of that ramshackle house.

The house had five rooms. My grandparents' bedroom was furnished with two huge iron beds and an immense ward-robe that reached up to the ceiling. Some of my abandoned aunts and various cousins slept in another room. A third room was shared by an uncle, who had had several women but finally was left alone, and my great-grandmother. A fourth room had belonged to my great-uncle, a bachelor who ended up hanging himself with a liana. My mother and I slept in that little room, next to the passageway. On the other side of the passageway, close to the palm-frond wall, slept the pigs, who would grunt all night. Sometimes when I got full of chiggers and could not sleep, I spent the night scratching my feet against the wire bedspring.

EROTICISM I think I always had a huge sexual appetite. Not only the mares, sows, hens, or turkeys but almost all animals were objects of my sexual passion, including dogs. There was one particular dog who gave me great pleasure. I would hide with him behind the

garden tended by my aunts, and would make him suck my cock. The dog got used to it and in time would do it freely.

Those years, between the ages of seven and ten, were a time of great eroticism, of a sexual voracity that, as I said, was all-embracing. It involved all of nature, including trees. I would carve out a hole in a soft-stemmed tree, like papaya, and stick my penis into it. It was great fun to fuck a tree. My cousins also did it, with melons, pumpkins, and soursops. But one of my cousins, Xavier, confided that his greatest pleasure was to fuck a rooster. One morning the rooster was found dead; I think it was not as a result of the size of my cousin's penis, which was really quite small; I think the rooster died of shame from getting fucked when normally he was the one to fuck all the hens in the yard.

Anyway, one must remember that life in the country is lived close to nature and, therefore, to sexuality. The animal world is always ruled by sexual urges. Hens are always getting laid by the rooster, mares by stallions, sows by boars. Birds fuck in the air; pigeons, after much clamor and dancing around, end up in a kind of violent tangling with their partners. Lizards stay stuck together for hours, flies are constantly fornicating on the dining table; guinea pigs have litters every month; bitches, when they get fucked, make such a fuss that they are capable of exciting the most pious nuns. Cats in heat howl all through the night with such passion that they awaken the most hidden erotic impulses. . . . There is no truth to the theory, held by some, about the sexual innocence of peasants. In the country, sexual energy generally overcomes all prejudice, repression, and punishment. That force, the force of nature, dominates.

In the country, I think, it is a rare man who has not had sexual relations with another man. Physical desire overpowers whatever feelings of machismo our fathers take upon themselves to instill in us.

An example of this is my uncle Rigoberto, the oldest of my uncles, a married, serious man. Sometimes I would go to town with him. I was just about eight years old and we would ride on the same saddle. As soon as we were both in the saddle, he would begin to have an erection. Perhaps in some way my uncle did not want this to happen, but he could not help it. He would put me in place, lift me up and set my butt on his penis, and during that ride, which would take an hour or so, I was bouncing on that huge penis, riding, as it were, on two animals at the same time. I think eventually Rigoberto would ejaculate. The same thing happened on the way back from town. Both of us, of course, acted as if we were not aware of what was happening. He would whistle or breathe hard while the horse trotted on. When he got back, Carolina, his wife, would welcome him with open arms and a kiss. At that moment we were all very happy.

V I O L E N C E The peasant world in which I grew up was not only a world of sexual encounters. It was also a world where violence was everywhere. Sheep would be hung by their legs to have their throats slit, and after the blood had been drawn, while they were still half alive, they would be cut into pieces. Pigs were stabbed with a long knife thrust into the heart, and before they were dead, alcohol would be poured on them and lit, to burn off all their hair before they were roasted. In order to kill young cows or heifers instantly, huge nails were hammered into their heads, and then they were quartered. Their meat would be hung in strips under a tree or in the pantry, where the flies also participated in the feast. The bulls that were to work in the fields were castrated, as were the horses. The castration of a bull was one of the most violent and cruel acts I have ever witnessed: The bull's testicles were tied with a thick wire and then stretched out onto an iron and stone anvil. With a hammer or a sledgehammer the testicles would be pounded until the tendons and connections to the rest of the body were severed. Only the bags remained hanging and in time would wither away. The pain suffered by those bulls was so intense that one could tell when the testicles had been destroyed because the animal's teeth would loosen. Many died, but others survived and were no longer bulls but oxen—that is, tame, castrated beasts used to pull the plow, while my grandfather would swear at them behind the plow, and prod them with a stick.

The world in which I grew up was pervaded with violence. The bulls that had not been castrated would crack each other's heads by butting each other with their horns to assert their sexual supremacy over the herd. The stallions would kick each other savagely as soon as they saw or scented a mare.

Once my mother and I were on our way to Arcadio Reyes's temple on my aunt Olga's mare (in the country, women rode mares and men rode stallions). Suddenly, a stallion appeared out of nowhere and followed us, giving clear signs of his passionate intentions. We were still on the mare when the stallion tried to mount her. My mother spurred her on, but the mare refused to budge; evidently she preferred to be hacked by the spurs rather than give up her chance of being possessed by that formidable beast. She was already spreading her legs and raising her tail. We had to jump off and allow them, right in front of us, to complete their copulation, a sexual encounter that was both powerful and violent and really so beautiful that it would have aroused anybody.

After the battle, my mother and I rode in silence to the temple. Probably she, as well as I, would have liked to be the mare, who now trotted so lightheartedly over Arcadio Reyes's land.

There was also violence in the struggle for life. At night you could hear the screeches of the frogs as they were slowly swallowed by small snakes; you could hear the squeak of a mouse being torn to pieces by a gnome owl; the desperate cackle of a hen being throttled and swallowed by a Cuban boa; the kicking and muffled cry of a rabbit quartered in the air by an owl, or the bleating of sheep cut to pieces by wild dogs. The noise, the desperate clamors, the dull stamping, all those sounds were familiar companions in the countryside where I grew up.

THE MORNING FOG

But there was also a dimension of serenity, of peacefulness, that I have found nowhere else. Among those very special moments, the arrival of the morning fog was especially intense and full of wonder, those mornings when everything seemed shrouded in a great white cloud that softened all outlines. There were no distinguishable shapes or bodies; the trees were immense, white silhouettes; even my grandfather, as he walked in front of me on his way to the barn to milk the cows, was a white ghost. The fog covered and ennobled this rather desolate and barren land, giving it a kind of aura. The hills and slopes became huge snowy mountains, and the whole land was a misty, fresh expanse in which we all seemed to be floating in space.

THE NIGHT, MY GRANDMOTHER

But perhaps even more impressive and mysterious than the morning fog was the night. It would be very difficult for anyone who has not experienced night in the open country to have a clear understanding of the splendors of nature, much less of its mystery. Night was not only infinite space above. Night in the countryside where I grew up (a coun-tryside that no longer exists, except in these recollections) was also a musical realm, a magical and endless orchestra-tion, vibrating everywhere, chiming into infinity. And the sky's radiance was not constant but an unending blaze of changing hues and streaks, stars that burst and disappeared (after having existed for millions of years) just to enrapture us for a few moments.

My grandmother could find the most important stars, and even the lesser-known ones, at any time of night. Whether by sheer instinct or because she had observed the skies for so many years, she could quickly indicate the position of those stars, as well as name them, although the names she gave them were certainly not the ones used by astronomers. For example, they had names like the Cross of May, the Seven Kids, the Plow. There they were, in that immense darkness shining for my grandmother, who would show them to me and not only be able to name them but, in accordance with their position and brightness, forecast the day's weather and also predict the future: whether it would rain the next day; whether the harvest, in two or three months, would be good or bad; whether it would hail; whether the dreaded hurricanes would come. . . . My grand-mother would try to drive away hurricanes by making crosses with ashes. When the storm was approaching, she would come with a bucket full of ashes from the stove and spread them in the four corners of the house, throw fistfuls of ashes into the air, and make crosses in the passageway and near the roof supports of the house. In this way she would try to appease the forces of nature.

What literary influence did I have in my childhood? Prac-tically none: no books, no teaching, with the exception of the school assemblies we called "Kiss to the Homeland." But regarding the magical, the mysterious, which is so es-sential for the development of creativity, my childhood was the most literary time of my life. And this I owe, in large measure, to that mythical figure my grandmother, who would interrupt her housework or throw down her bundle of firewood in the woods and start talking with God.

My grandmother knew the medicinal powers of almost all herbs, and prepared brews and infusions for all kinds of diseases. With a clove of garlic she would take care of indigestion by massaging not the stomach but a leg. By means of a system she called *las cabañuelas*, which consisted of twelve heaps of salt that she would uncover on the first of January, she would forecast the rainy season and the dry season of the year to come.

Night also came under my grandmother's domain; at night she ruled. She understood that family gatherings in the evening acquired a transcendence not readily explainable; she would therefore invite the whole family under any pretext: sweets, coffee, a prayer. Thus, in a circle of candle-light, my grandmother would officiate. Beyond, there was the infinite night of the countryside, but she had created a space against the darkness and was not about to give it up easily.

My grandmother would tell me stories of apparitions, of men who walked with their heads under their arms, of treasures guarded by the dead tirelessly pacing their place of hiding. She of course believed in witches, although she never considered herself one; the witches would come at night crying or swearing, and would perch on the roof of the house; their demands had to be satisfied. My grandmother knew of some exorcism that prevented witches from doing too much harm. She knew that the hills were sacred places full of mysterious creatures and animals, not only those used for work or food. There was something above and beyond the realm of our senses; every plant, every tree could exhale a mystery that she would know about. When she walked around she would question the trees and, in fits of anger, sometimes slap them. I remember my grandmother, in a rainstorm, hitting a palm tree. What could that tree have done to her? Some betrayal, some slight, and she would answer back by slapping the tree. My grandmother also knew old songs probably sung in our family for generations. She would sit me on her lap and sing them to me; I do not remember ever getting such tenderness from my mother. My grandmother could afford to be affectionate, perhaps because to her I was not the embodiment of frustration, nor the reminder of failure. She could give me affection without resentment or shame. For my mother I represented the fruit of a love betrayed; for my grandmother I was just another child who had to be entertained with an adventure, a story or a song, as she had done with her own children. My grandmother was undoubtedly wise; she had the wisdom of a peasant woman who had given birth to more than fourteen children, none of whom had died. She had suffered the beatings and vulgarities of a drunken, unfaithful husband; she had gotten up every morning for over fifty years to prepare breakfast and then work all day, moving the animals to where the heat would not suffocate them and where they would not starve, carrying firewood to prepare dinner, digging up some fleshy root to eat. My grandmother was wise; that is why she understood the night and did not ask me too many questions; she knew that nobody is perfect. Surely there were times when she saw me playing with the behind of a sow and even with the bitch Diana, a very unfriendly animal that I could never get close to. But my grandmother never reproached me; she knew those things were normal in country life; perhaps her sons and even her husband had done them. My grandmother was illiterate, but she made all her children go to school, and if they did not want to, she would tear a branch from any thorny tree and, to the beat of the lashes, would take them to school; all of her children could read and write. It was my mother who really taught me to write. By the light of the kerosene lamp, she would write long sentences, very faintly, which I had to trace over with a heavier stroke.

My grandmother's world was much more complex than my grandfather's. My grandfather claimed to be an atheist and apparently believed in nothing; he therefore had no deep metaphysical obsessions. My grandmother believed in God and at the same time considered herself cheated by that very God; she would besiege Him with questions and requests. Her world was one of anxiety and helplessness. All this came together in an illiterate woman who interpreted the stars at night but, at the same time, had to scrape a living from the earth every day. The kitchen and the stove were also the center of her life, and all of us, when we got up, would have breakfast by the warmth of the fire that she had kindled and tended.

THE EARTH In time my aunts realized that they would not be able to get another man. My mother also understood, perhaps even before my aunts did, that her lover would never return. They all became more pious, turned into mediums, and went once a week to the temple of Arcadio Reyes, where they ended up being possessed and shaken by violent spirits. Even my grandfather's house became a sort of branch of Arcadio Reyes's spiritualist temple. People from every nearby neighborhood, and from some remote ones, would come to be cleansed of evil spirits by my aunts. All my aunts would gather around the person to be exorcised. Often people would be freed of their ills after one visit, but at times their problems were so terrible that they had to come again and again and submit to a number of exorcisms.

Once, while one of those spiritual séances was taking place, my cousin Dulce María and I took a handful of dirt and threw it against the wall; immediately one of my aunts came down in a trance. My grandmother's parents had recently died and the heirs were having a feud over the distribution of the land. To my aunt, in her trance, that handful of dirt was surely a message from a spirit requesting that the land be distributed fairly among the heirs, or otherwise terrible disasters would come to plague the family. At the time, my cousin and I laughed at those predictions; however, many misfortunes certainly did occur later and the land was lost. Perhaps our hands had been tools of some prophetic and prankish spirit. In any case, back to the earth: One of the first things I ever did in life was to eat dirt. My first crib was a hole in the dirt, dug by my grandmother. In that hole, which was waist-deep, I learned to stand up. My grandmother had used the same technique with all her children; stuck in that hole, I would crawl around on the dirt floor. Later I would throw dirt against the walls, and one of my solitary diversions was to build mud castles. I would mix dirt with water that I had fetched from the distant well. A favorite game for me and my cousins was to throw dirt at one another. To dig out the earth was to discover unusual treasures like pieces of colored glass, snail shells, and shards of pottery. To water the earth and see how it absorbs the water we provide is also a unique experience. To walk on the earth after a rainstorm is to be in touch with absolute fulfillment: the earth, satisfied, floods us with its well-being, while its many aromas saturate the air and fill us with life-creating impulses.

When we were born, the local midwife who cut the umbilical cord would rub dirt into it. Many children died of infection, but no doubt those who survived had accepted the earth and were ready to bear almost any future calamity. In the country we were attached to the earth in an ancestral way; we could not do without it. The earth was there when we were born, in our games, in our work, and of course, at the moment of our death. The corpse, in a wooden box, would be returned directly to the earth. The coffin would soon rot and the body had the privilege of dissolving in that earth and becoming a vital, enriching part of it. The body would be reborn as a tree, as a flower, or as a plant that one day, perhaps, someone like my grandmother would smell and be able to divine its medicinal properties.

T H E S E A My grandmother was also the one who first took me to the ocean. One of her daughters had managed to get a permanent husband, and he worked in Gibara, the seaport closest to our hometown. For the first time, I took a bus. I think that for my grandmother, who was already sixty, it was also the first time. We went to Gibara. My grandmother, and the rest of my family, had never seen the ocean, although it was only twenty or thirty miles from where we lived. I remember that once my aunt Carolina came to my grandmother's house crying and saying: "Do you realize what it means that I am forty years old and have never seen the ocean? I will soon die of old age without ever having seen it." From then on, I thought of nothing else but the sea. "The sea swallows a man every day," my grandmother would say. And I felt then an irresistible urge to see the ocean.

How could I explain what I felt the first time that I saw the sea! It would be impossible to describe that moment. There is only one word that does it any justice: the Sea.

P O L I T I C S My grandfather had political ambitions, or at least he wanted to participate in politics, but the politicians paid him scant attention. He was a member of the Orthodox Party [a liberal reformist party], which was then led by Eduardo Chibás. Once, around Christmas, someone wanted to take a picture of the entire family. My grandfather pulled out a huge poster with Chibás's picture on it. The poster was so large that it crowded everyone out of the photograph.

My grandfather opposed religion and was an anticommunist liberal. He could read with ease and, within that peasant milieu, this was a rare privilege. Once a week he went to Holguín to buy *Bohemia* magazine, edited by Miguel Angel Quevedo, which was in a way the source of our political education. My grandfather would lean against one of the house support poles and read the magazine out loud. If anyone uttered so much as a sound, my grandfather would make such a fuss that as soon as he opened the magazine, even the animals would retreat in silence. In those days *Bohemia* was one of the best magazines published in Latin America. It had everything: literature, politics, sports, news; it was against all dictatorships, including, of course, those that were communist.

What made my grandfather sense that communism would not solve Cuba's problems, when he had really never suffered under that system but had, in fact, endured all the calamities of capitalism? I would say it was his peasant intuition. I also think that my grandfather was influenced by the reports of farmers being shot in communist countries, which made him reject communism while he still passionately hated the right-wing dictatorship that we were enduring, had endured, and would continue to endure for several years. For my grandfather, those who ruled before Batista had also been a bunch of crooks. That is the reason why he felt a great deal of respect for Chibás, who denounced corruption and whose motto was "Integrity Against Greed." My grandfather's hero was not to become president of the Republic; a few months before the election, he shot himself. According to several commentators, Chibás's suicide was related to the fact that he had denounced the corruption of an important government official, Aureliano Sánchez Arango, but was unable to submit conclusive proof when required to do so.

The same day that Chibás died, so did my great-grandmother; she also died suddenly, hit by lightning. In our area lightning struck frequently, supposedly because the earth was very rich in nickel. At my great-grandmother's wake everybody dissolved in tears. I walked up to my mother, who was crouched in the kitchen by the stove, and she said, "I'm not crying because of my grandmother, but because of Chibás." I think the whole family was crying for that reason.

My great-grandmother's death was actually somehow related to the death of Chibás. Years ago my grandfather had installed a crystal radio receiver so he could listen to Chibás when he spoke. This receiver was wired to an antenna installed high on bamboo poles. The antenna had served as a lightning rod, and my great-grandmother, who at that moment was next to the radio, was struck.

We all used to gather around the radio because it had only one earpiece, through which my grandfather usually listened and then relayed the news to us as he heard it. Sometimes, when my grandfather was upset with my grandmother, he would interpolate phrases that were not part of the radio program; they were insults or else chauvinistic comments against women, which my grandmother would listen to impassively because she thought they came from the radio.

One of my aunts had the privilege of being allowed to listen to a soap opera; while she listened, she would pass the story on to her sisters. My aunt would summarize the love affairs of a woman in a soap opera called *Divorced*, broadcast at noon. The title and the story itself bore a close resemblance to the lives of my aunts and my mother, all abandoned women who, as the announcer would say at the beginning of the program, either "dreamed of an ideal marriage or had known happiness." Sitting on my mother's lap, I remember, while my aunt was describing the erotic scenes she heard, I would feel my mother's legs quivering; I would feel the sexual tension in this young woman, probably anxious to make love.

Part of the house burned down as a result of the lightning bolt that killed my great-grandmother, and now we kept on crying, not because of those burnt palm fronds, which could be replaced, but because of the death of a man who had promised us Integrity Against Greed.

After the death of Chibás, things got easier for the political crooks who always managed, one way or another, to control the island of Cuba. In 1952 a military coup led by Fulgencio Batista brought him to power again, and it became impossible for the Orthodox Party, or any other party, to win elections. Batista's dictatorship was repressive from the start, not only politically but morally as well.

One day we were preparing *ñame* [a tropical tuber] cuttings to be planted on the farm, when we saw a couple of county policemen coming our way. That filled us with dread; the police never made social calls. They came to arrest my uncle Argelio, who had had a sexual encounter with an underage peasant girl whose father had notified the police. My uncle was arrested and taken to jail. It was proven later that the girl had taken on several lovers before my uncle, and he was released. He nevertheless decided to act on his long-held plan to emigrate to the United States. In those days of extreme poverty, the dream of all who were down-and-out in Cuba was to go "north" to work. My uncle Argelio did go, and from the United States he sent us a photo in which he was steering a luxurious motorboat, his hair impeccably groomed even though the boat seemed to be moving at great speed. Many years later I discovered the trick: One would go to a special photographic studio and have one's picture taken while sitting in a cardboard boat with a cardboard ocean as background. In Cuba everybody thought my uncle was driving his own boat.

In time some of my relatives decided to let my uncle start immigration procedures for them so they could go to the United States. It was not easy; thousands wanted to emigrate, and a visa was difficult to obtain. My aunt Mercedita made over twenty trips to the consulate in Santiago de Cuba to request a visa to the United States, which was for many years denied her. She was finally able to leave with Dulce María, and my "doctor games" behind the bed came to an end. Later my mother emigrated. Apparently she went as a tourist without permission to work but did work illegally, taking care of the children of those lucky enough to get a job in a factory. I can imagine my mother in some run-down apartment in Miami in the fifties, taking care of crying babies who were possibly more unbearable than I was. I imagine her trying to comfort them in her arms, trying to give them the love and affection she so seldom had time to give me, or perhaps was ashamed to show.

HOLGUÍN While Batista's dictatorship continued to oppress the country, the economy deteriorated, at least for poor peasants such as my grandfather or my uncles, who could seldom find work at the sugar mills as cane cutters. My uncle Rigoberto once left us for four months and we all thought he had managed to get a job at a sugar mill. He returned without a penny, sick and running a high fever. He had roamed around most of Oriente province without finding any work as a sugarcane cutter. My grandmother cured him with a special infusion.

Things got so bad that my grandfather decided to sell the farm, about a hundred acres, and move to Holguín, where he planned to open a small vegetable and fruit stand. For years my grandmother and grandfather had been wanting to sell the farm, but they could never agree on the timing. So finally they did sell it to one of my grandfather's sons-in-law, who at the time sympathized with Batista and was well-off.

A truck came from town and everything was loaded up: bedsprings, stools, the living room rocking chairs. How my grandmother, grandfather, aunts, mother, and even I cried! In that hut with its thatched roof, where we had suffered so much hunger, we had no doubt also lived the best moments of our lives. This was perhaps the end of our period of absolute poverty and isolation, but also the end of a kind of enchantment, exultation, mystery, and freedom that we would never find again, least of all in a town like Holguín.

Holguín was for me, by then a teenager, absolute boredom. The town was flat, commercial, square, with absolutely no mystery or personality. It was hot and there was no place where one could enjoy some shade or simply let the imagination roam. The town rises out of a desolate plain, crowned at one end by a barren hill, the Hill of the Cross, so called because an enormous concrete cross had been built on its top. There were many concrete steps leading to the cross. Holguín, with that cross standing out above it, seemed like a cemetery to me; on one occasion a man was found hanging from the cross. I saw Holguín as a gigantic tomb; its low houses looked like pantheons punished by the sun.

Once, out of pure boredom, I went to Holguín's cemetery and discovered that it resembled the entire city; the crypts were like the houses, bare and flat, only smaller; they were concrete boxes. I thought of all the people in that town, and of my own family, living so many years in those house-boxes, only to end up in these smaller boxes. I think right then I promised myself to leave that town as soon as I could, and if possible, never to return. To die far away was my dream, but to make that dream come true was not easy.

Where could I go without any money? On the other hand, like so many other sinister places, the town had a certain fatal attraction; it bred a certain dispiritedness and resignation that prevented people from leaving.

I was working in a guava paste factory. I got up in the morning and started making wooden boxes into which boiling guava jam was to be poured, there to harden into bars that were later labeled "La Caridad Guava Paste" and decorated with an image of Our Lady of Charity. I do not think there was much charity on the part of the factory owner, who made us work up to twelve hours a day for one peso. On payday I would go to the movies, which was the only magical place in Holguín, the only place where one could escape from the city, at least for a few hours. On those days I went alone because I liked to enjoy the movies without having to share my excitement with anybody. I would sit in the *gallinero*, or top balcony, the cheapest seats, where I could sometimes see up to three movies for five cents. It was a great joy to see those people galloping over the prairies, hurling themselves down mighty rivers, or shooting each other to death, while I was dying of boredom in a town that had no ocean, no rivers, no prairies, no forests, nothing that could be of interest to me.

Perhaps influenced by those movies (mostly from the United States and Mexico) or God knows why, I started to write novels. Whenever I wasn't going to the movies, I went home and, to the sound of my grandparents' snoring, began writing. Sometimes dawn would come, and from the typewriter that my cousin Renán had sold me for seventeen dollars, I would go straight to the guava paste factory and continue thinking about my novels while making those wooden boxes. Often I would hammer my fingers, which quickly brought me back to reality. The boxes I made were getting worse and I was writing long and horrendous novels with titles like "How Tough Life Is" or "Good-bye, Cruel World." As a matter of fact, I think my mother still has them in Holguín, and she claims they are the best I have ever written.

My aunts and my mother, once settled in Holguín, managed to get an electric radio. Now they could all listen at once to the same soap opera they used to hear in the country. I think those radio dramas, which I also listened to, influenced the novels I wrote when I was thirteen.

THE RUB PUB Holguín had a totally macho atmosphere which my family shared and in which they raised me. Nevertheless, my love life at thirteen was somewhat ambiguous. I fell in love with Carlos, a kid from the factory, with whom I had a lot in common; we even looked alike. We had both been abandoned by our fathers and were only children, closely attached to our mothers. I used to go to the movies with Carlos, but our relationship was limited to sitting next to each other in the theater and letting our knees touch, as if by accident; with our knees in close contact, we would sit for hours watching ferocious Indians parade or listening to Pedro Infante sing. Perhaps influenced by the prevalent attitude in town, I also had girlfriends: Irene, Irma, Lourdes, Marlene; and I had fistfights with other boys who were after them, or with the ones whose girlfriends I had taken away. I remember fighting it out with a very good-looking boy, Pombo, who actually punched me hard in the face. Looking back, I think I was more in love with Pombo than with Lourdes, the girl I "took away" from him; perhaps I kept her as my steady just to annoy him.

At the time, I was still attracted to Carlos. He was the one who first took me to Eufrasia's Rub Pub, which was a big whorehouse with a grand dance floor. It was located on the top of a red dirt hill we used to call the Frontier, a very appropriate name since beyond it there was a neighborhood with no pretensions of civilization, no hypocrisy, and where anything could happen. Almost everyone who lived there was a thug or a prostitute. For me, visiting that place was a great revelation and an irresistible attraction. The name Rub Pub came about because the women who danced there would sway their hips in such a way that, rather than dancing, they would rub against the men's genitals in a circular motion. Once the music stopped, the man would make the arrangements to have sex with the woman, and for two or three dollars they would get a room in the house across the street. Each dance, by the way, cost five cents. When the organ music started, Eufrasia, the owner, dressed all in red and with her huge white handbag, would tap each man on the shoulder in order to collect his five cents. Two of those five cents went to the woman. Eufrasia kept track mentally of how many times each whore had danced and how much to give her as her share. I danced with Lolín, a young mulatto girl with powerful thighs. In the end, encouraged by some friends, Carlos among them, I went to the house across the street to fuck Lolín. We did it by the light of a kerosene lamp, and I remembered my mother in the country. I was nervous and could not get an erection, but Lolín was so adept that she finally got me aroused. Or rather, was it my thinking of Carlos's face while he waited for me outside? In any case, it was the first time I ejaculated inside a woman.

My grandparents' house was not really theirs. Ozaida, one of their daughters, had helped them buy it. She was planning to leave for the United States with her husband. They had a daughter who died, and Ozaida had never completely gotten over the tragedy. Perhaps Florentino, her husband, thought she would feel better living in the United States. I don't think she has. It seems to me that over time Ozaida has felt even unhappier in the loneliness and horror of the Miami swamps.

The house was still too small for us—there were only

two bedrooms for ten people—and so I sometimes went over to my aunt Ofelia's to sleep. No one, of course, had the privilege of sleeping alone. We slept two or three to a bed. My grandparents, who were able to sleep separately in their country house, and therefore hate each other at a respectful distance, now had to share a bed. Perhaps that was why they started making love again. Sometimes while I was writing, I would hear them in their bed, engaged in pretty noisy sexual embraces. I would take advantage of the opportunity and slide under the bed in which they were fornicating to snitch some money from his wooden box. My grandfather would bring that box from the store every night. It was, one might say, his cash register.

Usually when I spent the night at my aunt's I shared the bed with my cousin Renán, who was sixteen years old and, it was said, already a Don Juan. After some minor erotic adventure, Renán would get home and masturbate in the same bed where I was sleeping. I enjoyed those episodes and like to think that sometimes, pretending to be asleep, I assisted him.

When I had time, I attended a sort of junior high school, where I had an anatomy teacher who made us recite, commas and all, the entire text of an awful book on anatomy, physiology, and hygiene. You could not pass unless you could recite it by heart. At that school I also fell in love with my grammar teacher. So my platonic love then was divided between Carlos, who was fourteen, and an old professor, who was around seventy. As a result, when my cousin masturbated thinking of one of the girls that perhaps he had kissed in one of the few scrimpy parks in town, I would do the same thinking of the grammar teacher who never paid any attention to me, although the students claimed he was homosexual and many even bragged about having fucked him.

In 1957 my cousin Dulce María and her mother came from Miami to spend some time in Holguín. Dulce María had turned into a very beautiful girl. It was just then that my friendship with Carlos had reached its deepest level; every night we went to the movies together. My cousin sensed something unusual in that friendship, and maybe that is why she fell in love with Carlos. Everything changed for me. No longer were Carlos and I going to the movies together; it was the two of them, and I was their chaperon. They sat next to each other in the theater and I would see them kissing. My cousin was now doing, right in front of me, all the things I had longed to do with Carlos, and I was just supposed to make sure nothing "bad" happened, according to my grandmother's instructions. The romance lasted for a month, until my cousin returned to Miami. Carlos tried to go out with me again, but I wanted no part of it; secretly he had betrayed me, and I didn't need to explain anything; he understood. Carlos would sit on the porch and talk with my grandparents, waiting for me to come out but, stubbornly, I would remain in the dining room. I had started writing another terrible novel, "The Cannibal," which fortunately was later lost. Never again did I go to the movies with Carlos.

In those days I made my voice sound deeper, pretended to be tough, and increased the number of my girlfriends. I even managed, I think, to convince myself that I liked one or another of the girls. In school I courted them all and took pains to keep anyone from even imagining that I did not like women. But one day, while the anatomy teacher was repeating her litany, one of my classmates sat next to me and with absolutely diabolic sincerity said, "Look, Reinaldo, you are a faggot. Do you know what a faggot is? It's a man who likes other men. A faggot, that's what you are."

C H R I S T M A S One of the greatest joys of my childhood was to hear my grandfather say the word *Christmas*. He pronounced that word with such resonance that Christmas seemed almost there. He would say it with a laugh, something most unusual in him, and that word contained all the happiness in the world.

When Christmas came in 1957, my grandfather did not even mention the word; there was no Christmas. It was only "the Bloody Christmas," as *Bohemia* magazine described it, because of the numerous political murders that the government committed that month. We could hear shootings every day; terror was now commonplace. Most of Oriente province was against Batista, and there were rebels in the mountains. Sometimes, from a distance, they would attack Batista's army, which fled because the soldiers were mostly very poor and hungry people who did not want to die for such a trivial cause. But no one can really speak of a battlefront between Fidel Castro's guerrillas and Batista's troops. Most of the dead were those killed by Batista's henchmen—students; members of Castro's partisan group, the 26th of July Movement; or simply Castro sympathizers who were captured in the towns and then tortured, murdered, and thrown into the gutter in order to intimidate the people, especially the conspirators. But among Castro's troops there were not many casualties, nor were there in Batista's army. After the Revolution took power, Castro talked about twenty thousand dead, and that became a sort of mythical, symbolic number. The names of those twenty thousand casualties were never published and never will be, because that many deaths just did not occur in the war. Really there was no war, rather a widespread discontent between the people and their dictator. The people committed acts of sabotage and were especially successful in spreading rumors that there were thousands of rebels and that they were everywhere; the only thing that was everywhere was contempt for the Batista regime, and thus flags of the 26th of July Movement sprang up all over. Even I once posted one of those flags. Batista was, moreover, a clumsy dictator who was not in control of the situation, and whose power continued to erode due to the pervasive corruption of his closest allies and the flight of the more honest ones. One must admit there was also a popular campaign against Batista, and it sometimes reached the media. *Bohemia* magazine published photos and interviews with the rebels in the Sierra Maestra as well as photos of the young men killed by Batista. *The New York Times* openly supported Fidel Castro from the beginning, and in general, the United States was where Castro and most of his agents could conspire openly. Besides, the Cuban middle class also hated Batista, who was black, and supported Castro, the white son of a Spanish sugar mill owner and the product of a Jesuit school. It was none other than Cuba's most prominent bishop who, on one occasion, saved Castro's life. Before resigning and leaving the country for good, Batista was already demoralized. He had been living high, and what he most wanted to save was his millions. On the eve of fleeing the country, he threw a party at the Tropicana, the most lavish nightclub in Havana. Some years later, in Paris, it was said that Batista had made some profoundly cynical comments referring to his last years in power in Cuba. He was reported to have said, "*Yo entré por la posta, salí por la pista y dejé la peste.*" ["I came in through the guardhouse, exited from the tarmac, and left the plague behind."]

R E B E L Around 1958 conditions in Holguín were becoming more and more unbearable, with little food and no electricity. If life there had been boring, now it was simply impossible. For some time I had considered the idea of leaving home, of joining the rebels. I was fourteen and there seemed to be no other solution. I had to join the guerrillas in the mountains. Perhaps Carlos and I might even go together, take part in some battle, and either lose our lives or find a better life; at least we'd be doing something. I told Carlos of my plan and he agreed; I should wake him up at dawn, and we would go to a town called Velasco, which was said to be in rebel hands already.

I got up at dawn, went to Carlos's house, and called him from outside his window several times. Carlos did not answer, and apparently did not want to answer. But since I had already decided to leave everything behind, I started walking toward Velasco. It took me a whole day to get there. I expected a warm welcome from a large group of rebels. But there were no rebels in Velasco, nor were there any of Batista's soldiers. There was a town—mostly women—dying of hunger. I had only forty-seven cents, with which I bought some local pastries, then sat on a bench to eat them. I sat for hours on that bench, with neither desire to return to Holguín nor enough strength to walk back. At dusk, a man who had been watching me for a while approached and asked me if I wanted to join the rebels. Yes, I told him. He said his name was Cuco Sánchez; he was about forty years old. All his brothers, seven of them, were with the rebels. He was the only one who had stayed behind to take care of his mother and of his wife. He took me home. His wife looked desolate, perhaps because all she had to offer was some beans, which they had to share with me. I was ashamed, but too hungry not to accept. Cuco Sánchez's mother encouraged me to stay the night with them. She told Cuco to take me the following day to the Gibara mountains, where the rebels were entrenched. She had a small country store that had been looted first by the rebels and then by Batista's soldiers. The week before, one of Batista's most notorious henchmen, Sosa Blanco, had passed through. He had devastated the town, burned a man alive, and taken what little was left in the store of Cuco Sánchez's mother. Then he had shot the shop window to pieces. Nothing remained but a scale, and that was also smashed. "Look what they did to it!" Cuco's mother said to me, both anger and terror in her voice. Yes, I had to join the rebels, she said, as if it were up to me to avenge her smashed scale. Cuco Sánchez's brothers were in the area, and it would not be difficult for Cuco to take me to them. Cuco was in charge of casting bullets for the rebels. While at his house, I helped him make ammunition. We finally went to the rebel headquarters in the Sierra Gibara.

I was interviewed by the guerrilla commander. His name was Eddy Suñol, and he had been wounded, shot when Sosa Blanco was in the area, he told me. One side of his waist was still covered by a large, primitive bandage; I think he had a broken rib. A peasant from Velasco, he seemed to like me but refused to take me on. I was very young and had no weapon. "We have plenty of guerrillas; what we need is weapons," he said. I did all I could to stay, and Cuco also helped me. We convinced Suñol to let me stay for a week, after which a contingent of troops would leave for the Sierra Maestra and I could join them. Whether they accepted me there or not was no longer his responsibility. In the meantime I could help in any way possible: cooking, carrying water, gathering firewood.

After I had spent about ten days waiting for orders to leave, a group of forty-five men and seven women returned from the Sierra Maestra. They had been sent earlier by Suñol, but Castro had no use for guerrillas without rifles. I could stay no longer; I had to go back to Holguín, kill a guard, and take his rifle. "If you bring a rifle or shotgun we'll take you at once," Suñol told me. One of the rebels, a young man of about eighteen, gave me his only knife, saying I should not leave without a weapon, and I should stab one of Batista's guards in the back, and return. "I'll be waiting for you right here," he said, probably to encourage me, to have me leave with some hope. So, back to Holguín I went.

I was in a truck with a number of people who had permits to go to Aguas Claras, a town near Holguín. These people were known to Batista's soldiers, but I was not. The driver warned me that taking me was very risky, because if they found out that I was a rebel or was not from that neighborhood, everyone in the truck would be shot. We finally got to Aguas Claras without any trouble. There, about six miles from Holguín, we parted company. I hid until dark and then started walking.

By midnight I was back home, knocking on the door. My grandmother opened it and let out a scream, which my grandfather immediately silenced with a slap. "If they catch you here they'll kill you, and everyone in this house will go to jail," he said.

I had made the mistake of leaving a note on my bed stating that I was going to join the rebels, asking them not to tell anybody. The loud voices of those ten women in the house spread the news all over the neighborhood. Now Batista's police were looking for me. I had to return to Velasco and, of course, I could not even dream of stabbing a policeman in the back with the knife I had. Even so, on the night of my departure I did approach a policeman. I looked at him and he looked at me, but the only sign he gave me was to grab his testicles, conspicuous under his uniform and almost as big as my grandfather's. I walked away as fast as I could, while he kept on rubbing his magnificent testicles.

I bushwhacked my way back to Velasco, got to the rebel encampment, and they had to accept me; they could not let me go back to Holguín. So I stayed, helping in any way I could. One of my aunts, the one who had bought my grandfather's farm, lived a few miles from there. Crossing over the mountains, I visited her once in a while and she would give me something to eat; since her husband had not been a rebel-sympathizer, it was to their political advantage that I, a rebel, would visit them.

During my whole time with the rebels I never took part in any battle; I never even witnessed a battle; those battles were more myth than reality. It was, rather, a war of words. The press and most of the people were saying that the countryside had been taken by thousands and thousands of rebels armed to the teeth. Not true. The few arms in rebel hands either were taken from the *casquitos* [little helmets]—as they called Batista's soldiers—or were old shotguns, made a century ago and now held together with wires, that had been used by the *mambises* [Cuban soldiers during the war of independence against Spain].

While with the rebels, I saw some injustices that to some extent made me doubt the goodwill of those people. One day a group of rebels went to arrest a peasant who lived with his mother. She was crying and screaming desperately. Her son had been reported to be an informer. He was taken and executed; in other words, even before Fidel Castro rose to power, the executions of people who were against his movement or who conspired against him had already begun. He called them traitors. That was, and still is, the word.

Eddy Suñol, in charge of the executions in that area, ended up by shooting a bullet through his own head fifteen years later. Suñol's death was just one more suicide in our political history, which is an endless history of suicides.

Most of us rebels did not expect Batista's dictatorship would fall so soon. When we got the news that Batista had left, many of us did not believe it. Castro himself was one of the most surprised; he had won a war that had never been fought. Castro must have been rather grateful to Batista; the dictator had departed, leaving the Island unharmed and Castro without even a scratch. For his part, Fidel Castro had never even tried to have Batista assassinated. A group of students made an attempt with insufficient weapons, and most died on the spot. The ones who survived were never allowed later into positions of power under Castro. It should also be remembered that Fidel Castro's brother-in-law had held a position of power with Batista—that of minister, no less. Although Batista fled on December 31, 1958, it took Castro many days to come down from the Sierra Maestra and get to Havana. The rest is part of the legend. He arrived in Havana on one of the huge tanks that were not part of his arsenal, surrounded by a large army, and hailed by soldiers and by masses of people who had had enough of Batista's dictatorship.

The rebels were, moreover, good-looking, young, and manly, at least apparently so. The world press was fascinated by those handsome, bearded men, many of whom also sported splendid long hair.

We came down from the hills and received a heroes' welcome. In my neighborhood in Holguín I was given a flag of the 26th of July Movement and for a whole block I walked holding that flag. I felt a little ridiculous, but there was a great euphoria, with hymns and anthems ringing out, and the whole town in the streets. The rebels kept coming, with crucifixes hanging from chains made of seeds; these were the heroes. Some, in fact, had joined the rebels only four or five months earlier, but most of the women, and also many of the men in the city, went wild over these hairy fellows; everybody wanted to take one of the bearded men home. I did not have a beard yet because I was only fifteen.

THE REVOLUTION Castro's
Revolutionary government started in 1959.

There was a surge of enthusiasm, great fanfare, and a new terror. A veritable hunt had started, against Batista's soldiers, against supposed informers, against military men of the fallen regime, and against the Masferrer "tigers." Masferrer was a Cuban politician as well as a gangster, not mutually exclusive occupations. In the last few years he had organized a private army; most of his soldiers were killed on the streets or in their homes, or on the Hill of the Cross, where many had fled in a desperate attempt to get out of town. By this time, Masferrer was already on a boat making his escape to the United States. In those first days, many people were murdered without any kind of trial. Later, the so-called Revolutionary Tribunals were set up and people were quickly executed; an informer's accusation before a provisional judge of the new regime was enough. The trials were a kind of theatrical entertainment where people would enjoy watching how some poor devil was condemned to be shot, whose worst crime may have been that he had slapped someone who now was taking advantage of the circumstances in order to get even. The innocent died with the guilty. Many more were dying now than during the war that never was.

In spite of the euphoria, many did not agree with those executions. I vividly remember this: A man was being taken to be executed for having killed a young rebel. The man was marched along the highway under an escort of rebel soldiers who were to prevent the mob from tearing him to pieces, so that he would at least get to the place of execution alive. Suddenly a woman in black appeared and stopped the march. She started shouting that the man should be punished but not put to death, that she was the mother of the rebel this man had murdered. Nobody paid any attention to the woman; her plea for mercy did not count; there was only the new order and the need for vengeance, so long repressed. The man was escorted out of town and shot. Those executions were a daily occurrence.

In Holguín the trials took place in the auditorium at La Pantoja, a huge military academy built by Batista and now occupied by the rebels. The trials, often shown on television, were oral, spectacular, and summary.

More than thirty years have gone by, and Fidel Castro is still staging those show trials and, of course, televising some of them. But now Castro is no longer executing Batista's henchmen; instead, he executes his own soldiers and sometimes even his own generals.

Why is it that we, the great majority of the people, and

even the intellectuals, did not realize that this was the beginning of a new dictatorship, even bloodier than the previous one? Perhaps we did realize it, but the enthusiasm of knowing that now one was part of a revolution, that a dictatorship had been overthrown and the time had come for vengeance, outweighed the injustices and the crimes that were being committed. Not only were injustices being inflicted; the executions were being conducted in the name of justice and freedom, and above all, in the name of the people.

There was still a lot of collective rejoicing during 1960. "Henchmen" were still being executed, but we must admit that in the midst of that euphoria nearly everybody approved of the executions. Who can forget that impassioned multitude of over a million people marching at Revolutionary Square (which, by the way, was not built by the Revolution but by the tyranny just overthrown), yelling the words "Execution wall!" In those days I was part of the Revolution; I had nothing to lose, and it seemed then that I had much to gain. I could study, get away from my home in Holguín, start a new life.

A S T U D E N T I was awarded a scholarship at La Pantoja, the Batista military camp that had been converted into a polytechnic institute. I was sixteen when the school opened. We would graduate as agricultural accountants in a new program that the government needed, as it already had secret plans to confiscate all land. I think these were among the first scholarships created by the Castro government, because this was a center for the training of young communists. Most of us did not realize, at the beginning, why we were really there. We had been carefully "trapped" from all over the Island.

I was one of the adolescents locked up in an encampment, together with over two thousand other young men, who were not permitted to go out. One would think, as I do now, that this was the opportunity for me to develop my homosexual tendencies, and to have many erotic relationships. I had none. In those days I endured all the prejudices typical of a macho society fired up by the Revolution. In that school, overflowing with virile militancy, there seemed to be no place for homosexuality, which, even then, was severely punished by expulsion and even jail. Nevertheless, homosexuality did occur among those young men, although very covertly. The boys caught in such acts had to march with their cots and all their belongings on the way to the warehouse, where, by order of the administration, they had to return everything. Their comrades were supposed to come from their lodgings and throw stones at them and beat them up. It was a sinister expulsion because it also included a dossier that would follow each person for the rest of his life and would bar him from admission to any other state school, and the state had started to control everything. Many of those young men who walked with their cots on their backs seemed quite manly. Witnessing that spectacle made me feel ashamed and terrified. "A faggot, that's what you are." I kept hearing the voice of my classmate back when I was in high school, and I realized that being a "faggot" in Cuba was one of the worst disasters that could ever happen to anyone.

There were already political as well as moral purges. All the teachers were communists and, needless to say, one of the most important courses was on Marxism-Leninism. We had to master the *Manual of the USSR Academy of Sciences*; the *Manual of Political Economy* by Nikitin; *Foundations of Socialism in Cuba* by Blas Roca. Of course, we also had classes in accounting, and as part of the course, we had to climb Turquino Peak in the Sierra Maestra at regular intervals. The Sierra Maestra was like a holy place which we, in a rite of passage, had to visit every now and then. It was, and I believe still is, a place of pilgrimage, like Mecca or the Holy Sepulcher. The Sierra Maestra was where Fidel Castro hid until Batista fled. To get a degree as an agricultural accountant, six climbs up Turquino Peak were required, and those who were unable to do it, because of a physical handicap or for any other reason, were considered lacking in character and could not graduate. It was really a privilege to have to climb the peak only six times to become an agricultural accountant. I remember once, on one of my climbs, I met a young fellow who was dragging himself along. He was studying for the diplomatic service and his graduation requirement was twenty-five climbs up that peak. I do not know if he ever made a good diplomat, considering his limited talents as a mountaineer.

For me, a peasant raised in the scrubby hills, it was an adventure to climb mountains with all those boys, sleeping in hammocks in the open and swimming in the rivers. As we went singing our way up the mountains, none of us suspected the sordid plans behind those excursions. After a few months we were told that we were not simply students but the vanguard of the Revolution and, therefore, communist youths and soldiers of the army. During the last hikes we could no longer sing what we wanted, but instead had to sing the "Internationale" and other communist hymns. The school's director was Alfredo Sarabia, an old militant of the Communist Party. So in 1960, while Castro was assuring the world that he was no communist and that the Revolution was "as green as our palm trees," Cuban youth was already receiving communist indoctrination in addition to military training. We were also given classes in military matters and were even taught how to handle long-range weapons.

One of the professors composed a hymn for the agricultural accountants with this opening line: "We are the vanguard of the Revolution." In fact, we, as well as the volunteer teachers in the Sierra Maestra, were the first "cadres of the Revolution." We were going to be in charge of the accounting and administration of the People's Farms, that is, the state farms, because they never ever belonged to the people. Many of my classmates later rose to become directors in Castro's regime; others committed suicide. I remember one of my friends from Holguín who blasted his head off with his machine gun. Those of us who prevailed were the new men, the young communists who would control the economy of the country.

It was not easy to survive all of the moral, political, religious, and even physical purges, and in addition, pass the various tests covering technical subjects. Of the two thousand students, fewer than one thousand remained. I was, naturally, not the only one who managed to hide his homosexuality and his rejection of communism. Many of the students who were homosexual managed to survive; others simply denied their orientation. Those who were anticommunists, like myself, would repeat the manuals on Marxism by rote. Early on we had to learn to hide our desires and to swallow the urge to protest. At one meeting in the large school auditorium, the same one where the trials to execute counterrevolutionaries had been held, someone told the director, Sarabia, that within the grains of rice there were grubs and worms. The director got up, furious and red in the face, and accused that young man of being weak and a counterrevolutionary, and of lacking, in his view, the spirit of sacrifice. Sarabia ended his speech by saying that soon we would have to learn to eat the worms and forget about the rice. The young man who had objected was of Chinese extraction and he was expelled from the school. But expulsions were selective, and a few people were untouchable.

It must be admitted, however, that there was still more enthusiasm than disenchantment.

Some of the professors, if not the majority, had sexual encounters with their students; there was one, Juan, who had relations with close to a hundred students. Sometimes the young men lined up by his room to fuck him; I actually saw this. In addition, a classmate of mine, reputed to have one of the largest penises in school, told me that he was a favorite of that professor of Marxism.

I think many of the young men who were at the school on scholarships were homosexuals who played the male role. In their view, fucking other youths did not make them queer; queers were the ones who got fucked. There was once a big scandal when it was discovered that every night more than a hundred of the students were jumping over the school fence to fuck a queer who came on foot from Holguín to take care of his suitors. When Sarabia arrived, with an army of his most trusted teachers, the boy ran away and disappeared in the hills. The students, under cover of darkness, returned to their quarters. That night Sarabia summoned the entire student body to the theater and made a speech full of slogans and threats. Afterward a movie was shown, *The Life of Lenin* no less. Almost every night we went to the theater to see a Russian movie; we also ate a lot of Russian meat. Undoubtedly we were being indoctrinated, but we were also being fed, and our studies were free; the government dressed us, educated us in its own fashion, and determined our fates.

H A V A N A In the summer of 1960 I went to Havana. On July 26 Fidel Castro would always deliver a mammoth speech in Revolutionary Square and he needed people to fill the square. Over a thousand of us young men were packed into a sugarcane train and we arrived in Havana after a trip of almost three days. Most of us were sexually aroused on that train; all those sweaty bodies pressing together. I was also aroused, but obstinately persisted in my absurd macho posture, which I found difficult to abandon because of the prevailing prejudice.

By then I had two girlfriends: Irene, whom I had known before entering the school, and Marlene, who was now generally considered my steady girlfriend. They took turns coming to the school on Sundays, which were visiting days. I was very "macho" then, or tried to be, although sometimes I had platonic relationships with other boys. These were manly relationships which included tests of strength, simulated wrestling matches, and horseplay.

We arrived in Havana and the city fascinated me. A real city, for the first time in my life. A city where people did not know each other, where one could disappear, where to a certain extent nobody cared who you were. We were lodged at the "Habana Libre" Hotel, that is, the Havana Hilton, which had suddenly become "liberated." We slept six or seven to a room.

Needless to say, the "queers" in Havana had a ball with us students, who after six months without sex suddenly found ourselves in the middle of the city. Monzón, a friend of mine, told me that one night he fucked more than twenty queers, at ten bucks a head. He made a small fortune during his stay for the Revolutionary parade. He was a strikingly handsome man who later held various positions with the Revolutionary government. I once met him again on the street, over ten years ago, and he told me he was directing some state company, constantly traveling to Bulgaria and other socialist countries.

The fact is that this first trip to Havana was my initial contact with another world, a world of many faces, immense, fascinating. I felt that Havana was my city, that somehow I had to return. Anyhow, during our short time there, our job was to parade and, of course, parade we did, all day, in Revolutionary Square, applauding, repeating the slogans of the moment, even with a certain enthusiasm. I also had a brief romance with another girl; she was from

Havana, eager to conquer some revolutionary "hero": a student, a Rebel Army soldier, or a peasant. Later she sent several letters to me at school, which I did not answer. In her last letter she sounded angry and wrote that she was coming to the school to see me. I showed the letter to several of my friends and they laughed, but I was terrified by the thought that the woman would show up and cause a scandal. She wrote that she was pregnant and that the baby was mine, which was preposterous, since all we had done was rub against each other on the public square; that baby was as likely to be mine as Fidel Castro's.

F I D E L   C A S T R O And speaking of Fidel Castro, that night after the assembly, or perhaps the following evening, he came to the Habana Libre Hotel to talk with us. He showed up all of a sudden, as he usually does. We were attending a sort of political seminar in one of the largest ballrooms of the hotel, and he arrived to thundering applause. His physical presence kindled our enthusiasm; it was an honor for us, lowly agricultural accountants, to be visited by the Commander in Chief. He told us that we were the vanguard of the Revolution, that we had an enormous responsibility because we would manage the first people's farms. He said we had to be very honest, and absolutely politicized and Revolutionary. The speech ended with explosive applause; I, of course, applauded too, but later found out that he gave such speeches almost daily; some of my friends in Holguín suffered similar speeches by Fidel Castro or by other leaders whom he had sent. The objective of some of the speeches was to incite young men to fight against Trujillo's dictatorship in the Dominican Republic; many died in those battles.

Before entering my scholarship program, I had enlisted

with my girlfriend Irene, of all people, in one of the groups that were to join an expedition to the Dominican Republic to kill Trujillo. But Trujillo killed most of those who went there to get him. He was waiting at the landing beach, and promptly wiped out practically the whole expedition. I escaped from that death, as I had escaped when I approached one of Batista's soldiers with a knife and all he did was rub his testicles. I also escaped death when I was with the rebels and Sosa Blanco's troops were in the area. Up to now I always managed to keep a few millimeters ahead of death; now things are different. In any case, how could I have thought of death then? I was sixteen, and surrounded by a thousand young men as vital and brave as I was, or much more so.

H Y M N S We returned to Holguín, singing the same hymns we had sung in Revolutionary Square. Some of us had letters or photographs of the girlfriends we had suddenly acquired during that parade. And again we climbed the Sierra Maestra, with our hammocks, our packs, our chocolate bars, our hymns. We swam in the river near Turquino Peak, scaled the peak, enjoyed the temperature that to us seemed almost polar, and came running down, like mountain goats, elated and lighthearted. No doubt we had found meaning in life; we had a plan, a project, a future, beautiful friendships, great promises, a huge job to be done. We were noble, pure, young, and our conscience was clear. It was wonderfully pleasant to breathe that mountain air, the smell of pine trees, of fresh earth, of food prepared under the open sky. We usually made a rest stop at a camp for voluntary teachers called Minas del Frío. I think that was one of the few communist recruiting stations that came into being before La Pantoja, our school of agricultural accounting. Those young people had come in for training as voluntary teachers but were actually receiving communist indoctrination. I remember a young man crying on that mountain, alone. He was a Rebel Army veteran, but he was cold and afraid. He told me he was not learning any teaching skills, that he was being indoctrinated. He was afraid he would flunk out, that he would not be able to take the climate and treatment and therefore would be expelled from the camp. He did not flunk out; I saw him once when they came down from the Sierra and spent a night at La Pantoja. I don't know what became of him, but I began to see a certain disenchantment in some people, including my own mother.

My mother had returned from Miami, tired of taking care of other people's shitty and squealing babies. Back in Holguín, still beautiful and young, my mother lived in absolute chastity. She came to see me at school and told me that most products had disappeared from the market; there was no soap, no food, no clothes. I was boarding in the school and wearing the uniform supplied by the Revolutionary government; I did not need any other clothes and did not pay much attention to my mother's complaints.

We had already learned some accounting when Fidel Castro's government decided to change the country's currency; that is, all the existing money was declared void and new bills were printed. It was a masterful political coup. By recalling the old bills, the government in fact took away from those who opposed the Revolution all the power that money could offer them, and gave them in return a new paper currency of limited value, useless for international transactions. Moreover, whoever had a lot of money received only a small portion. In place of the balance, a bond or voucher was issued; the rest was supposed to be paid back in monthly installments.

In what could be called a cruel twist of fate, I was chosen as one of the employees to exchange the old money for the new currency at a bank in the town of Velasco. Naturally, the first thing I did when I got there was to inquire about

Cuco Sánchez and his family. Nobody would talk to me about them, until finally someone said that he was in jail, that the government had taken control of the family's store, that most of the men in the family were against the regime and some had taken up arms. This was early 1961 and already there were rebels, among them men like Cuco Sánchez.

When I was sixteen I sang the hymns of the Revolution and certainly studied Marxism; I even got to be one of the directors of Marxist study groups and was, of course, a fledgling communist. I thought then that all those men who took up arms against Fidel were either wrong or crazy. I believed, or wanted to believe, that the Revolution was something noble and beautiful. I could not imagine that the Revolution which was giving me a free education could be sinister. I firmly believed there would be elections and Fidel Castro would be elected in a democratic way. But the only facts were that we were being indoctrinated and no real aggression from the United States had started yet. In other words, the Revolution was communist right from the beginning. I have to confess this because I was one of the first people who received communist texts, which I had to study in order to teach them to others. The government had already taken control of a great number of private properties. Communism simply was being implemented although this could not be officially acknowledged. All our teachers were communists, the command cadres were communists, the whole school was nothing but a communist indoctrination center, just like the center for volunteer teachers at Minas del Frío. Even the books used to teach the peasants how to read were communist. But we were so full of enthusiasm that we could not believe, or did not want to believe, that anything seriously bad might happen. It is almost impossible for human beings to imagine so many calamities befalling them at the same time; we had suffered continuous dictatorships, incessant abuse, and unrelenting mistreatment by those in power. This was our opportunity, the opportunity for the lower classes.

I had not forgotten my literary ambitions, in spite of an environment that was so politicized and certainly not literary at all. I would write long poems inspired by what, I don't know; perhaps the weather, the rain or the morning mist—as they happened or maybe as I remembered them. Deep down I was still the lonely boy who would walk in the woods, half naked, singing grandiose, almost operatic songs. Now I did write them down, in notebooks that I eventually lost.

Finally I graduated as an agricultural accountant. But before my graduation something happened that filled me with great sorrow and reminded me of my grandfather's words. He used to say that communism was the end of civilization, that it was a monstrosity. His happiest day was when Stalin died. "At last that bastard is dead," he said with joy.

THE FIRE When the attack began at Playa Girón [Bay of Pigs] in April 1961, we were recruited immediately and boarded on trucks headed for the battle zone to fight, of course, on Fidel Castro's side. We never got there because during the time it took for us to be recruited and deployed, the invaders had been defeated. We returned to school, and in the great theater where all the events took place and where Soviet movies were shown to us every night, a television set had been readied so we could both watch and hear Fidel Castro's speech. There I heard him confirm what he had denied previously, that we had carried out a socialist revolution, that we were socialists. Suddenly, what had been hidden for two years was out in the open; we were socialists, we were simply communists.

What impressed me most was the reaction of those in the theater. The thousand youths, the hundreds of teachers and employees of that school rushed out to the esplanade and the main road in the school complex, and started shouting communist slogans. The most popular of these was:

> *We are socialists,*
> *and for socialism we shall toil,*
> *and whoever doesn't like it,*
> *let him swallow castor oil.*

Undoubtedly all this had been planned since the beginning of the Revolution: the communist slogans, the communist texts, and the most convenient time to declare the communist nature of the Revolution. And in the midst of that wave of young men shouting slogans, I suddenly saw myself participating, carried away, marching and singing like all the others. At first I did not join in, but I did not protest either. I thought I could read in the faces of some of my friends from Holguín the same anguish or disenchantment that I felt, but naturally we did not talk about it. A few minutes later we were swept up by the parade, repeating slogans, which became more and more vulgar and offensive, against "Yankee imperialism" and against untold thousands of enemies suddenly discovered. Little by little the march turned into a sort of conga, into a grotesque carnival, where everybody, while moving their buttocks, began gesturing in an erotic and obscene manner. In a strange way that crowd, in less than a minute, had passed from socialism on to communism.

Heading the procession were the professors, the indoctrinators, the ideological guides, and Alfredo Sarabia. I understood that in reality we had been locked up for a year, as if in a monastery, where new religious ideas, and therefore new fanatic ideas, prevailed. We had been indoctrinated in a new religion and after graduation we were to spread that new religion all over the Island. We were the ideological guides of a new kind of repression, we were the missionaries who would spread the new official ideology among all the state farms in the Island. The new religion had in us its new monks and priests, and also its new secret police.

The atmosphere of the Revolution admitted no dissent whatsoever. Fanaticism and faith in a "brilliant" future, as our leaders incessantly hammered home, prevailed. This fanaticism reached its peak with the creation of the so-called ORI, that is, Integrated Revolutionary Organizations. Vulgarity and rabble behavior, encouraged by the Revolution, were logically a part of those organizations. One of the slogans was: "ORI Is Fire, Don't Say ORI, Say Fire." And everybody wiggled their butts, turned round and round, and sang to the conga beat of those songs and chants.

In fact, the Communist Party was, naturally, behind the ORI, and Fidel Castro became aware that those "Integrated Organizations" wanted to get rid of him and seize power; that is, the communists of the old guard wanted to remove Castro and take charge. But if Fidel Castro was ever loyal to anybody, it was to Fidel Castro. Later on, trials took place and some of those gentlemen received thirty-year sentences. And Castro affirmed that he was a Marxist and had always been a communist, that his political education had been Marxist-Leninist. So he became "the Fire," he became the ORI, the head of the "Integrated Organizations."

I finished my studies and became an agricultural accountant. I was assigned to the William Soler farm near Manzanillo, in the southernmost part of Oriente province. Before leaving for the farm, I spent some days in my grandfather's house.

THEATRICS AND THE CHICKEN FARM

My grandfather's grocery store, which had been his livelihood, had already been taken over by the government, and he now spent his time on a stool next to the closed store, talking to himself. He did not read the newspaper or *Bohemia*, which no longer was the liberal, irreverent, critical magazine that he used to read to us in the country. By this time it was but another instrument in the hands of Castro and his new regime. The press was now almost completely controlled. Freedom was something constantly talked about but not practiced. There was freedom to say that there was freedom or to praise the regime, but never to criticize it.

Probably one of the most monstrous events of the time was the notorious trial of Marcos Rodríguez, a young man suddenly accused of having been a Batista informer. This trial implicated several leaders of the Revolution who, in order to save their necks, attacked Marcos Rodríguez viciously. It will never be known whether Marcos Rodríguez really informed on some students at the University of Havana who were murdered by Batista's police. What became obvious by the middle of the trial was the grandiloquence and theatricality so characteristic of Fidel Castro. Those trials in which someone was condemned to death were really theatrical spectacles. We had returned to the times of Nero, the times when the masses rejoiced in watching how a human being was being condemned to death or murdered right before their eyes.

Fidel Castro was (and is) not only the maximum leader but also the chief district attorney. In one instance, in which an honest court did not want to condemn a number of air force pilots accused of bombing the city of Santiago de Cuba, which they actually never did, Fidel set himself up as district attorney and judge, and sentenced them to twenty and thirty years in prison. The judge, who had a long rebel beard and had declared them innocent, shot himself. All this had already given us an inkling of what the new regime was about. There was still some hope, however. There is always some hope, especially for cowards. I was one of them, one of those cowardly or hopeful young men who still thought the government had something to offer.

Toward the end of 1961 I went to my first chicken farm to count chickens and to inventory the new properties that the State had taken over and to keep their books, where no one even knew the price of anything, or who had owned those properties before. Apart from that, the constant pilferage by the very officials who ran the farms made it impossible to update the books, whose figures never balanced. Only one thing was ever clear: that the losses were much greater than the earnings.

The farm was a huge, boring place where, amid the egg-laying hens and the incessant crowing of the roosters, the prevailing mood was one of tedium, typical of people working for miserable wages. It was a bit pathetic to see the farmers working land they no longer owned; they were no longer farmers, much less owners. They were now day laborers who did not care about the efficiency or quality of their work. Some other laborers commuted in trucks back to the towns where they lived. But it is not possible to do farm work or raise animals with people uninitiated in the mysteries of reproduction or the raising of crops. A plant knows who takes care of it with loving hands and who does not; it does not grow and bear fruit if tended by someone who is unskilled. Only people who have lived in the country, love nature, and know its secrets are qualified to cultivate the land. To farm the land is an act of love, a legendary act. There is a tacit complicity between the plant or seed and the person who is caring for it.

At that farm I made seventy-nine pesos a month, and gave part of it to my mother. At home there were still serious money problems, especially after the government took over my grandfather's store. They had promised to indemnify him with a monthly payment of thirty pesos, I believe, but countless forms had to be filled out and one never knew how long it would take. Once more, our constant companion was hunger.

—

People would come to the chicken farm begging permission to buy eggs or chickens, but the farm could not sell any. Some people offered to pay whatever was asked, but a "People's Farm" could not sell to individuals. Once a man drove up in a car, and when he was not allowed to make any purchases, he opened his mouth and said, "Look here, I have a cancer." His tongue looked awful, huge and purple. I think the manager of the farm sold him two chickens.

R A Ú L On weekends I would return to Holguín. The trip from the farm to Holguín was pretty complicated; the farm was in a remote area bordering the Sierra Maestra. I had to walk to a main road, and then hitchhike my way to Bayamo in any kind of vehicle I could get on. From there I had to take a bus, or whatever was available, to Holguín. I was lucky that day and near the park I found a boat. "Boats" were private taxis, still available then, that would load up as many passengers as possible. Later, in a long speech, Castro condemned the "boaters," saying that they belied socialism, that by earning thousands of pesos a day they would become millionaires and therefore counterrevolutionaries. A passenger in that boat was a fairly good-looking young man who started a conversation with me while the driver was looking for more customers to fill his boat. He said that his name was Raúl and he lived in Holguín but worked in Bayamo. When the taxi was full, Raúl sat pressed against me. It was getting dark. Raúl placed his hand on my leg and slowly let it slide up to my penis. I removed his hand violently and he, perhaps terrified that I would make a scene, did not look at me again or say another word during the entire trip. But as we were approaching Holguín, I took Raúl's hand and placed it on my penis. I think he was somewhat surprised; I was completely aroused, and he started to rub my penis right there in the car full of people. I do not know if they noticed what was going on and just enjoyed watching, but it was already pitch-dark, and there was no electricity along the highway. I ejaculated before we reached Holguín. I must confess it was a liberating experience. The moment had finally come, so long awaited and so long rejected by me. I remember Raúl, in the dark car, wiping my pants with his handkerchief.

At the Calixto García Park, which was the final stop for the taxi, I got off and so did Raúl. He tried to talk to me, perhaps to arrange a meeting or give me his telephone number or something, but I turned away and ran without stopping until I got home, which was pretty far away, in a neighborhood on the outskirts of Holguín called Vista Alegre.

When I arrived, my mother, my cousin Marisela (who was an invalid), my grandparents, and my aunts were all there. I was afraid they would read in my face what had happened. I was elated and had a feeling of joy that my mother did notice because, after all, there was nothing to be happy about. I was even in a joking mood, and ravenously hungry. In fact, I was content; I had found a fulfillment I had never experienced before.

The next afternoon I went to Central Park in Holguín, where all the young people usually gathered. I thought Raúl might be there, and after walking around the park two or three times, I saw him. He greeted me as if nothing had happened and invited me for a drink at a nearby bar on Liberty Street. This bar was a revelation to me, a bar just for homosexuals. It was crowded with men, some very macho, others extremely feminine, but the atmosphere was one of absolute camaraderie and fellowship. Such places still existed then in Holguín and in the rest of the Island. Later they disappeared.

My erotic encounters with Raúl took place every weekend at the local hotels. In those days two men could still rent a room in a hotel and spend the night together. The Petayo, Tauler, and Expreso hotels witnessed our adolescent passions. We enjoyed ourselves in those creaky beds that sometimes had dirty sheets; in our moments of passion we did not pay attention to such things.

My family started to notice that my absences were rather mysterious; if I came to Holguín only once a week and did not even spend the night at home, something was going on. I think that is when they began to suspect, though without any proof, that I was having a relationship with a man. Perhaps what bothered my mother most was my good mood when I returned home, that even my face seemed to have changed a little; it was smoother. My happiness was like an insult in that house filled with abandoned women and a somewhat embittered old couple. But my nights were intense and I could not hide my joy. I fell in love with Raúl, but he was not in love with me; for him I was a whim, a peasant boy whom he had initiated in sex, so to speak, considering that my childish sexual contacts with my cousin Orlando were just games, quite far from reaching a climax and all the mysteries of erotic love. Raúl tired of me though, and at some point he said or at least suggested as much. It was a hard blow for me; he had been my first lover, and the whole affair lasted only three or four months. In those days I had a different idea about sexual relations; I loved someone and I wanted that person to love me; I did not believe that one had to search, unceasingly, to find in other bodies what one body had already provided. I wanted a permanent love, wanted what perhaps my mother had always yearned for; that is, a man, a friend, someone we could belong to and who would be ours. But it was not to be, and I do not think this is possible, at least not in the gay world. The gay world is not monogamous. Almost by nature, by instinct, the tendency is to spread out to multiple relationships, quite often to promiscuity. It was normal for me not to understand this at the time; I had just lost my lover and felt completely disillusioned. Besides, my job at the farm was getting more and more boring, and now I lacked even the expectation of meeting Raúl and making love. I did not believe I could find another lover, nor did I even want one.

GOOD-BYE TO THE CHICKEN FARM

One day the Revolutionary government published an announcement calling for interested agricultural accountants to take part in a planning course at the University of Havana. We merely had to send in an application and, if approved, we would receive a telegram of acceptance. I received the telegram requesting me to report at the Hotel Nacional in a week. I had no second thoughts. I was leaving behind a farm full of noisy chickens; a world full of malcontent, smelly, ragged, underpaid people; a frustrated love; and Holguín, a town totally devoid of either spiritual or architectural beauty.

At the Hotel Nacional I learned that most of the young men who had graduated as agricultural accountants were there; all had opted for the planning course in the hope that it would provide a way out of the farms where they were working as accountants, some already as administrators. And with good reason: life in those farms was ghastly. Payday always turned into a big commotion, with workers claiming that they were being ripped off, that the timekeeper had not reported all their hours of work. By the way, a Russian technician was assigned to every one of those farms. Ours was Vladimir, a typical Soviet peasant; I don't know how much he knew about chickens, but he was the ideological director of the farm. Vladimir, I think, was completely chaste; he lived in a chalet with other Russians. In fact, the whole setup of the People's Farms was run by Russians; we did the work, but the Russians decided what was or was not to be done. Without speaking a word of Spanish, those Russians had quite often become the ruling class for the Cuban peasants.

At the Hotel Nacional we were scheduled to take entrance exams since only about fifty of us were to be selected. Fortunately, I was one of the fifty admitted to the planning course at the University of Havana. We were lodged at the Habana Libre Hotel. I was assigned to share a room with Pedro Morejón, a somewhat misshapen and extremely radical student, and Monzón, the handsome expert in pimping homosexuals. He continued with his life-style, telling me of his adventures with dancers from the Ballet Nacional de Cuba, who would pay him up to thirty pesos to suck his cock. It surprised him that he was paid so well to enjoy himself.

I was still faithful to Raúl's memory, and also very much afraid that my homosexuality might be discovered in Havana, although there was no excessive surveillance as yet. Classes at the university, moreover, took all day; there were classes in political economy, trigonometry, mathematics and planning. The course director was Pedro Marinello, who I think was either a nephew or a brother of Juan Marinello, the famous Communist Party leader. After some time Pedro Marinello disappeared; he was said to be a CIA agent, the label pinned on anyone who shows any disagreement with Fidel Castro's regime.

We had a great professor of economic geography who talked, nevertheless, about everything except the subject he was supposed to teach. He would tell us about his trips all over the world; to Africa and the desert, and how he tried to ride a camel that refused to move. He talked about his loves in Paris, of the women who had loved him, or about literature, with quotes from the great writers. He was a humanist, a man of artistic sensibility. His name was Juan Pérez de la Riva. He later lost favor and tried several times, unsuccessfully, to commit suicide. Born a millionaire, he had become a cadre of the Revolution, and one of the few in his family who accepted the social changes and remained in Cuba. He was permitted to visit his family in Paris, but on each trip he would jump from one of the bridges, always trying to kill himself. He was forever in love with his female students but never had any luck with them. His wife, Sara, was also a professor as well as a librarian at the university; I think she loved him and therefore put up with his infatuations. Finally he found a girl who fell in love with him, and then, suddenly, Pérez de la Riva got throat cancer; he no longer wanted to die, but die he did. He did not have to kill himself.

Fidel Castro's government discovered that it was not practical to have us stay at the former Havana Hilton, now Habana Libre, while there were much more distinguished guests to be put up in those rooms. Then again, most of us were peasants and did not know how to turn off a faucet or how to mix hot and cold water. Some rugs got soaked, some floors almost became swimming pools. Probably the furthest thing from Mr. Hilton's mind was someday to have his luxurious hotel full of peasants who did not even know how a shower head worked.

We were transferred to new lodgings at Rancho Boyeros, and from there we were taken every day by truck to the University of Havana. I saw that many of my fellow students had sexual relations with each other, and some were quite open about it; a sort of silent toleration existed. We discussed Sartre, and I recall lying on a cot and reading Virgilio Piñera's *Aire frío* [Cold Air] for the first time.

One of my best friends was Rafael Bolívar, son of Nancy Bolívar, an old socialist stalwart who, of course, was very much part of Castro's Revolution. Bolívar openly confessed to me that he was gay and told me about his adventures with young men at Rancho Boyeros, inviting me to join him. I flatly refused; I did not want to declare myself a homosexual, and I still thought that perhaps I could "regenerate," the word I used to convince myself that I had a defect that had to be overcome. But nature and my real self asserted themselves over my prejudices.

One day I went with Bolívar to the National Library. In the music department he introduced me to all his gay friends. Some of them propositioned me; I was shocked and rejected them. Yet the following evening I returned to the Library.

The Revolutionary government not only wanted us to study "planning"; it also made us work so that in some way we could pay for our classes. I was to work for INRA, the National Institute for Agrarian Reform, which occupied a building erected in Batista's time, as was the Palace of the Revolution, the National Library, and every other building around Revolutionary Square, where Fidel Castro delivered his speeches.

I started working as an accountant in one of the offices of INRA. At first, the director was Carlos Rafael Rodríguez, and later, Castro himself. Rafael Bolívar* and I rented a room in a boardinghouse not too far away. Men slept there three or four to a room; it was like a place in one of the picaresque novels of Quevedo or Cervantes. There was a continuous flow of people, in and out; transients who could be easily picked up at the corner and brought home for sex. Sometimes the erotic sounds coming from Bolívar's bed made sleep impossible. He would always find some gay near home and spend the night gasping and warbling in the most fantastic manner.

* Some names have been changed.

We were always hungry, because on seventy-nine pesos a month we could not afford to have both lunch and dinner on the same day. So we would get up at night and secretly raid Cusa's refrigerator. Cusa was the owner of our boardinghouse. She quickly found out and put a lock on the refrigerator, but we were able to pick the lock and eat whatever we found inside. Finally, Cusa had the refrigerator fitted with little wheels so she could hide it in her room. Cusa was a huge old white woman who could easily pull that giant refrigerator into her room every night.

Our lack of money also forced us to move frequently. I remember moving eleven times in one year. It was 1963, and the persecution of homosexuals was getting worse. Many of Rafael Bolívar's friends had already been sent to one of the UMAP [Military Units for Aid to Production] concentration camps, but I was not yet a confirmed homosexual. I had no sexual involvement with anybody and was very repressed; all alone, listening to the heavy breathing and gasps of pleasure coming from Rafael and his *partenaire*, I masturbated.

In Cuba we had a typical "cruising" routine, no different perhaps from that of any other country. You walked a few blocks and a young man would follow; you would stop briefly at a corner and he would stop also. You started walking again and so would the young man. Finally, a match, the time, the weather, or the usual question of whether you lived nearby. I met a young man this way and took him to my room. He was good-looking, about eighteen to twenty-one, and more experienced than I myself was. Up to that moment, in my few sexual encounters I had been the active partner, but this young man was not willing to submit. He wanted to "possess" me, and being really so masterful, he did just that and I liked it. His name was Miguel, and we began to see each other often. He even had a car, which was not easy in those days, and we visited friends or drove to the countryside. A hotel room for two men had become very difficult in Havana.

We made love wildly, and Miguel always took the active part. I had switched from possessor to possessed and enjoyed it fully.

Through Miguel I became acquainted with a circle of performers and entertainers in Havana, such as the big-time whores who danced at the Tropicana nightclub show or at Nocturno, another cabaret located then where the Coppelia ice cream parlor is now. Those women, some of whom were very beautiful, had liaisons with high military commanders or government officials, and could get an apartment or a house near the Malecón Shore Drive or in Miramar. I remember a party at the home of one of these women, on the feast day of Saint Lazarus. It was a huge party, and all sorts of performers were there. Even ballerina Alicia Alonso came and touched the huge, brightly lit statue of Saint Lazarus. Famous singers such as Elena Burke were there too. Miguel was well known in that crowd, and I felt sort of strange being the lover of such a popular person.

At night we would go to some cabaret, either the Tropicana or any of the nightclubs at the Capri, Habana Libre, or Riviera hotels. Martha Estrada was the big star of the moment and, of course, Miguel was her friend.

We spent New Year's Eve 1963 together. At midnight Miguel embraced me, and weeping, he said, "It's hard to believe that Fidel has been in power for four years already!" The poor fool! He thought four years were too many. He was finally arrested and taken to a UMAP concentration camp. I never saw him again, nor have I heard of him since my exile. Sometimes I think they killed him at the concentration camp. He was short-tempered, undisciplined, and loved life.

After losing Miguel I went back to cruising on the streets of Havana. One day I met a well-mannered older man who took me to his home. His name was Luis Gómez and he was a painter. He became my lover, and I switched back to being the active sexual partner, which is what Luis wanted, though I felt good either way if I liked the person. Luis was sort of a father figure for me; he opened new windows in my appreciation of art, painting, literature. He lived with a man who had been his lover and was now his friend: a second-rate playwright in favor at the time because he had written some monotonous pieces praising the political system. His name was Néstor Bardo.

I stayed with Luis and Néstor. Luis also had a painter's studio at La Casa de las Américas, where I visited him, and there, among the canvases, we made love, only a few steps away from the office of Haydée Santamaría. She ended up shooting herself, but at the time she ruled in that building.

T H E   L I B R A R Y I was still writing poetry, taking advantage of the typewriters at INRA in those free moments that always occur where bureaucratic activities take place. I filled pages and pages with poems that I think were really bad. I showed them to Luis, who was knowledgeable in literary matters, and he confessed that the poems were, in fact, horrible. But that did not stop me from writing.

In 1963 the National Library organized a storytelling competition. During my lunch period I would always go and do some reading at the Library, which was close to INRA, and I saw the notice. Anyone who wished to participate had to memorize a story by some well-known author and tell it. The committee entrusted with the selection would choose on the basis of the storyteller's skill. I looked for a story that would not take more than five minutes in the telling (which was the maximum time allowed), but did not find any. So I decided to write one myself. I named it "The Empty Shoes."

It was only two pages long and took three and a half minutes to read. I went before the committee, consisting of five very respectable-looking men and an old lady who was blinking all the time, and told my story. They were impressed, not by my skill in telling the story but by the story itself. They asked me who the author was, and I told them that I had written it the day before. I pulled the paper with the story out of my pocket and gave it to one of them.

The next day I received a telegram saying that they were very much interested in talking with me and would I please come to the National Library. It was signed by a man named Eliseo Diego. I went, and met Eliseo Diego. I also met the blinking old lady, María Teresa Freyre de Andrade, who was the director of the National Library. Cintio Vitier and his wife, Fina García Marruz, were also present. They constituted a sort of cultural aristocracy. At the time, all of them (including Salvador Bueno) were considered somewhat unsympathetic to the government, and María Teresa, who was a magnanimous woman, was protecting them. She had given them jobs at the Library and there they worked, or pretended to work, and while drawing a salary, they could go on writing their poetry.

María Teresa then instructed the assistant director of the National Library, a huge and butchy woman by the name of Maruja Iglesias Tauler, to contact the director of my section at INRA and arrange for my transfer to the Library. To transfer an employee from one place to another involved complicated bureaucratic maneuvering, even in those days. Fortunately, Maruja Iglesias was very adept at such formalities. I think today she is a high official in the Ministry of Foreign Affairs. This woman, by the way, had been the owner of the Tauler Hotel in Holguín, where Raúl and I used to make passionate love.

The transfer went through and suddenly I left Fidel Castro's sphere, the accounts, the numbers, the adding machines, and the endless list of names and figures that had to be repeated and corrected. I had joined the magical world of the National Library, which still enjoyed an aura of splendor under the leadership of María Teresa Freyre de Andrade.

This woman belonged to an aristocratic family of old revolutionary tradition. She had been educated in Paris and had created the National Library, which functioned splendidly under her direction. My transfer there was decisive for my literary education. My job consisted in looking for the books people requested, but there was always time to read. Moreover, on the nights when I had guard duty, by then a requirement at all work centers, I enjoyed the magical pleasure of picking any book at random. Walking among those shelves, I saw, radiating from each book, the scintillating promise of a unique mystery.

Eliseo Diego tried to direct me in my reading of children's books, and Cintio Vitier told me to stay away from the works of Virgilio Piñera and other similar authors. I was subjected to a refined and gentle censorship. At that time they were all against the government and said terrible things about Fidel Castro and the tyranny he had imposed; they wanted to leave the country, but they either had too many children or were not able to for other reasons. Eliseo Diego said: "The day I have to write an ode in praise of Fidel Castro or of this Revolution, I will stop being a writer."

Some time later, however, both Cintio and Eliseo became spokesmen for Fidel Castro's regime. Eliseo has written not one but dozens of odes in homage to Fidel Castro and his Revolution. Cintio has done the same, and perhaps worse. Maybe that is why they are no longer writers. But in those days, they were sensitive men who undoubtedly influenced my literary development. Eliseo gave me a copy of his book *En la Calzada de Jesús del Monte* [On Jesús del Monte Avenue], which I consider among the best in Cuban poetry. Cintio was a critic with a rather monastic approach, but he was a man of culture and it was still worthwhile to talk with him. Fina was a much better poet than her husband, but she always assumed a subordinate role to him, in accordance with the Spanish Catholic tradition. She was the patient, submissive, resigned, chaste woman; the one who shone was Cintio, while she just stayed in the background as the obedient wife.

I used the Library to the utmost. María Teresa, in her wisdom, required only five hours of work. My working day started at one, but I would come in at eight and, taking advantage of the empty halls, write. There I wrote *Celestino antes del alba* [Celestino Before Dawn, published in the United States as *Singing from the Well*]. I read a great many of the books on the shelves in that huge library.

But things began to change, for the worse of course. It was said that the National Library was a center of ideological corruption, that María Teresa was not strong enough and the place had been taken over by lesbians. I do not know whether it was true or not, but rumor had it that María Teresa herself was a lesbian, along with all the women who worked there. Some of them actually did appear to be rather masculine, but I think their lesbianism was more platonic than anything else. They would meet at Maruja Iglesias's rather luxurious apartment, or at the home of María Elena Ross (married to a relative of Fidel Castro) and have some refreshments, enjoy the swimming pool, or discuss the literary idol of the time: Alejo Carpentier and his novel *El siglo de las luces* [published in English as *Explosion in a Cathedral*].

And then one day a big scandal erupted at the Library. Two well-known women employees had been caught in the ladies' room, undressed, and making love. The women were brought before María Teresa, who pardoned them, saying that this was none of her business and concerned only their husbands, and that there was nothing for her to do. Precisely for being so generous, María Teresa could not avoid having more and more "enemies" infiltrate the Library: resentful people who could not forgive her for the fact that they owed their jobs to her. One of them was María Luisa Gil, who hated María Teresa with a passion simply because she wanted the job of director for herself. She was a Stalinist Spaniard, married to an old stalwart of the Communist Party. She was filled with bitterness, which she covered up with an apparent sweetness. Little by little those enemies started to make headway, saying that María Teresa was a lesbian, an aristocrat, and a counterrevolutionary, and they finally managed to get her replaced. Lisandro Otero was the one to tell María Teresa that she had been ousted. Like a good partisan custodian and enemy of culture, he took great pleasure in firing the person who had created that institution. The new director was none other than a captain of Fidel Castro's police, Captain Sidroc Ramos. María Teresa left the Library in tears.

A few days later I decided the Library was no longer a place for me either. Any book that could be deemed to be "ideological diversionism" disappeared immediately. Of course, any book dealing in any way with sexual deviation also vanished. An eight-hour workday schedule was introduced, which became ten hours because we had two hours for lunch and there was no place to go.

Fortunately for me, about this time I received a literary award for my novel *Singing from the Well*, which I had submitted to the [1965] competition sponsored by UNEAC [Cuban Writers and Artists Union]. The novel was published sometime later. One of the members of UNEAC came to interview me. He had liked my novel very much, and not only interviewed me but asked me to share his bed as well. I did not appreciate his offer; he was not my type. But in those days I was neither monogamous nor selective. His name was Rafael Arnés and he lived in the Vedado [an affluent suburb of Havana]. I stayed with him for several months. He had a sense of humor, was not an altogether bad poet, and in those days still had a rebellious spirit. This was the period between 1964 and 1966, when young men were persecuted for having long hair or wearing tight pants. He had rather long hair himself and wrote an ode to my hair, in which he criticized the current inquisitorial attitude toward long-haired youths.

In 1966 I submitted my second novel, *El mundo alucinante* [This Hallucinatory World, published in the United States as *The Ill-Fated Peregrinations of Fray Servando*] to the UNEAC competition, where *Singing from the Well* had won first honorable mention. My new novel won second place again. The jury was made up of Virgilio Piñera, Alejo Carpentier, José Antonio Portuondo, and Félix Pita Rodríguez—more or less the same group as when I received the previous award, except that the first jury included Camila Henríquez Ureña, an exceptional woman who fought hard to give first prize to *Singing from the Well* while Alejo Carpentier and José Antonio Portuondo, a longtime militant in the Communist Party, applied their influence to have the prize given to *Vivir en Candonga* by Ezequiel Vieta. *Vivir en Candonga* was an apologia of Fidel's struggle in the Sierra Maestra and a denunciation of the so-called escapist writers who, according to the author, spent their time chasing butterflies with their hats, in the fields around Bayamo and elsewhere.

Now Carpentier and Portuondo refused to award first prize to *El mundo alucinante*. Apparently there was no other novel to merit the prize, so they decided not to award it and to give my retelling of the story of Fray Servando first honorable mention.

At the awards ceremony I met Virgilio Piñera and he said to me point-blank: "Portuondo and Alejo Carpentier deprived you of first prize. I voted for you. Here is my phone number, call me; we have to work on that novel. It looks as if you typed it in one night." He was almost right. The deadline for the competition had kept getting closer, and with my eight-hour job at the Library I did not have much time. I would lock myself in my room and write thirty or forty pages at a stretch.

THE CUBAN
BOOK INSTITUTE With

two of my novels (although not yet published) winning awards, and thanks to the influence of my then lover Rafael Arnés, I was able to get a job at the Cuban Book Institute, directed by Armando Rodríguez. He had a lover, and by the way, I have never met a more strikingly handsome man than Armando's lover. His name was Héctor. He was one of those men who radiated such overwhelming beauty that it was impossible to continue writing after he had passed through the hallways. I do not know how Armando, an important official of the regime, managed to hold on to such a handsome lover without inciting the envious, who did not have access to Héctor, to disrupt that relationship or to arrange to have Armando removed from his position. But Armando was a friend of Fidel Castro's, just like Alberto Guevara, whose scandalous homosexual life was well known all over, especially in Havana. These people never had to face the consequences of their behavior, while others had to pay such a high price. At the height of his splendor, Héctor died in an accident while riding his motorcycle.

THE FOUR
CATEGORIES
OF GAYS Noting the substantial differences

among homosexuals, I established some categories. First there was the *dog collar gay*. This was the boisterous homosexual who was constantly being arrested at the baths or the beach. As I saw it, the system had provided him with a permanent "collar" around his neck. All the police had to do was hook him by the collar and take him to one of the forced-labor camps. A typical example of this kind of gay was Tomasito La Goyesca, a young man who worked at the National Library, to whom I had given that nickname because he looked like a figure out of a Goya painting; he was a grotesque dwarf, walked like a spider, and had a boundless sexual appetite.

After the collar gay came the *common gay*. This is the type of homosexual who has made his commitments; who goes to the film club, writes a poem now and then, never takes great risks, and sips tea with his friends. A typical example of this category was my then friend Reinaldo Gómez Ramos. Common gays generally have relations with other gays and never get to know a real man.

Next after the common gay was the *closet gay*. Nobody knew he was gay. He married, had children, and then went to the baths surreptitiously, still wearing the wedding ring his wife had given him. Closet gays were hard to spot; many times they were the ones who censured other gays. There are thousands in this category, but one of the most typical is the dramatist Nicolás Díaz, who once, in an act of desperation, stuck a light bulb up his anus; this man, who was a militant in the Communist Youth Organization, had no way of explaining how the bulb ended up in that portion of his anatomy. His expulsion from the organization caused a great scandal.

Then came the *royal gay*, a species unique to communist countries. The royal gay is the one who, because of close contact with the Maximum Leader or especially important work with the state security apparatus, or any similar reason, can afford to be openly gay, to have a scandalous life, and at the same time to hold an important public office, travel freely at home, leave the country and come back, cover himself with jewels and clothes, and even have a private chauffeur. Alberto Guevara is a prime example of this type of gay.

VIRGILIO PIÑERA

Virgilio Piñera, in spite of his extensive published work and all his renown, fell under the category of collar gay; in other words, he had to pay a high price for being homosexual. He was picked up at the beginning of the Revolution and imprisoned at El Morro. He was released thanks to the intervention of highly influential people (among whom, I believe, was Carlos Franqui). After that, he was always treated with suspicion and constantly censored and persecuted. As a collar gay he was a really genuine person and one willing to pay the price of being genuine.

I would visit Virgilio Piñera at his home at seven in the morning. He was a man who worked incessantly. He would get up at six, make coffee, and then we would work on my novel *El mundo alucinante*. We would sit facing each other. The first thing he said was, "Don't think I am doing this because of some sexual interest; I do it for reasons of intellectual honesty. You have written a good novel, but there are some things that need fixing." Virgilio, sitting there in front of me, would read from a copy of the novel, and where he thought a comma should be added or a word changed, he would tell me. I will be forever grateful to Virgilio for that lesson; more than a lesson in writing, it was a lesson in editing. This was really important for a wildly impulsive writer such as I have been, lacking a good college background. He was my college professor as well as my friend.

Virgilio wrote nonstop, although he did not seem to take literature very seriously. He hated to have his work praised; he also despised high rhetoric. He detested Alejo Carpentier with a passion. He was a homosexual, an atheist, and an anticommunist. He had dared, at the time of the Republic, to praise the complete poetry of Emilio Ballagas, which was basically homosexual. Virgilio had dared to refute Cintio Vitier's foreword when Vitier tried to cover that profoundly sensual and erotic poetry under a cloak of religion. Virgilio expressed it clearly. Vitier never forgave Virgilio for his daring approach.

Around 1957 Virgilio parted from the literary magazine *Orígenes* and, together with José Rodríguez Feo, started another one, almost entirely oriented to homosexuals and much more irreverent, right under the eyes of Batista's reactionary and bourgeois dictatorship. The first thing Virgilio did in the new magazine, *Ciclón*, was to publish *The Hundred and Twenty Journeys from Sodom and Gomorrah* by the Marquis de Sade.

From the start of the Revolution, Virgilio was already marked for his homosexuality and his anticommunist reputation. He wrote and published in *Ciclón* "El muñeco" [The Puppet], a lucid anticommunist story of dire foreboding. This story was systematically deleted by the Fidel Castro government from all anthologies and collections of stories by Virgilio Piñera.

Virgilio was also ugly, gaunt and ungainly, unromantic. He did not take part in typical literary hypocrisies of the Vitier kind, where reality is always shrouded by a sort of violet cloud. Virgilio saw the Island with terrible, desolate clarity; his poem "La Isla en peso" [The Island Up in the Air] is one of the masterpieces of Cuban literature.

During the time of the Republic and, according to Virgilio, as a result of poverty and the cultural restlessness in the country, he emigrated to Argentina, where he lived for more than ten years, working at minor bureaucratic jobs, as sort of a Kafka of underdevelopment. There he met the Polish writer Witold Gombrowicz. Both emigrés, they became friends and buddies in cruising and erotic adventures. Gombrowicz, as Virgilio used to say, was very handsome then; to survive he became a male prostitute at the Buenos Aires baths, letting himself be fucked for a few coins. According to Virgilio, on one occasion his friend met an Argentine with a huge penis; the man had already paid and insisted on fucking him and, of course, he did. But, as Virgilio told it, the man ruptured Gombrowicz's anus to such an extent that he came home all bloody. Virgilio filled the bathtub with hot water, took the clothes off his friend, and got him into the tub to ease his pain. Virgilio said Gombrowicz spent two days in the tub until his wounds started healing.

I think this friendship influenced Virgilio considerably, making him more daring, more irreverent. Or perhaps they influenced each other. Their lives were similar, uprooted and grim; they did not believe in institutionalized culture, or in taking culture too seriously, in contrast to Jorge Luis Borges who, even then, was already the most important Argentine writer. They made fun of Borges, perhaps a little cruelly, but they had their reasons. When Gombrowicz finally left Argentina to settle in Europe, someone asked him what advice he would give to the Argentines. He answered, "Kill Borges." It was, of course, a sarcastic reply; when Borges died, Argentina stopped existing. Gombrowicz's reply was his revenge for all he had suffered in Argentina.

According to Guillermo Cabrera Infante, Virgilio was unlucky in love. I do not happen to think so. Virgilio had a preference for black men, and I am witness to the fact that he had opportunities to enjoy relations with formidable blacks. One day a black man with a cart full of lemons walked by, offering them for sale even though such street vendors and their cries were already illegal. Virgilio brought him up to his apartment, bought all the lemons, and then they made love. I think that black man kept coming back with the pretext of bringing more lemons, and Virgilio always took him to his room.

Another black man with whom Virgilio had a pretty deep sexual relationship was a cook who, according to Virgilio, had a huge penis. Virgilio enjoyed being fucked by him even while the cook kept moving pots and pans around and did not stop cooking. Virgilio was really a fragile gay, who could be impaled and held up by that powerful Negro's penis.

Even before the Revolution, Virgilio's sex life in Cuba had

been intense. He had a house in Guanabo Beach and frequented the male brothel that José Rodríguez Feo operated in the town. It was a brothel where strong men worked as bartenders and, on the side, engaged in such other activities as clients might request. Tomasito La Goyesca also worked there.

Rodríguez Feo belonged to a wealthy family that had left for the United States after the Revolution took over. He gave his properties up to the Revolution and stayed, perhaps feeling that he would be regarded as an important person. In fact, he ended up becoming an informer for State Security, a culture policeman, and had a small apartment next to Virgilio's. Rodríguez Feo, mediocre and degraded, had refused to talk to him when Virgilio lost favor with the regime, and did not even attend his funeral.

Rodríguez Feo and Virgilio shared the same balcony to the street. The story goes that Rodríguez Feo once had several friends over and Virgilio went to the balcony to put something out to dry. When someone asked, "Is that Virgilio Piñera?" Rodríguez Feo replied, "No, that *was* Virgilio Piñera." That is why he did not attend the funeral; once Piñera lost favor with the Castro regime, he was dead for Rodríguez Feo.

These things happen because under a sinister political system a lot of people turn sinister as well. Not many can escape that wild, all-embracing evil which destroys those who are not part of it. Before the Revolution, Rodríguez Feo was a sort of Maecenas; he financed Piñera's *Cuentos fríos* [*Cold Tales*]; he bankrolled *Orígenes* magazine, and later *Ciclón*. Of course, there were personal interests and small vanities on his part, but there was also generosity. Other Cuban millionaires never paid for the publication of a magazine or helped writers.

LEZAMA LIMA The other Cuban writer besides Virgilio with whom I had a great friendship was José Lezama Lima. We became acquainted in connection with the publication of my novel *Singing from the Well*. I had seen him before at UNEAC; he was a huge, corpulent man, with a big cross on a chain always protruding from one of his pants side pockets. His showing off that cross at UNEAC, a center of communist propaganda, was undoubtedly a provocation. Fina García Marruz let me know one day that Lezama wanted to meet me; I never would have dared to call him because I was terrified by a man of such vast culture. I had met Alejo Carpentier, but it had been a distressing experience; he was a man who manipulated information, dates, styles, and numbers like a refined but dehumanized computer. Meeting Lezama was an entirely different experience. Here was a man who had made literature his very life; here was one of the most erudite human beings I had ever met. He did not use his knowledge to show off; it was simply something to hang on to for survival, something vital that fired his imagination and at the same time reflected on anyone who came close to him. Lezama had the extraordinary gift of radiating creative vitality. After talking with him I would go home and sit down at my typewriter to write, because it was impossible to listen to that man without being inspired. In him, wisdom and innocence met. He had a special talent for giving meaning to the life of others.

Reading was Lezama's first passion. He also possessed the very Cuban gifts of laughter and gossip. Lezama's laughter was unforgettable, contagious; it prevented you from feeling totally unhappy. He could switch from the most esoteric conversation to the gossip of the moment; he could interrupt his discourse on Greek culture to ask whether it was true that José Triana was no longer a sodomist. He could also dignify the commonplace and make it extraordinary.

Virgilio and Lezama were very different but had one thing in common: their intellectual integrity. Neither was capable of endorsing a book for the sake of political gain or out of cowardice, and they were steadfast in refusing to promote the communist regime. They were, above all, honest toward their work and honest with themselves.

From a literary standpoint, the publishing in 1966 of Lezama Lima's *Paradiso* was a truly heroic event. I do not think Cuba had ever witnessed the publication of a novel so explicitly homosexual, so extraordinarily complex and rich in imagery, so idiosyncratically Cuban, so Latin American, and at the same time, so unique.

Virgilio Piñera also accomplished the heroic by submitting his theater piece *Dos viejos pánicos* [Two Old Terrors] to the 1968 competition of La Casa de las Américas. This work mirrors the fears and terrors of living under the regime of Fidel Castro.

Both writers, of course, suffered ostracism and censorship, and lived in a sort of internal exile. But neither of them allowed his life to become bitter or resentful, and neither stopped writing, not for a moment. They worked until death claimed them, knowing that most likely their writings would end up in the hands of State Security, and that perhaps the only person to read them would be the policeman assigned to filing or destroying them.

Lezama's life centered in his home; there, at 164 Trocadero Street, he would officiate like a magician, like a strange priest. He would talk, and whoever listened, like it or not, was completely changed. Virgilio preferred to spread his vitality all over Havana; he loved literary gatherings away from home, conversations at the corner café or on buses. His sexual tastes weren't as particular as Lezama's. Virgilio liked tough men, blacks, and truck drivers, while Lezama's preferences were Hellenic: the extremes of Greek beauty and, of course, adolescents. Virgilio diligently converted his sexual needs into practical reality, while Lezama was much more inhibited, perhaps because he had lived with his mother for so many years.

On one occasion Lezama and Virgilio met by chance in a sort of men's brothel in Old Havana. Lezama said to Virgilio: "So you come here to hunt the boar," and Virgilio answered, "No, I just came to fuck a Negro."

Both men had European influences, especially French. They both admired French literature. Their differences, however, were manifold: Lezama was a Catholic humanist, Virgilio an atheist. Even so, both felt such a great love for the Island, and especially for Havana, that it was impossible for them to leave it. Once, Lezama landed a job in the city of Santa Clara; all he had to do for a while was give some lectures. He returned the following day because it was impossible for him to be away from Havana. At the beginning of the Revolution, Virgilio could have stayed abroad; he already knew about the persecution of homosexuals and had been in jail himself. Nevertheless, he returned to the Island. To quote Virgilio: "The cursed condition of being surrounded by water on all sides" cast a spell that these men were unable to break.

I was privileged to have the friendship of both men at the same time. When Rodríguez Feo distanced himself from *Orígenes* magazine and *Ciclón* was born, Lezama and Virgilio became somewhat estranged, but their greatness brought them together again. Their intellectual integrity transcended any personal differences. The publication of *Paradiso* earned Lezama official repudiation from the government and a ban on all his later works, as well as *Paradiso*, which had an almost clandestine circulation in Cuba and was never reprinted. Virgilio, who was no close friend of Lezama then, was the first to acknowledge the literary worth of that novel and the first to praise it openly, even before Julio Cortázar's famous article.

Lezama was also able to acknowledge the great poet and dramatist that Virgilio had always been. On the occasion of

Virgilio's sixtieth birthday, Lezama wrote one of his most profound poems, "Virgilio Piñera Reaches the Age of Sixty."

In the end the two men were drawn together, perhaps because of the persecution, discrimination, and censorship both suffered. Virgilio used to visit Lezama every week. Lezama had married a friend of the family, María Luisa Bautista, as his mother, moments before her death, had begged him to do. María Luisa was an extraordinary woman, brave, refined, and very outspoken; she would insult government officials who came to request information on Lezama, and she typed his handwritten manuscripts (he never learned to type). This woman came to love Lezama deeply, even though theirs was not a sexual relationship.

María Luisa, because of the mystery of friendship, of shared loneliness, of mutual devotion, of survival in terrible times, would go out with a large white plastic handbag to stand in food lines all over Havana, in order to find Lezama something to eat. He would say, "There goes the tousled doe." She would always return with some cream cheese or yogurt—something to satisfy the voracious appetite of that man. In the evening, at nine, Maria Luisa would make tea; she always managed to find some, God knows where. If the tea was a minute late, Virgilio would remind her, "María Luisa, are we having tea?" There was a symbolic significance in the meetings of those three people in that already somewhat run-down house, which would sometimes get flooded. It was the end of an era, of a life-style, of a way to perceive and transcend reality by artistic creativity, always faithful to art itself, regardless of circumstances. It was also, in a way, a secret conspiracy to give one another the essential support they needed.

But when María Luisa turned her back to make tea in the kitchen, Virgilio and Lezama would share their more or less erotic adventures, which were, by then, more platonic than anything else. Lezama, for instance, would confess to Virgilio that Manuel Pereira, the novelist and Alberto Guevara's lover, would visit him and sit on his lap, sometimes bringing on a powerful erection. And Virgilio would tell Lezama that he was having a love affair with one of the black actors who were part of the cast of Virgilio's drama *Electra Garrigó*. When María Luisa returned, the conversation would stop.

Once I mentioned to Eliseo Diego my admiration for the work of Virgilio Piñera. Eliseo looked at me and said exactly these words: "Virgilio Piñera is the devil." When I became Virgilio's friend, I realized that in Cuba there was only one intellectual whose innocence might surpass Virgilio Piñera's. That man was Lezama Lima.

At the National Library in 1969, Lezama gave a reading of perhaps one of the most extraordinary essays of Cuban literature, under the title of "Confluences." It reaffirmed the creative force, the love of language, the struggle for an integrated image against all those who opposed it. A sense of beauty is always dangerous and antagonistic to any dictatorship because it implies a realm extending beyond the limits that a dictatorship can impose on human beings. Beauty is a territory that escapes the control of the political police. Being independent and outside of their domain, beauty is so irritating to dictators that they attempt to destroy it whichever way they can. Under a dictatorship, beauty is always a dissident force, because a dictatorship is itself unaesthetic, grotesque; to a dictator and his agents, the attempt to create beauty is an escapist or reactionary act. That is why Lezama, as well as Virgilio, ended their lives in ostracism, abandoned by their friends.

Lezama himself finally forbade Rafael Arnés and Pablo Armando Fernández to visit him. He understood that these men were not poets but vulgar policemen who came to pry from him any kind of information that might earn them a little trip abroad.

MY GENERATION

Besides my friendship with Lezama and Virgilio, I had contacts with many writers of my generation and enjoyed more or less secret get-togethers where we would read our latest works to one another. We wrote incessantly and would read anywhere: in abandoned houses, in parks, at beaches, while walking over rocks. We would read not only our own works but also those of great writers. There was Delfín Prats, talented and satanic; Coco Salas, misshapen in body and soul; René Ariza, somewhat crazed, though less so than nowadays; José Hernández (Pepe el Loco), whose talent was as big and unrestrained as his madness; José Mario, who had just been released from the concentration camp; and there were Luis Rogelio Nogueras, Guillermo Rosales, and many more. We would read aloud for everyone to enjoy. These men, my generation, would read the poems, banned under Fidel Castro, of Jorge Luis Borges, and we recited from memory the poems of Octavio Paz. Our generation, the generation born in the forties, has been a lost generation, destroyed by the communist regime.

The best part of our youth was wasted cutting sugarcane, doing useless guard duty, attending countless speeches (in which the same litany was repeated over and over), in trying to get around repressive laws; in the incessant struggle to get a decent pair of jeans or a pair of shoes, in hoping to rent a house at the beach to read poetry or have our erotic adventures, in a struggle to escape the constant persecution and arrests by the police.

I remember that once during a Varadero Song Festival, as soon as we arrived at the beach, we were picked up by the police and sent back to Havana; many foreign visitors were expected, and apparently our presence was not welcome on display for such prominent guests.

What did happen to most of the talented young men of my generation? Nelson Rodríguez, for example, author of *El regalo* [The Gift], was executed. Delfín Prats, one of the best poets among us, became a dehumanized alcoholic; Pepe el Loco, the bold chronicler, ended up killing himself; Luis Rogelio Nogueras, a talented poet, recently died under suspicious circumstances, it being unclear whether from AIDS or at the hands of Castro's police; Norberto Fuentes, storyteller, was first persecuted, then converted into an agent of State Security, and is now out of favor; Guillermo Rosales, an excellent novelist, is wasting away in a home for the handicapped in Miami. And what about me? After having lived thirty-seven years in Cuba I am now in exile, waiting for an imminent death but still suffering all the sorrows of exile. Why this relentless cruelty against us? Why this cruelty against all of us who did not want to be part of the banal tradition and dull daily existence so characteristic of our Island?

I think greatness and dissidence have never been well tolerated by our governments nor by a great many of our people. It is not in our tradition. The objective has always been to reduce everything to the lowest, most vulgar level. Those who would not conform to that accepted level of mediocrity have always been looked at with hostility and have always been pilloried: José Martí had to live in exile, and even there he was persecuted and harassed by many of his fellow exiles. He returned to Cuba not only to fight but to die. Even Félix Varela, one of the most important Cuban intellectuals of the nineteenth century, had to live in exile until his death. Cirilo Villaverde was condemned to death in Cuba and had to escape from jail to save his life, and in exile tried to reconstruct the Island in his novel *Cecilia Valdés*. Heredia was also banished, morally destroyed, and dead at thirty-six. He had in vain requested from the dictator of the moment an official permit for a return visit to the Island. Lezama and Piñera also died under suspicious circumstances and absolute censorship. Yes, we have always been victims of the dictator of the moment, which may be not only part of our Cuban tradition but also part of our Latin American tradition, the Hispanic heritage we have had to suffer.

Ours is a national history of betrayals, uprisings, desertions, conspiracies, riots, coups d'etat; all of them provoked by infinite ambition, abuse, despair, false pride, and envy. Even Christopher Columbus, on his third trip, after he had discovered all of America for Europe, was returned to Spain in chains. Two attitudes, two personalities, always seem to be in conflict throughout our history: on the one hand, the incurable rebels, lovers of freedom and therefore of creativity and experimentation; and on the other, the power-hungry opportunists and demagogues, and thus purveyors of dogma, crime, and the basest of ambitions. These attitudes have recurred over time: General Tacón against Heredia, Martínez Campos against José Martí, Fidel Castro against Lezama Lima and Virgilio Piñera; always the same rhetoric, the same speeches, always the drums of militarism stifling the rhythm of poetry and life.

Dictators and authoritarian regimes can destroy writers in two ways: by persecuting them or by showering them with official favors. In Cuba, of course, those who opted for favors also perished and in an even more deplorable and undignified manner: People of unquestionable talent, once they embraced the new dictatorship, never wrote anything worthwhile again. Whatever happened to Alejo Carpentier's work after he completed *El siglo de las luces*? His writing became slipshod, dreadful, impossible to read to the end. What happened to the poetry of Nicolás Guillén? After the sixties his work became irrelevant or, worse, deplorable. What happened to the brilliant essays, though always somewhat reactionary, of the Cintio Vitier of the fifties? What happened to the great poetry written by Eliseo Diego in the forties?

None of them are what they used to be; they are dead

although, unfortunately for UNEAC and even for themselves, they are still living.

I now see the political history of my country as I saw the river of my childhood, which dragged everything along with a deafening roar; a turbulent river that has been gradually destroying us all.

In spite of everything, youth in the sixties managed to conspire, not against the regime but in favor of life. We still had clandestine meetings at the beaches, at somebody's house, or we simply enjoyed a night of love with a passing recruit, a female scholarship student, or some desperate young man looking for a way to escape the repression. For a time, a great sexual freedom developed in Cuba, although not openly. Everybody was desperate to make love and young men grew long hair (of course, they were pursued by menopausal women with long scissors), wore the tight clothes and embroidered patches fashionable in the free world, listened to the Beatles, and spoke of sexual liberation. A great number of us young people would get together at Coppelia ice cream parlor, at the Capri cafeteria or the Malecón Sea Wall, and would enjoy the tropical nights in spite of the patrol car sirens.

A T R I P Hiram Prado and I undertook a somewhat difficult trip through the Island and went as far as Guantánamo. We traveled in a run-down train, which stopped in every town and sometimes backed up to the point of departure. At one of the stops we saw a lot of oranges scattered on the ground, possibly fallen off a truck. We jumped through the train window, eager to eat those oranges; we were ravenously hungry. There was a fierce struggle with all the other passengers who had also jumped from the train, just as desperate to get at the fruit.

The train was full of recruits; everybody was sexually aroused and having sex in the bathrooms, under the seats, anyplace. Hiram used his foot to masturbate a recruit who seemed to be sleeping on the floor. I was lucky enough to be able to use both hands.

It was an extraordinary trip. In Santiago de Cuba we would spend the night under bridges and in culverts. One night we went to sleep on the rear seat of a bus at an intercity terminal, assuming the bus would be there at least two or three days. When we woke up the next day, we were in El Caney, many miles from Santiago, and we had no idea how to get back.

A certain erotic rebelliousness pervaded our youth. I see myself naked under a bridge in Santiago de Cuba with a young recruit, also completely naked, while cars crossed over the bridge at full speed, shining their headlights on us. Hiram Prado left Santiago in the back of a truck with a black man, and a few minutes out of town he was already sucking his cock while the truck moved at top speed on the highway. I can imagine the surprise of the peasants at the spectacle displayed in that truck.

To get to a beach was like entering paradise because all the young people wanted to make love, and there were always dozens of them ready to go into the bushes. Many young men made love with me in the changing stalls of La Concha public beach, desperate with the knowledge that this instant was, perhaps, unique and had to be enjoyed to the fullest, because at any moment the police could come and arrest us. After all, those of us who were not yet in a concentration camp were privileged; we had to take advantage of our freedom. We looked for men everywhere and we found them.

On our erotic adventure, Hiram and I went as far as the Isle of Pines, where we could enjoy entire regiments. The recruits, desperate for sex, woke up the entire camp when we arrived. The young men, covered with blankets or naked, came to meet us. We would go into some abandoned tanks and cause a terrible commotion.

One day we began to take inventory of the men we had slept with until then; this was sometime in 1968. I came to the conclusion, after complicated mathematical calculations, that I had sex with about five thousand men. Hiram arrived at approximately the same figure. Of course, Hiram and I were not the only ones carried away by this kind of erotic rage; everybody was: the recruits who spent long months of abstinence, and the whole population.

I remember a speech by Fidel Castro in which he took it upon himself to lecture men on how they should dress. At the same time, he also criticized the young men who had long hair and roamed the streets playing the guitar. All dictatorships are sexually repressive and anti-life. All affirmations of life are diametrically opposed to dogmatic regimes. It was logical for Fidel Castro to persecute us, not to let us fuck, and to try to suppress any public display of the life force.

E R O T I C I S M Sometimes our adventures did not end as we would have liked. I remember that traveling on a bus one day Tomasito La Goyesca grabbed at the fly of a very handsome young man. The young man had actually signaled Tomasito several times and had touched his own evidently erect penis. When Tomasito grabbed it, the man reacted violently, beat him up, and called him, and all of us, queers. The driver opened the door of the bus and we ran across Revolutionary Square while a crowd of "chaste" men and women followed us yelling insults. We took refuge in the National Library, through a back door, and hid in María Teresa Freyre de Andrade's office.

Tomasito's face was swollen, and Hiram Prado discovered that the wallet Tomasito was holding was someone else's. In the melee, he had grabbed the wallet thinking it was his own; it actually belonged to the man who had beaten him, an official of the Ministry of the Interior, no less. Tomasito had lost his identification card and now it was in the hands of the aroused man who had hit him. A few hours later, the man came to the National Library in a rage, looking for Tomasito. Since Tomasito did not want to come out of his hiding place, Hiram and I talked with him. He told us to bring the wallet to his home at midnight or he would have us all arrested.

At midnight the three of us arrived at his house, trembling. The young man had been taking a shower and came out naked and drying himself with a towel, which he then wrapped around his waist. He had drawn up a long, strange affidavit for us to sign, stating that we had returned all his documents and that he had returned ours. While we read and signed the affidavit, he was touching his penis, which again was giving signs of life. At the same time, he was insulting us, calling us immoral. In questioning us, he found out that Hiram had been in the Soviet Union and he wondered how one could be gay after having been in that country. He also said that he would do everything in his power to have us expelled from the National Library. When he found out that I was a writer, he looked at me indignantly. But his penis was still erect, and every now and then he touched it.

He finally asked us to sit down and tell him about our lives. The towel gave us ever-increasing evidence of the man's excitement. We exchanged glances among ourselves, astonished, wishing to reach out and touch the promising bulge. We left at around four in the morning; the man dismissed us with his penis still in a state of arousal under the towel. We did not dare touch that wonderful area. We feared that it might be a trap, that the house could be full of cops to catch us in the act. But this was probably not the case. The man, who was persecuting us for being gay, probably wanted nothing more than for us to grab his penis, rub it, and suck it right then. Perhaps this kind of aberration exists in all repressive systems.

I remember another adventure with a young soldier. We met in front of UNEAC; I gave him my address; he came by and sat on my only chair. There was no need for much talk; we both knew what we were after, because at the Coppelia urinals he had already given signs of urgent desire. We tangled in a pretty memorable sexual battle. After he had ejaculated and fucked me passionately, he dressed quietly, pulled out his Department of Public Order ID, and said, "Come with me. You are under arrest for being queer." We went to the police station. All the officers there were young, like the one who had fucked me. He declared that I was gay, that I had made a grab at his dick. I told them the truth, and that I still had his semen in my body. We were accusing each other face-to-face. Perhaps he thought that by being the active partner he had not done anything wrong. Or perhaps he saw himself as having lost his virginity to a sexually depraved person. The fact is that he had enjoyed himself like a real bastard and now wanted to put me in jail. The officers were amazed at the confession; the offense was too blatant. They ended up saying it was a shame that a member of the police force would engage in such acts, because I, after all, had my weakness, but for him, being a man, there was no excuse for getting involved with a queer. I believe a record of the proceedings was drawn up and he was expelled from the police, or at least transferred to another station.

I had other such problems with army officers. Once I went into the Barreto Woods in Miramar with a soldier. We were open with each other from the beginning. He was aroused and so was I. When we found a convenient place he said, "Kneel down and touch me here," and pointed to his belly.

I tried to touch his penis, which he had taken out of his pants, but he moved my hand farther up to his waist, and what I touched was a pistol. He took the pistol out and said, "I'm going to kill you, you faggot." I bolted, heard some shots, yelled out and threw myself into the bushes. I stayed there the whole day. I heard patrol cars; the police were looking for me. Evidently the soldier, once his sexual arousal was under control, was trying to hunt me down, fortunately to no avail.

At dawn I returned to my room in Miramar. There was a terrific-looking boy waiting for me, one of my many lovers at the time who would come back again and again. He had waited for me all night. We went up to my room and between his legs I found refuge, as I had done before among the bushes when the soldier was searching for me.

My friends also had disappointments in love and with their erotic encounters. During a really dazzling carnival celebration in Havana, Tomasito La Goyesca entered one of the portable urinals set up on Prado Boulevard. Nobody went there to pee, except perhaps those who had been drinking and needed to go. They then became excited and ended up entangled with other men; there were dozens of men standing around while others sucked their cocks; some were being fucked right there. At first you could not see anything; then you could make out the bright penises and the sucking mouths. When Tomasito walked in he felt someone caressing his buttocks and his legs; he felt hands rubbing and touching him all over. Finally, completely sated and unable to bear it any longer, he went out to the street, only then realizing that someone in the bathroom had picked up shit and smeared it all over his body. It was an incredible scene to watch; a queer, full of shit from head to toe, right on Prado Boulevard, in the midst of the carnival and surrounded by thousands of people. Actually, he had no trouble making his way through the crowd; the stench coming from him was so bad that as he ran, a breach opened up to make way for him. He got to the Malecón and plunged, fully clothed, into the ocean. He swam beyond El Morro and, following him closely, I lost sight of him and feared a shark might have finished him off. He swam for hours and did not come ashore until daybreak, when he no longer smelled of shit.

Walking back to Prado Boulevard, we made up for all this. We picked up two fabulous sailors and went to the house where Tomasito lived with his mother. She was a tolerant old lady who did not mind if he came home with men, provided he did it quietly. We enjoyed those young men as much as they enjoyed us.

Pepe Malas also had numerous tragic encounters when he tried to satisfy his erotic urges. Once he was infatuated with a great example of masculine beauty who worked the night shift at the pharmacy. Pepe liked to stick his head through the small window that was left open at night, and then order ten cents' worth of aspirin while he stared at the pharmacist's fly. One night the man, tired of this game, yelled that he did not have any aspirin and yanked the window down with such force that Pepe's head got caught as if in a guillotine that had jammed at the crucial moment. People walking by on the street were somewhat astonished to see a man stuck in the little window, while the pharmacist slept peacefully on the other side.

Another one of his adventures turned out to be a little more costly. He took a hoodlum to his room on Monserrate Street, which was on the fifth floor of an old building and had a balcony above the street. The hoodlum told Pepe to take his clothes off and then pushed him onto the balcony, locking him out. The hoodlum filled a suitcase with the queer's belongings and left. Pepe, naked on the balcony above the street, did not know what to do. It would have been ridiculous to call the police; there was no way Pepe could explain how that delightful hoodlum was able to walk away with all his clothes, including the ones he had been wearing.

Hiram Prado always got into trouble in theaters. He had been sent to the Soviet Union as a young communist student, but was expelled after he was caught sucking the cock of a young Russian during a Bolshoi Theater performance.

Some time later, on one of our literary and erotic excursions to the Isle of Pines, Hiram Prado met a young man who was part of a grapefruit-picking brigade. At the height of their erotic encounter, while Hiram was sucking the young man's penis behind a theater curtain, the curtain was suddenly pulled open and there they were, on center stage. The response to their performance was not exactly applause; rather, it was a deafening roar. The young man was only sixteen years old. Hiram was arrested, shaved to the scalp, and jailed. For a week I roamed the Isle of Pines trying to find out which jail he had been taken to. When I was finally about to catch the boat back to Havana, I saw Hiram and behind him the beautiful boy, who had also been arrested, being led under guard to a ship. Hiram was deported from Havana and sent to a farm in Oriente, his place of birth. We kept writing to each other for quite some time.

Once in a while our lovers had criminal intentions or mental quirks that made them commit acts of unjustified violence. The case of Amando García is a good example. He met a beautiful young judoka and took him home. The young man told him to lie down and then he looked at Amando García and said, "You have such a beautiful neck. Stretch it out a little more." Then the beautiful Adonis ordered, "Now, close your eyes." Amando, his neck outstretched and eyes closed like a swan in ecstasy, was desperately awaiting the caress, when the young man gave out one of those terrifying judo yells, pounced on Amando, and with open hand struck him on the neck. The young man was actually trying to break Amando's Adam's apple and kill him. Amando, a very strong queer, screamed so loud that his neighbors at the boardinghouse came to his assistance. They took him immediately to the hospital, spitting blood. The young man had disappeared, shouting insults.

Several of Amando's erotic adventures ended in the hospital. I recall one occasion when I introduced him to one of my regulars, a recruit. I had a sort of special army; I would meet a recruit and the next day he would bring one of his friends, who in turn would bring one of his, so at times there were fifteen or twenty recruits in my room. This was too much of a surplus. And besides, we were generous and would share our lovers with our friends, who would also feel stimulated by meeting new guys. So I took this recruit to Amando. The man was really beautiful but his penis was smaller than Amando expected. Unsatisfied, he asked the recruit to stick a baseball bat (which he kept for such purposes) up his anus. The recruit went too far and shoved almost the entire bat into Amando, causing intestinal perforation and peritonitis. For a long time he had to live with an artificial anus. (His nickname changed then from Gluglú to "Double Ass.")

We would also become victims of the jealousies of those buggers, as they called themselves. Sometimes they were jealous of one another. Once I got a very good-looking youth into one of the changing booths at La Concha Beach, and another guy, apparently in love with him, called the police, saying that two men were fucking in the booth. Needless to say, all homosexual acts were illegal and punishable, and to be caught in the act could mean years in jail. But that malicious guy brought the cops right to the booth where we were, naked and sweaty. They demanded we open the door; from above they had already seen us coupled. It seemed there was absolutely no escape: two naked men, inside a booth and sexually involved—there was just no way of justifying this to the police. I quickly wrapped my belongings in my shirt, making a tight little bundle, then opened the door, and before the police could lay hands on me, gave out a yell and ran at top speed down the stairs at La Concha, jumped into the ocean, and started swimming away. That day nature was my ally; suddenly there was a tropical downpour. It was almost a miracle; I saw the police looking for me in a patrol boat along the shore, but the rain was so heavy they lost sight of me. I was able to swim, naked, to Patricio Lumumba Beach, which was one or two miles from La Concha. It had stopped raining, and there were three boys jumping from the diving board. They were beautiful. In their full view I climbed up the diving board and put on my bathing suit. Then I started talking with them. I don't know if they noticed something odd about me, but they did not ask any questions. We swam awhile, and a few minutes later they were already with me in my room, which luckily was a short walk from Patricio Lumumba Beach. They really made up for my distressing experience at La Concha. For several months I had to stop going to that beach; there were so many men wanting to fuck other men. But La Concha had been famous since the days of the Republic as a place where everybody went to fuck; you could lock yourself in those booths and do whatever you wanted. Besides, whether naked or in bathing suits, all those men were truly irresistible.

Men would go to the beach with their wives, and sit on the sand to relax; but sometimes they would go to the changing booths, have erotic adventures with other young men, and then return to their wives. I remember a particularly good-looking man playing with his son and wife in the sand. He would lie down, lift his legs, and I could see his beautiful testicles. I watched him playing with his son for a long time, lifting his legs and showing me his testicles. Finally he went to the changing-booth building, took a shower, and went up to get dressed. I followed him; I think I asked him for a cigarette or a match, and he invited me in. For five minutes he was unfaithful to his wife in the most astonishing way. Later I saw him again with his wife on his arm and his son, a beautiful family picture. I think that image prompted the idea for my novel *Otra vez el mar* [The Sea Once Again, published in the United States as *Farewell to the Sea*], because the sea really provided us with the greatest sexual excitement, that tropical sea full of extraordinary young men who swam either in the nude or in bikinis. To be by the ocean and look at the sea was always a wonderful feast; we knew that somewhere in those waves an anonymous lover would be waiting.

Once in a while we made love underwater. I became an expert at this. I managed to get a face mask and flippers. It was wonderful to dive and swim underwater and be able to feast my eyes on all those bodies. Sometimes I would make love underwater with someone who also had a face mask. Occasionally he was not alone, and while he was up to his neck in the water, I would suck his penis powerfully until he ejaculated, and would then swim away with the help of my flippers. The person he was talking to at a little distance would notice no more perhaps than a deep sigh at the moment of ejaculation.

We usually had to stand in long lines to get a booth at La Concha, but if we were unsuccessful, we would perhaps make love up in the almond trees that surrounded the beach. These were luxuriant tropical trees of dense foliage; adolescents could easily climb them and then, up there amid the warbling of birds, we would perform erotic maneuvers worthy of professional tightrope walkers.

Our greatest joy, though, was being able to rent a house at Guanabo Beach, always a difficult proposition. Nevertheless, during the sixties one friend or another would usually manage to get one. He would not rent the house himself; it would have to be a woman or a married man. But somehow we would get a house for the weekend or, at times, for the whole week. It was a great feast. We would all bring our notebooks and write poems or chapters of our books, and would have sex with armies of young men. The erotic and the literary went hand in hand.

I could never work in pure abstinence; the body needs to feel satisfied to give free reign to the spirit. In the afternoons

I would lock myself in my little room in Miramar, and sometimes write until late into the night. But during the day I roamed all the beaches, barefoot, and enjoyed unusual adventures with wonderful guys in the bushes, with ten, eleven, twelve of them sometimes; at other times with only one, who would be so extraordinary he would satisfy me as much as twelve.

Many of the guys would come back to me, but the problem was that the house was not mine; I lived in the maid's room of my aunt Agata's house. She was, moreover, an informer for State Security and therefore it was dangerous for those young men to pay me a visit, especially if I was not home and they started pounding on the door. My aunt had many cats. I told my lovers not to enter through the front door but through the patio, and to do this they had to jump a wall on the ocean side. Unfortunately, they would sometimes land on one of my aunt's numerous cats. The cat would let out incredible howls and my aunt would scream louder. On many occasions the youths were so terrified that they did not come to my room as we had agreed. Others were more daring and would climb in from the roof or onto the balcony on the street side. Sometimes there were four or five, and while I fucked one, the others would masturbate awaiting their turn. At times we had group sex, which was like having a party.

I would tell Lezama about my adventures. As soon as María Luisa left to prepare tea, he would ask me how I was doing and how my love life was going. I was doing all right, although occasionally I suffered from the violence of some of my lovers, an experience shared by all of us.

I remember once, getting off the bus, I approached a muscular adolescent. We didn't waste words. One of the advantages of a pickup in Cuba was that not much talk was needed. Things were settled with a look, asking for a cigarette or saying you lived nearby and would he like to come with you. If he accepted, everything else was understood.

The young man accepted, and once inside my home, surprisingly asked me to play the role of the man. Actually that gave me pleasure too, and the man went down on me. I fucked him and he enjoyed it like a convict. Then, still naked, he asked me, "And if anybody catches us here, who is the man?" He meant who fucked whom. I replied, perhaps a little cruelly, "Obviously, I am the man, since I stuck it into you." This enraged the young man, who was a judo expert, and he started to throw me against the low ceiling; thank God, he would catch me in his arms on the way down, but I was getting an awful beating. "Who? Who is the man here?" he repeated. And I, afraid to die on this one, replied, "You, because you are a judo expert."

Two blocks away from my aunt's house there was a huge school called INDER.* Thousands of young men on scholarship trained there in cycling, boxing, pole vault, and other sports. Almost all the students went through my room—sometimes a number of them, sometimes only one. Once a professor and a student met by coincidence; they looked at each other in surprise. The professor belonged to the Communist Youth Organization, and when he arrived and knocked at my door, I did not open it because I had the student in my room. He climbed onto the balcony, however, pushed the window open and came in, finding his naked student there. How could he explain to that student why, at three in the morning, he was bursting into a queer's room? The truth is, I don't know how he managed it. He left that night and returned the following day when, fortunately, the student was not there.

My erotic adventures were not limited to beaches and military camps; they also occurred in universities and university dorms where hundreds of students slept. Once I met a student whose name was Fortunato Granada. He was Colombian and had come to Cuba in the hope of studying

* *Instituto Nacional de Deportes y Recreación*—R.A.

BEFORE NIGHT FALLS

medicine. In those years the Revolutionary government had invited many young people from all over Latin America to study at Cuban universities. Once enrolled at the universities, they were subjected to political indoctrination and finally they were told that their country had to be liberated, that it was a victim of U.S. imperialism, that they had to return home as guerrillas.

Fortunato told me all this while we were making love on a bunk mattress in the dorm basement. He wanted to be a doctor—his reason for coming to Cuba—not to go back as a guerrilla. When he refused, his passport was taken away, and now they were threatening to expel him from the university. He was trying desperately to figure out what to do in Cuba after being expelled from the university and deprived of any ID.

We continued making love for a year; he finally had to enlist as a guerrilla fighter. I don't know if he got killed, because I never heard from him again. When I wrote *The Palace of the White Skunks*, I wanted to pay tribute in a small way to this great lover of mine; the hero's name in my novel is Fortunato.

The guerrillas who were lucky returned to Cuba. One of them, Alfonso, had met Fortunato. One day Alfonso knocked at my aunt's door asking for me, and he identified himself as Fortunato's friend. I realized right away what he wanted. We became good friends and excellent lovers. He had belonged to the guerrillas and now worked for the Ministry of the Interior in Cuba. He had an official role at diplomatic affairs attended by Fidel Castro, as part of his security guard. Perhaps his homosexual inclination was forgiven because he was a foreigner; or perhaps the government didn't find out about it. He kept coming to me for years. Of course, he came only now and then and, frankly, behaved in a very masculine way. Then suddenly he disappeared; maybe he was transferred to another country on a special mission. God knows where he is now.

In addition to the pickups during the day, which generally took place at the beaches, there was another powerful homosexual scene in Havana, underground but very visible. There were pickups at night all over La Rampa, at Coppelia, on Prado Boulevard and along the Malecón Shore Drive, and at Coney Island in Marianao. These areas were full of recruits and students, single men who were locked up in barracks or schools and went out at night eager for sex. They were willing to settle for the first thing that came along. I always tried to be one of the first they met in these places. Hundreds of them ended up in my room. Sometimes they did not want to go that far, in which case we had to risk going downtown, to Old Havana, where we would walk up some stairway to the top floor and lower our pants. I think that in Cuba there was never more fucking going on than in those years, the decade of the sixties, which was precisely when all the new laws against homosexuals came into being, when the persecutions started and concentration camps were opened, when the sexual act became taboo while the "new man" was being proclaimed and masculinity exalted. Many of the young men who marched in Revolutionary Square applauding Fidel Castro, and many of the soldiers who marched, rifle in hand and with martial expressions, came to our rooms after the parades to cuddle up naked, and show their real selves, sometimes revealing a tenderness and true enjoyment such as I have not been able to find again anywhere else in the world.

Perhaps deep down they realized they were breaking into the realm of the forbidden, the dangerous, and the damned. Perhaps that is the reason why, when that moment came, they showed such fullness, such radiance, and enjoyed every instant in the awareness that it might be their last, that it could cost them many years in jail. There was, moreover, no prostitution. It was pleasure for pleasure's sake, the craving of one body for another, the need to find fulfillment. Sexual pleasure between two men was a conspiracy, something that happened in the shadows or in plain daylight, but always forbidden; a look, a wink, a gesture, a sign, was enough to start the sequence that resulted in such full enjoyment. The adventure in itself, even if fulfillment did not come with the desired body, was already a pleasure, a mystery, a surprise. To enter a movie theater was to figure out whom we would sit next to, and whether that young man over there would stretch out his leg toward us. To reach over slowly with one hand and touch his thigh, and then to dare a little more and feel the part of his pants where that penis wanted to break through the fabric; to masturbate him right then and there during an old American movie, to see how he would ejaculate, and then leave before the movie ended; and perhaps I would never see him again, after having seen his face only in profile. What does it matter, he was surely a wonderful guy.

People would really get sexually aroused on interstate trips. If you took one of those buses crowded with young men, you could be sure that some erotic games would take place during the trip. The driver would turn out the lights, and the bus would be moving on those highways full of potholes; with each lurch of the vehicle one had the opportunity for contact, for touching an erect penis, a young thigh, a strong chest; hands could move over a body, feel for the waist, unbuckle the belt, and then, cautious and eager, reach for the spot where that terrific member lay hidden. Those adventures, and the people with whom one had them, were great. Those men enjoyed their roles of active males; they wanted to be sucked and even to fuck right on the bus.

Later, in exile, I found that sexual relations can be tedious and unrewarding. There are categories or divisions in the homosexual world. The queer gets together with the queer and everybody does everything. One sucks first, and then they reverse roles. How can that bring any satisfaction? What we are really looking for is our opposite. The beauty of our relationships then was that we met our opposites. We would find that man, that powerful recruit who wanted desperately to fuck us. We were fucked under bridges, in the bushes, everywhere, by men who wanted satisfaction while they penetrated us. Either conditions here are different, or it is just difficult to duplicate what we had there. Everything here is so regulated that groups and societies have been created in which it is very difficult for a homosexual to find a man, that is, the real object of his desire.

I do not know what to call the young Cuban men of those days, whether homosexuals who played the male role or bisexuals. The truth is that they had girlfriends or wives, but when they came to us they enjoyed themselves thoroughly, sometimes more than with their wives, who often would refuse to suck or had inhibitions that made lovemaking less pleasurable.

I remember an extraordinary mulatto, married and with several children, who escaped his family once a week to fuck me on the iron chair in my room. I never saw a man enjoy sex so much. He was, nevertheless, an excellent father and exemplary husband.

I think that the sexual revolution in Cuba actually came about as a result of the existing sexual repression. Perhaps as a protest against the regime, homosexuality began to flourish with ever-increasing defiance. Moreover, since the dictatorship was considered evil, anything it proscribed was seen in a positive light by the nonconformists, who in the sixties were already almost the majority. I honestly believe that the concentration camps for homosexuals, and the police officers disguised as willing young men to entrap and arrest homosexuals, actually resulted in the promotion of homosexual activities.

In Cuba gays were not confined to a specific area of a club or beach. Everybody mingled and there was no division that would place the homosexual on the defensive. This has been lost in more advanced societies, where the homosexual has had to become a sort of sexual recluse and separate himself from the supposedly nonhomosexual society, which undoubtedly also excludes him. Since such divisions did not exist in Cuba, the interesting aspect of homosexuality there was that you did not have to be a homosexual to have a relationship with a man; a man could have intercourse with another man as an ordinary act. In the same way, a real gay who liked another gay could easily go out and live with him. But the gay who liked real macho men could also find one who wanted to live or be friends with him, without in any way interfering with the heterosexual life of that man. It was not the norm for one queer to go to bed with another queer; "she" would look for a man to fuck "her" who would feel as much pleasure as the homosexual being fucked.

Homosexual militancy has gained considerable rights for free-world gays. But what has been lost is the wonderful feeling of meeting heterosexual or bisexual men who would get pleasure from possessing another man and who would not, in turn, have to be possessed.

The ideal in any sexual relationship is finding one's opposite, and therefore the homosexual world is now something sinister and desolate; we almost never get what we most desire.

That world, of course, also had its dangers. Along with other homosexuals, I was robbed and blackmailed a number of times. Once, after I received my monthly pay from the National Library, just ninety pesos, which was not much but had to cover all of my expenses for the month, I was foolish enough to go straight to the beach. I met a marvelous youth who had caught a crab, tied it to a string, and was walking it on the sand as if it were his dog. I praised the crab while looking at the legs of the youth, who then quickly came with me to my booth. He was wearing a tiny bathing suit. I don't know how he did it, but during his sexual gymnastics, which he handled with practiced skill, he managed to steal all my money from my pants pocket and hide it in his small bathing suit. The truth is that after he left I realized that I had been cleaned out; I did not even have a nickel for the bus fare home. I looked for him all over La Concha Beach. In one of the open booths I found a smashed crab. He was evidently a violent person. The carapace was all that was left of the crab. The beautiful adolescent had disappeared without leaving a witness: not even a crab.

That afternoon I walked home. Once in my room, I continued writing a long poem. I entitled it "Morir en junio y con la lengua afuera" [To Die in June, Gasping for Air]. A few days later I had to stop working on the poem because somebody had entered my room through the window and stolen my typewriter. This was a serious theft; to me that typewriter was not only the one object of value in my possession but also the thing I treasured the most. To me, sitting down at the typewriter was, and still is, something extraordinary. I would be inspired (like a pianist) by the rhythm of those keys and they would carry me along. Paragraphs would follow one another like ocean waves, at times more intense, at others less so; sometimes like huge breakers that would engulf page after page, before the next paragraph. My typewriter was an old iron Underwood, but to me it was a magical instrument.

Guillermo Rosales, then a good-looking young writer, lent me his typewriter and I finished the poem.

Some time later a mulatto police officer, rather handsome in fact, showed up at my home. He told me my typewriter was at the police station. The thief had been caught burglarizing another home, and his house had been searched. They found many stolen items, my typewriter among them. Apparently the thief himself told the police that the typewriter was mine. After many bureaucratic formalities, it was returned and I had to carry it home in a bus full of people; it seemed to weigh a ton, but I got it back where it belonged. I was afraid it would be stolen again, and my friend Aurelio Cortés had the bright idea of bolting it to its metal table.

A number of times hoodlums—that is, the boys with

whom I had made love—entered my room and tried to steal the typewriter, but to no effect; it was impossible to carry both typewriter and metal table. From then on I felt safer, better able to continue my love life without endangering the rhythm of my literary production. That rhythm has always been part of me, even during periods of the most intense lovemaking or of the greatest police persecution. Writing crowned or complemented all other pleasures as well as all other calamities.

There were three marvelous things that I enjoyed in the sixties: my typewriter, at which I sat as a dedicated performer would sit at his piano; the unique youth of those days, when everybody wanted to break away from official government policies and be free and make love; and lastly, the full discovery of the sea.

As a child I had already been in the town of Gibara for several weeks with my aunt Ozaida, whose husband, Florentino, worked there as a bricklayer. I was able to get into the water then but not to experience the magic of the sea as much as I could later, at twenty-something. During the sixties I became an expert swimmer. I would swim out into the open sea in those crystal-clear waters, look back at the beach as if it were something very remote, and enjoy being rocked by the ocean waves. It was marvelous to dive in and behold the underwater world. The views are incomparable, no matter how much you have traveled and how many other undoubtedly interesting places you have seen. The island platform surrounding Cuba is a world of rock and coral, white, golden, and unique. I would come up glistening, smooth, full of vitality, toward that dazzling sun and its immense reflection in the water.

The sea was then my most extraordinary source of pleasure and discovery; to see the raging waves in winter; to sit looking at the sea; to walk from my home to the beach and there to experience the sunset, the twilight. Those late afternoons by the sea are unique in Cuba, particularly in Havana, where the sun falls into the sea like a giant balloon; everything seems to change at dusk, cast under a brief and mysterious spell. There is the smell of brine, of life, of the tropics. The waves, almost reaching my feet, ebbed and left a golden reflection on the sand.

I could not live too far from the sea. Every morning when I woke up, I would go to my little balcony to look at the blue, scintillating expanse reaching to infinity, at the lavishness of that extraordinary glittering water. I could not feel despair, because no one can feel despair when facing such beauty and vitality.

Sometimes I would get up at night to look at the sea. If the night was dark, the thundering of the surf would comfort me; it was the best company I ever had, then and always. In me the sea reverberated with erotic resonance.

While sitting at Patricio Lumumba Beach one day, I watched a teenager walk toward the wall and then disappear behind it. I followed the youth; he had lowered his bathing suit and was masturbating looking at the sea.

I was familiar with all the nooks and crannies of the seashore around Havana, the places where a sudden deepening would attract fish of unexpected colors, the areas covered with red coral, the big rocks, the huge sandbanks where one could stand to rest. After my swim I would return home and take a shower. I generally ate little and not well. Rationing was very severe, and besides, I was registered in my aunt's rationing book. She gave me only part of my share, and usually the worst part. I once heard her say to my uncle, "I told him the chicken was spoiled so that there would be more for us." Chicken was available once a month and my aunt had a husband and three children, in addition to various lovers; because of that, I suffered more than others under the rigorous rationing quotas imposed by Castro. But after taking a shower or, rather, after dumping a bucketful of water over me (there was not enough pressure for the water to rise to my shower), I would go to UNEAC feeling so alive that all those hours of bureaucratic work seemed bearable. I had to check galleys of horrendous publications like the UNEAC magazine, where I was supposed to be an editor but was actually only a proofreader, allowed to have neither an opinion nor the right to publish. But after my ocean swim I could imagine all of it was only a nightmare; real life started near the shore in the glittering sea that would be waiting for me the next day, and into which I could vanish, at least for a few hours.

Even to own a diving mask and flippers was a privilege in Cuba. I had them thanks to Olga, the French wife of a friend of mine. Those flippers and face mask were the envy of all the young men around me at that beach. Jorge Oliva trained with them many, many times, until one day he was able to swim to the Guantánamo Bay Naval Base, and freedom. La Ñica, Jorge Oliva's girlfriend, trained with my swim fins too and was also able to leave Cuba secretly, via the U.S. naval base.

One day an adolescent, a really splendid creature, asked to borrow my flippers. I saw no danger in this and gave them to him. I don't know how he managed to disappear the way he did; he must have come out of the water several miles from there. The fact is that I never saw that young man or my beloved swim fins again.

Hiram Prado, who was with me and knew the youth, said that we could pay him a visit. I did not hesitate and ventured with Hiram into one of the most dangerous neighborhoods in Havana. It was known as Coco Solo, and was not far from Marianao. When we knocked at the young man's door he was so confused that he asked us to wait for him at the corner, where he showed up with more than twenty-five hoodlums armed with sticks and stones. We had to retreat at top speed.

All we could hope for was that Olga would bring us a new pair of flippers on her next trip to France. Olga was an incredible woman; she liked gays and found it impossible to have sex with anyone else. I assume that her life was unfulfilled, but I have met many women with such a preference. Her husband was always on the prowl for gays; they had to be passive gays who would also want to possess Olga, indeed a beautiful woman. Many heterosexuals were eager to possess her, but to no avail; she wanted to go to bed only with passive and openly gay men. Miguel asked all of us to make love to Olga and I think we all made love to his wife, out of friendly loyalty.

Miguel, however, claimed to be heterosexual, although his friends were monuments of masculine beauty. One afternoon at the beach a fierce storm broke out and Miguel and two of his friends, José Dávila and a very handsome judo expert, who I think was a member of State Security, had to take shelter in my room. Night came and they stayed over. Around midnight the judoka had an enormous erection; I had never seen a man with such a powerful penis. Miguel and José Dávila were sleeping or pretending to be asleep. The judoka, who according to Miguel and José was one of the most womanizing men they had ever met, engaged me in a memorable encounter.

A few days later Miguel came to visit and could not believe it when I told him. In any case, he soon told me that he felt the need to be possessed and prodded me to do it; I had to comply. He came to my house several times with the same request, and I always obliged. After getting dressed, he would say, "I don't do it for the pleasure; I just need a prostatic massage, which is most important to maintain a healthy equilibrium."

This kind of thing happened quite often. I remember a tanned, charming young man, very masculine, who would come to my room wanting to get laid. I confess I enjoyed possessing the type of youth who appeared to be very masculine. Even if one eventually got bored, at the beginning it was an adventure. That young man, after being possessed and enjoying himself more than I did, would get dressed, give me a strong handshake, and say, "I've got to go, I have to see my girlfriend." And I really don't think he lied; he was a handsome guy and his girlfriends were lovely too.

My friends and I always liked to get together by the sea. Hiram Prado would wait for me under some pines, near the surf. Whenever we could, our group would go to Guanabo, Santa María, and Varadero Beach near the Bay of Matanzas, or to the most remote beaches in Pinar del Rio. But our destination was always by the sea. The sea was like a feast and forced us to be happy, even when we did not particularly want to be. Perhaps subconsciously we loved the sea as a way to escape from the land where we were repressed; perhaps in floating on the waves we escaped our cursed insularity.

An ocean voyage, practically impossible in Cuba, was a major pleasure. Just to cross Havana Bay on the ferry to Regla was a marvelous experience.

As I said before, those times spent near the ocean inspired my novel *Otra vez el mar*. Like ocean waves, the manuscripts of this novel, which I had to write three times, kept vanishing and later landing, for various reasons, in the hands of the police. I imagine all those lost versions of my novel must be taking up a lot of shelf space in the Department of State Security in Cuba. Bureaucrats are very systematic and for that very reason, I hope my manuscripts have not been destroyed.

By the year 1969 I was already being subjected to persistent harassment by State Security, and feared for the manuscripts I was continually producing. I packed all my manuscripts and the poems I had written earlier—that is, everything I had not been able to smuggle out of Cuba—in an empty cement bag, and visited all my friends in order to find one who could hide them for me without arousing the suspicions of State Security. It was not easy to find someone willing to risk having those manuscripts; anyone found with them could spend years in prison.

Nelly Felipe kept them for me. For months my manuscripts were hidden in her house. One day she started to read them and was very honest with me: "I do like the novel but my husband is a lieutenant in State Security and I don't want him to find those manuscripts at home." Again I found myself walking along Fifth Avenue with my cement bag full of scribbled papers and no place to take them.

I finally took them back home. In my room there was a small closet, which I was able to camouflage by wallpapering it just like the rest of the room, with pages from foreign magazines, surreptitiously obtained. The closet disappeared; it was now part of another wall in my room, and all those sheets of paper I had scribbled over the years were perfectly hidden.

I really had to be careful. One day Oscar Rodríguez picked me up at UNEAC and took me to his home at H Street and Seventeenth, in the Vedado. After serving me some tea, he said, "Reinaldo, I am your friend but I am also an informer for State Security." He claimed that Security wanted to know exactly how I smuggled my manuscripts out of Cuba, who got them out for me, what other unpublished manuscripts I had, where I kept them, and who my foreign contacts were. By then, I had already published one novel abroad, *The Ill-Fated Peregrinations of Fray Servando*, and the next one, *Singing from the Well*, had already been announced.

The Ill-Fated Peregrinations of Fray Servando had been banned in Cuba, even though UNEAC had awarded it a prize. Oscar Rodríguez worked at the Cuban Book Institute and had been inducted into the State Security organization. Being an informer gave him certain privileges; if caught in a homosexual act, he would not end up in a concentration camp. He had also been promised a trip to one of the socialist countries and a possible transfer as a translator to the U.S. Interests Section in Cuba, where, indeed, he did work later.

Obviously, I did not tell Oscar how I had smuggled my manuscripts out, or what I was writing at the moment. His questions startled me, but I did not trust him. I could not be sure that this man, who had been my friend for so many years, was not also such a good cop that he would go to the extreme of pretending to betray his superiors in order to get the desired information from me, and thus do a more efficient job. After his confession, perhaps he expected me to do the same and tell him where I kept my cement bag. I did not do so; on the contrary, the next day I lugged the bag to the home of another one of my then intimate friends, Dr. Aurelio Cortés, who lived at 57 San Bernardino Street, in Santos Suárez.

JORGE
AND MARGARITA

The truth can now be told as to how those manuscripts got out of the country. In 1967 a famous and important event took place in Cuba, the so-called *Salón de Mayo*. The Revolution wanted to whitewash its image in a bath of Western liberalism; and the great majority of European intellectuals and, naturally, the Latin Americans, still had respect for the Revolution. To that end, an extensive exhibition of paintings, even including works by Picasso, was organized. It is usually held in Paris but this time it was transferred to Havana.

Fidel Castro had the bright idea of exhibiting some cows together with the paintings. The cows ruminated almost next to the works of Picasso and Wilfredo Lam. The only one of my novels that was ever published in Cuba, *Singing from the Well*, had just come out, and I was still working at the National Library. One day I received a call at the Library from someone who identified himself as Jorge Camacho, a painter. I did not know him. He had left Cuba in 1959 and his work was therefore not known in Cuba; certainly I knew very little about paintings produced before 1959. Camacho was now one of the painters whose work was on exhibit at the *Salón de Mayo* and he was staying at the Hotel Nacional with his wife, Margarita. He said he wanted to meet me, and invited me to the hotel for a drink. He had just bought a copy of *Singing from the Well* and liked it.

I went to the Hotel Nacional, very fearful of the consequences, because in those days hotels were places for foreigners only, and for every foreigner there were at least ten cops.

My meeting with Camacho and Margarita marked a new period in my life. They had the intuition (rare among official guests at events in socialist countries) to see the underlying truth, even when hidden by layers of praise and official attention lavished upon them. Their single concern was to find out what the real conditions were for artists in Cuba. Desiderio Navarro, Virgilio Piñera, and I brought them up to date: concentration camps, persecutions, censorship, jails bursting at the seams.

Camacho and Margarita actually sympathized so much with our situation that it was even difficult for them to leave Cuba. Naturally, they paid a visit to Lezama Lima, who was practically starving. They invited him to dinner several times at the Hotel Nacional. Camacho was amazed at the amount of food that Lezama could ingest. But Lezama was like a camel who had to store food until the next time such an invitation came along, which did not happen often.

Our friendship was one of those which, once begun, last forever. It was like meeting a loved one for whom we had always been yearning and who suddenly materialized. I did not have any brothers or sisters and had never experienced much family warmth, but I felt that this was a brotherhood that would last. For more than twenty years, one way or another, they have always managed to keep in touch with me every week; through a passing tourist, a coded message in a letter mailed via the usual channels, a postcard, the notice of an exhibit, a book, and hundreds of little attentions that helped to keep me going during the almost fifteen years I remained in Cuba after our first meeting.

When Margarita and Jorge Camacho left, they took with them, of course, *Singing from the Well* as well as my manuscript of *The Ill-Fated Peregrinations of Fray Servando.* Camacho took the published novel and the manuscript to Editions du Seuil in Paris, and submitted them to Claude Durand, who was one of the editorial directors of their Latin American list. Three days later I received a telegram advising me that they wanted to publish my novel immediately. This surprised me no end because just a few months earlier, at Rodríguez Feo's suggestion, I had submitted *Singing from the Well* to Severo Sarduy, who was a co-director of the same Latin American list, and Severo had sent me a mellifluous letter full of praise for the novel but concluding that the production schedules were such that it would not be possible to publish it.

Later I got to know Severo a little better. He is one of the many devious people so common in the literary world. You never really know what they are all about. *Fray Servando* was immediately translated by Didier Coste, one of the best translators (together with Liliane Hasson) I have had in years. The novel was very successful in France, and shared first prize as the best foreign novel with García Márquez's *One Hundred Years of Solitude.* If I had been living in the free world, this would have served me well; it would have enabled me to continue my work, and I would have become a respectable writer or something like that. In Cuba, the official impact of the reviews of the French version of *Fray Servando* was for me absolutely negative. I was placed under surveillance by State Security, not only as a controversial figure who had written novels such as *Fray Servando* and *Singing from the Well*, which were irreverent and did not praise the regime (they really were rather critical), but as one who had the nerve to smuggle his manuscripts out of the country and have them published without the authorization of Nicolás Guillén, president of the Writers and Artists Union [UNEAC]. I had also published a book of short stories, *Con los ojos cerrados* [With My Eyes Closed], in Uruguay.

It was logical for State Security to want to know how I had smuggled the manuscripts out of the country and who my foreign connections were, as well as what other manuscripts I had written.

After being assigned to question me, Oscar Rodríguez held other official positions. Now he is in exile and travels constantly. For whom is he working? Nobody seems to know. Anyway, being a peasant, I have always been very skeptical, which probably helped me safeguard my new manuscripts and not give Oscar any leads.

SANTA MARICA (SAINT QUEER) I could not hide information about my manuscripts from Aurelio Cortés, one of my greatest friends then. We used to wait together in long lines at restaurants in Havana in order not to starve. Aurelio was a good reader; he was a dentist, and had big long teeth but they were his own. I am not making a pun, he was a voracious reader. He lacked, though, something intrinsically Cuban: a sense of humor. When I told him of my conversation with Oscar, he panicked and took the more than one thousand pages of my manuscript to some old ladies at Guanabo Beach who were friends of his and

happened to be very religious. In spite of their piousness, the old ladies had no scruples about opening my bag and reading *Farewell to the Sea*. As they read on, they became more and more horrified, but they did not stop until they got to the part where their friend, Cortés himself, appears and is canonized as Saint Queer. This is one of the ways I pay homage to my friends through my writings, a funny and ironic homage perhaps, but irony and laughter are also a part of friendship. Cortés, who was seventy then, was a virgin; he was skinny and ugly, and had lived with his mother until her death only ten years earlier. His virginity had not interested any of the young men around him. I wanted to honor him in my own way and canonized him as Santa Marica, virgin and martyr, the patron saint of queers.

Cortés was furious about that canonization, and said he had instructed the old ladies to destroy the novel. He himself told me so. I had asked him about the manuscript because in Jibacoa Beach there was a tourist, a friend of Margarita and Camacho, who could perhaps take it out of the country. Cortés beat around the bush a lot before giving me the news; first he said it was in one place, then in another, and finally he told me it was no longer in his hands; he had given the manuscript to some people who would not return it because it offended the Catholic religion and him personally. This sounded so absurd to me that it made no sense. I tried to persuade Cortés to return the manuscript to me, and to that end several of my friends visited him at the Library, but to no avail. Cortés, seeing that I was upset by the loss of those manuscript pages, began to enjoy the situation; it was his moment of vengeance, and vengeance is sweet only when the victim obviously suffers the full consequences.

What seemed to have irritated Cortés most was that in my novel I described him as having very long teeth. But I really do not think I exaggerated much in that first version of *Farewell to the Sea*.

Ismael Lorenzo, another writer and friend of mine, began

making all sorts of schemes to recover the manuscript of the novel. His plans included kidnapping Aurelio Cortés. We would lock him up incommunicado in a room and force him to tell us where the manuscript was. The plan sounded too wild to me; we had to get a car, the man would have to be forced in, and we would have to take him somewhere, but we had no such place. And all this had to be done without alerting the police; they were the ones most interested in getting hold of that manuscript.

I had another conversation with Cortés, and this time he told me to forget about the manuscript because he had destroyed it. What could I do? Kill Cortés? Give up writing the novel?

For days I was totally disconcerted. It had taken me many years to finish that novel; it was one of my great acts of vengeance and one of my most inspired works. It was a gift from the sea, and the product of ten years of disappointments endured under the Fidel Castro regime. All my rage was in that novel.

One day at the beach, thinking of my lost book, feeling as if I had lost one of my children, the most beloved, I realized, all of a sudden, that I had to go back home to my typewriter and start again. There was no other way. It was the novel of my life and not only formed part of the *pentagonía* but was its center. It was not possible to continue the *pentagonía* without that particular novel. I started all over again.

In two years I had finished the novel for the second time. My great triumph came when, manuscript in hand, I went to Gibara with Hiram Prado and there, at the town docks, which were now completely abandoned, I again read to him the most furious of the "cantos" from *Farewell to the Sea*. I chose to read my novel in that particular town because it was there that I experienced the sea for the first time. Gibara was then one of the most vital towns of our island, full of fishermen, tourists, hotels, mansions, and churches with beautiful stained-glass windows. People would dance in great halls built on the higher rocks, from which the young men would jump into the water, come out glistening, and return to the dance. What happened to that town? It was totally destroyed and deserted. The port itself had been invaded by the sand; it had not been dredged for too long. The boats were gone, and the sand was gone from the beaches; there were only rocks and sea urchins.

While we were reading the novel, a few young guys came by; they were still as beautiful as the ones I remembered from my childhood, walking on the breakwaters in Gibara. These youths did look a bit more ragged and they were swimming in pants that they themselves had made into bathing suits. Naturally Hiram Prado and I, after reading the novel, enjoyed their company.

We slept in the park that night and the police came and arrested us. I was afraid for the manuscript, but fortunately it survived. It was very difficult to make photocopies in Cuba; there were no copying machines. I had no more friends I could trust to hide my manuscript; the ones I did trust lived in such difficult and uncertain circumstances that they could not keep it, aside from the fact that having it would have been much too risky for them.

I took all my papers and wrapped them in black plastic bags that I had stolen when planting coffee seedlings around Havana, in what was then called *El Cordón de La Habana* [Ring Around Havana]. This was one of Castro's harebrained ideas, which consisted in planting coffee seedlings all around the city and turning it into a sort of coffee plantation. Not one of those plants ever gave a single coffee bean, and millions of dollars were lost, plus the labor of thousands of workers who sacrificed their weekends to dig holes and plant the seedlings. The only use *El Cordón de La Habana* had for me was that I acquired a few plastic bags, which I was now able to use to wrap my manuscript and hide it in the roof at Agata Fuentes's house, where I was then staying.

Someday (I thought), when the time was right, I would smuggle all my manuscripts out of Cuba. I lifted some roof tiles and hid my novel under them.

THE ABREU BROTHERS

While working desperately on the second version of *Farewell to the Sea* I met the Abreu brothers (Juan, José, and Nicolás). They gave me a lot of support to write the novel again. I promised that every week I would read to them one more canto from the novel. We met in the most out-of-the-way places in Lenin Park to hold our literary gatherings. In those days, even while under surveillance and suffering persecution, we wrote indictments against the regime. Then we wrote mainly poetry; it kept us from going insane or falling into the sterility that had already dragged other Cuban writers down.

To get to Lenin Park was an odyssey. One had to take three or four different chock-full buses. It was the only park that had lakes and woods, in a huge section outside Havana's city limits. It was evidently a park for high officials of the government, privileged people who had cars and were able to drive there in order to buy chocolates and cream cheese, not available elsewhere. There was even a luxurious restaurant called Las Ruinas, a name singularly appropriate because any average person having a meal there would surely face financial ruin; the prices of the entrées were way beyond the reach of our pocketbooks. But Castro's high officials would arrive in their cars and eat at the restaurant. We would meet, not too far from there, to read poetry, novels, and plays. Those gatherings, which we held every Sunday for over four years, were attended by José Abreu, Juan Abreu, Nicolás Abreu, Luis de la Paz, and myself. It was undoubtedly a time of the most intense creativity for everyone in the group.

The police naturally searched my room now and then, but I did not let it bother me too much and I kept writing. There was no reason for them to lift the tiles on the roof where my manuscripts were hidden.

These gatherings in Lenin Park lasted until 1974. I remember reading there *El central* [*El Central: A Cuban Sugar Mill*], "To Die in June, Gasping for Air" and "Leper Colony," as well as all the rewritten cantos from *Farewell to the Sea*. One day, the five of us decided to start an underground magazine. We would type it, making six or seven carbons, and circulate it among ourselves and the few trusty friends we had left by then. We named it *Ah, La Marea* [Oh, The Tide], and in that first number, if I remember correctly, we included some of my translations of Rimbaud, poems contributed by everyone, and a chapter from a novel by Juan Abreu. Though we were only able to publish two numbers of the magazine and we were the only ones who read it, it was one of the few consolations available to us.

But we had little hope by then that the system would change, or that our works would be published or there would be any kind of opening. We had given up on that possibility years ago and, I believe, for good reason.

SUPER - STALINISM

One event that convinced me there was nothing left for me to do under the Castro regime occurred in 1968. I was traveling in a steamy bus to give a lecture at the Cultural Center in Pinar del Río. It amazed me that my friend El Beny (Evelio Cabiedes) had been chosen as coordinator of the lectures. I don't even know how he managed to get a job at the Ministry of Culture. Perhaps in that province they were not aware of his sex life and bohemian life-style, or of his having joined a group of hippies. The fact is that El Beny managed to get me invited, and this included the round trip and three days in Pinar del Río, all expenses paid. During the bus trip we were reading *Granma*, one of the few publications you could find to read in Cuba. We were surprised to learn about the Soviet invasion of Czechoslovakia and to see the way *Granma* was reporting that event without taking a position, merely quoting other opinions from different newspapers, and even the Pope's reaction. Some people felt that perhaps *Granma* had not taken sides because Castro intended to deliver a speech breaking with the Soviet Union; this might lead to an opening, to a more humane and democratic society.

For two or three days we were kept in the dark. *Granma* continued publishing news on the invasion of Czechoslovakia without taking sides. Finally, in Pinar del Río, we listened to Fidel Castro's speech: he not only vehemently approved of the invasion and congratulated the Soviet Union and its "heroes" who had crossed the Czech border with tanks; he asked that the Soviet Union invade Cuba should the United States threaten his regime.

There was no way out. The leader who had fought against Batista was now a dictator much worse than Batista, as well as a mere puppet of the Stalinist Soviet Union.

If *Granma* was publishing all the news without taking a position, it was undoubtedly because Fidel Castro was awaiting the pertinent guidelines from the Soviet Union in order to prepare his speech. Once the Soviet ambassador advised Castro as to what to say, Castro, following the script, took to the microphones and gave that speech, dedicating it to the heroic Soviet invaders.

My stay in Pinar del Río was deeply depressing. Any hope of a possible democratization of the system, of a possible break with the Soviet Union, had died then and there. Our only choice was to live under a despotic regime, in a despotic colony, which was, no doubt, more despotic than the metropolis from which all our orders emanated.

In spite of our government's official backing of the Soviet invasion, we did not remain indifferent. We organized a protest march in front of the Czechoslovak embassy; it was a march joined by a great number of Havana's youth; Soviet imperialism was openly condemned. I think it was one of the last protest marches organized in Havana. The march was ended by the police, and many of the participants were arrested. Hiram Prado, El Beny, and I fled through the bushes at Coppelia. Once more we had escaped the dragnet.

Czechoslovakia had evidently fallen into the fold controlled by the Soviet Union, and therefore there was very little to be done.

In the Czechoslovak Cultural Affairs building we had been able to see movies produced during the Prague Spring; they were excellent, but the communist regime considered them "diversionist." We were also able to meet there to read our books. The last one had been Delfín Prats's *Lenguaje de mudos* [Language for the Mute]. The Russian invasion of Czechoslovakia also deprived us of that small comfort: a place where we could hold our literary readings.

This started a period of Super-Stalinism for us Cuban writers. Forced "voluntary" work was intensified, and we could no longer enjoy a free weekend to read in Lenin Park or go to the beach; we had to participate, without reprieve, in agricultural work. It was the time when the entire nation was gearing up for the ten-million-ton sugarcane harvest. Forced labor camps had already been created by 1969. At UNEAC we constantly had meetings to force us to participate in the harvest; in the end, UNEAC "decided" to close altogether and send all writers to the sugar mills to cut cane. The Island became an enormous sugarcane plantation, sugarcane that we all had to help cut down.

UNEAC organized lectures, generally by official writers, but now and then they invited a controversial author. They were trying to sound out the cultural spectrum of the time so that they could then take the appropriate repressive measures.

Among the invitations issued that year by UNEAC was the one sent to the poet Heberto Padilla. Padilla arrived at UNEAC wearing a violet shirt, and started reading poems from his new, unpublished book, *Provocaciones*. Even the cultural attaché from the Chinese embassy, a strange character, was there, and poetry was almost certainly not his forte. The attaché was zealously tended to by the Cuban Security—that is, by Otto Fernández, José Martínez Matos, Gustavo Eguren, and a few others.

Padilla was then a sort of hero to our generation. In 1968 he had written *Fuera del juego* [*Out of the Game*], submitted it to the UNEAC competition, and won first prize. The jury was unanimous. The book was published with a protest note added by UNEAC in which Padilla was called a counterrevolutionary and anti-Soviet. But it was a triumph. The book had been published, even though almost nobody was able to purchase it because most of the copies of the limited edition were withdrawn from bookstores.

No one there had a tape recorder, of course, and young men wrote down in shorthand the poems being read, their intuition perhaps telling them that this book would never be printed, at least not in Cuba.

One of the most undignified and despicable readings ever held at UNEAC was one by Cintio Vitier in 1969. We, the underground writers, labeled that reading "the conversion of Cintio Vitier." All of a sudden this man, who had been criticizing the Revolution and had mostly refused to publish under the Castro regime, was now more revolutionary than Castro himself, and read long poems inspired by the coffee harvest and the cutting of the sugarcane. Cuban officialdom was there to support Cintio: Retamar, Guillén, Raúl Roa.

Undoubtedly, Cintio knew which way the political winds were blowing and wanted to make sure he was on the right side. It was the typical position of the reactionary Catholic, the typical position of the Catholic Church itself: always on the side of the powerful and betraying the downtrodden.

It was ironic that the same night on which Cintio declared himself a Revolutionary, one of the largest raids ever was taking place. It was a brutal action by State Security during which hundreds and hundreds of young men were arrested and beaten by the police and taken to concentration camps because hands were needed to cut cane. The sugar harvest was approaching, and those vital, long-haired young men who still dared to walk around the city were all dragged to the sugar plantations, just like the Indians and black slaves in the past. It was the end of an era, underground and defiant, but still full of creativity, eroticism, intelligence, and beauty. Those adolescents were changed for life; after all the forced labor and constant vigilance, they turned into enslaved ghosts. Moreover, they could not even go to the local beaches anymore because most were closed or becoming private enclaves for foreign tourists or for officers of Castro's army.

THE SUGAR MILL In 1970, I of course also ended up at a sugar plantation. Officials of State Security, among them the notorious Lieutenant Luis Pavón, were already in control of UNEAC, and they sent me to the Manuel Sanguily Sugar Mill to cut sugarcane and to write a book praising that odyssey as well as the ten-million-ton harvest. The sugar mill was west of Havana, in Pinar del Río. It was actually a huge military unit. All the cane cutters were young recruits being forced to work there. It was part of a scheme by the Castro regime to use the compulsory military service personnel in peacetime as an army of forced laborers, which would supply farmhands to agriculture. For any of those young men, to desert a plantation could mean from five to thirty years in jail.

The situation was almost intolerable. Unless you have lived through it, you could not possibly understand what it means to be in a Cuban sugar plantation under the noon sun, and to live in barracks like slaves. To get up at four in the morning and, with a machete and water bottle, to be taken by cart to the fields to work all day under a blistering sun, among the sharp leaves of the sugarcane, which cause the skin to itch unbearably. To be sent to one of those places was like entering the last circle of hell. Completely covered from head to foot, with long sleeves, gloves, and a hat (the only way to be in those infernal places), I came to understand why the Indians had preferred suicide to working there as slaves; I understood why so many black men had killed themselves by suffocation. Now I was the Indian, I was the black slave, and I was not alone. I was one among hundreds of recruits. It was perhaps more pathetic to see them there than to see myself, because I had already lived some years of splendor, even if underground; but those young men, sixteen and seventeen years old, were treated like beasts, had no future to hope for, nor a past to remember. Many would hack their legs or cut their fingers off with their machetes. They would do absolutely anything to be relieved of working in the sugarcane fields. The vision of all that enslaved youth inspired my long poem *El central*. I wrote the poem right there; I could not remain a silent witness to such horror.

I had been at the trials where young men were condemned to twenty or thirty years in jail, their only crime being that on a weekend they had gone to see their families, their mother, their girlfriend. Now they were being court-martialed for desertion. The only way out for those boys was to accept the "rehabilitation" plan, which meant returning to the sugarcane fields, but now in an undefined category, as slaves.

And all this was happening in the country proclaiming itself the First Free Territory of the Americas.

Every two weeks the young men had three or four hours of free time to rest and wash their uniforms. Still, in spite of the exhausting work schedule, we were alive; sexual activity was rampant in the camps. The kind of eroticism that became evident under the mosquito nets, in the obvious ostentation of an erect member under the rough fabric of the uniform. Yes, those young slaves were handsome, and it was beautiful to see them looking at each other in the showers, still apprehensive but, deep down, sexually aroused.

I remember a lieutenant who found out that I knew some French and who insisted that I teach him the language in my free time. Classes started when the lieutenant said, "Let's study French," and grabbing his testicles, he would place them on the table I used for teaching. That erect penis and those testicles were only inches from the copybook in which I would write down a few phrases in French. I stretched those classes as long as I could.

There was, in spite of everything, a certain magic in that environment, and it was the landscape around us. The land in the northern part of Pinar del Río is volcanic, mountains of blue rock that jut out from the ground. It is an airy landscape, with a light, thin breeze, such as I had never enjoyed in Oriente, a land of black earth and dark vegetation at the eastern end of the Island. Yes, without question and all the horror notwithstanding, it was a comfort to behold those airy mountains cloaked in a blue mist.

I started keeping a diary, "The Western Diary," in which I would record daily events: the conversation with one recruit; the story of another one, who cut his foot to get five days of rest; or of the one sentenced to ten years.

The barracks where we slaves slept was a place full of bunks, piled one on top of the other and made of wood and canvas, covered with mud, each with a small duffel bag where a recruit kept his few belongings. An ordinary can of condensed milk was a privilege; a notebook and a pencil were luxury items.

In the evening, it was a feast to be able to get some sugar (even though we were at a very productive sugar mill). We would improvise black coffee with grounds stolen from the kitchen, or make tea from orange leaves.

During the day the barracks became a sort of hospital; the only people allowed to stay there were the sick and the head of the barracks, the one who watched over the others. The patients were those who had lost an arm or were seriously ill and waiting for a transfer to a clinic or hospital, which sometimes took months, if it came at all. The recruits who trucked the cane at night were also allowed to sleep in the barracks during the day. They were a rather privileged group.

One day they sent me to the regional reporter; one was assigned to every sugar mill to report on progress in meeting set goals. I was asked to help him write some report. Luckily we finished early and I was able to stay in the barracks during the afternoon, take a shower, and lie down on my bunk under the mosquito net. One of the truckers was sleeping in the bunk next to mine. I watched his beautiful body, lifted the mosquito net to get a better view, and noted that, little by little, his pants began to bulge at the crotch. But the recruit kept on snoring rhythmically. I got up from my cot and picked up one of the undershorts that were all over the place, and nonchalantly dropped them on the legs of the recruit. This gave me an excuse for being so close to him: I had to pick them up. I did it and nothing happened. I dropped them again, and while I picked them up the young man, who was still snoring, stretched his legs voluptuously and his penis outlined itself through the rough fabric, in all its splendor.

There were not many possibilities for sex in that place, but I nevertheless went down on the young man and we had a brief though intense encounter.

A heavy downpour hit us that night, followed by clouds of mosquitoes and no-see-ums, making the barracks even more unbearable. And as if it were not enough to have to endure being in the scorching sugarcane fields all day, we had to help burn them down at night. The goals had to be accelerated, we had to achieve the ten million tons of sugar; the deadline was getting closer, and the possibility of reaching the goal was becoming more and more remote. So the official order was to burn the sugarcane in order to speed up the cutting process, once the leaves had been burned off.

The burning of a sugarcane field at night was a horrible spectacle. Millions of birds, insects, reptiles, and all kinds of creatures fled the flaming fields in terror. And in the meantime, we were trying to control the fire, our bodies sweaty, hot, and eroticized.

The next morning we had to enter the burnt cane fields, looking like medieval figures under new armor: boots, belts, helmets with wire mesh to prevent burnt spears from poking into our eyes. We had to do the cutting while the ground was still smoldering and some of the cane still burning.

Even if we just wanted a drink of water, we had to ask the lieutenant, who watched us like an overseer.

Sometimes on weekends an important visitor or high official would come, in his Alfa Romeo, to inspect the books and talk with the barrack chiefs; he would depart with a gloomy look on his face. We evidently would never reach the ten-million-ton goal. The recruits and peasants were already commenting that it would not be possible. Anyone who dared say so publicly, however, would be labeled a traitor. Even the head of the sugar industry, a man by the name of Borrego, was fired from his job by Fidel Castro because, a few months before the end of the harvest, he told Castro that it was technically impossible to reach the goal of ten million tons. But three months later, Fidel himself had to admit that the ten million tons of sugar had not been produced; all the sacrifices had been in vain.

The country had been devastated; thousands upon thousands of fruit trees and royal palms, and even forests, had been felled in the attempt to produce those ten million tons of sugar. The sugar mills, trying to double their production, were run into the ground; a fortune would be needed to repair the machinery and resume agricultural production. The whole nation, completely ruined, was now the poorest province of the Soviet Union.

Of course, as usual, Castro refused to admit his error, and tried to deflect attention from the failure of the sugar crop to other areas, such as his hatred of the United States, on which he placed the blame. A story was concocted about a group of fishermen kidnapped by CIA agents on some Caribbean island, and suddenly, the millions of people who had been cutting sugarcane for a year had to reassemble in Revolutionary Square or in front of what used to be the U.S. embassy in Havana, to protest the alleged kidnapping of the fishermen. It was grotesque to see those young men marching and yelling epithets against the United States (where perhaps no one even knew what had motivated such outbursts). I remember Alicia Alonso using obscene language against President Nixon, saying something like, "Nixon, you son of a bitch, return the fishermen to us."

The drama ended, as do most Cuban tragedies, in a sort of rumba; likenesses of President Nixon were burned to the beating of bongo drums. There was food and beer you could not buy at any market; the masses gathered in order to be able to eat a Cuban burger. Many had been assembled by their Committees for the Defense of the Revolution [CDR]. And so, all of a sudden, the populace forgot the failure of the harvest. Now the aim was to achieve the return of the allegedly kidnapped fishermen. A week later, the fishermen showed up, and Fidel gave a "heroic" speech stating that he had intimidated the United States into returning them. The whole thing was pathetic and ridiculous. If a problem ever existed for those fishermen, it was probably that they had entered the territorial waters of some British island, not even one belonging to the United States, and after an investigation the men were returned to Cuba. Castro always had a flair for theatrical strategies. In this way the fishermen returned as heroes who had escaped the clutches of Yankee imperialism.

That year there were great carnival celebrations in which the remaining scant economic resources of the country were invested. There were huge floats with all kinds of animals; some were big tanks full of tropical fish, topped by half-naked women dancing to the beat of drums. This lasted for over a month; there was beer everywhere, and food was distributed at almost every corner. It was absolutely necessary to forget, by any means, that we had been the butt of a bad joke, that the efforts of all those years had been useless, that we were a completely underdeveloped country, more and more enslaved every day.

Needless to say, we enjoyed the carnival festivities and although wearing masks or disguises was no longer permitted, at least we could laugh and get drunk. We knew that this occasion was one of a kind, and we had to make the most of it. After so much repression, excesses were rampant. Public urinals were great places for sexual encounters, and the smell of urine didn't deter anybody from sucking and fucking. The police came once, at the height of the carnival, and overturned the huge wooden urinals, surrounded by thousands upon thousands of people astonished at the sight of so many sexually aroused men.

O L G A   A N D R E U Naturally, many intellectuals were by then requesting exit permits. The actual departures were delayed indefinitely; in the meantime they had to do farm work to survive. Our clandestine literary gatherings were becoming ever more dangerous, and writers would meet in private homes where we could read sections of our work. One of those homes was that of Olga Andreu, who took such risks because, to her, literature was something sacred. I think that Virgilio Piñera continued writing during the last years of his life only because of Olga Andreu's encouragement: he knew that there was a place where he could count on an admiring audience. Olga was a good listener, a rare quality in Cubans, and since she had no literary pretensions, she would neither be the implacable critic nor offer opportunistic praise.

At Olga Andreu's home one could breathe and be oneself. I recently heard that this woman committed suicide a while ago by jumping off the balcony of her small apartment.

It was clear that these gatherings would not last. Some of the participants left the country, and others became officials of Fidel Castro's regime. Some, like Pepe el Loco, killed themselves while still on the Island; others, like writer Calvert Casey, in exile.

Olga Andreu's world, in the last years of her life, was mostly a world inhabited by beloved ghosts who had disappeared tragically. Her death was perhaps an act of affirmation. There are times when living means to degrade yourself, to make compromises, to be bored to death. Olga had wanted to enter that timeless world where State Security could no longer define her parameters, with all her sense of joy and her dignity intact.

But in those days the parameters of many artists had not yet been defined. The government knew conspiracies were going on, at least verbal ones. Literary meetings were always held at Lezama Lima's home, where this even-tempered man was always ready to give good advice or recommend a book. Virgilio Piñera also participated in the meetings at Olga Andreu's home, or he would read at the home of José Ibáñez, grandson of Juan Gualberto Gómez.

Ibáñez's house was isolated and outside Havana, one of

the few eighteenth-century homes that were still very well preserved, with huge gardens and luxuriant vegetation. When you entered that home it seemed as if Fidel Castro's Revolution had never taken place. The gatherings started at midnight. Undoubtedly those meetings had already been infiltrated by agents of State Security, writers turned informers, such as (we later found out) Miguel Barnet, Pablo Armando Fernández, and César López. Whatever was read in one of those places was reported to State Security by the next day.

As the persecutions intensified, the people were more and more eager to get to know the works of censored writers. Lezama became very popular, and some people knew Padilla's banned verses by heart. The greatest danger to the regime was the large number of young people who became followers of dissident writers, and for that reason, those writers had to be demoralized so they could not become symbols; they had to be humiliated and cut down.

THE PADILLA "CASE"

State Security chose Heberto Padilla as the sacrificial lamb. Padilla was the irreverent poet who had dared to submit a book critical of the Revolution, *Fuera del juego*, to an official competition.

Outside Cuba, Padilla had already become an international figure who therefore had to be destroyed, and with him, all other intellectuals in the country who had similar attitudes.

Padilla was arrested in 1971, as was his wife, Belkis Cuza Malé. He was locked up in a cell, intimidated, and beaten. Thirty days later he emerged from that cell a human wreck. Most of us Cuban intellectuals were invited by State Security, through UNEAC, to hear what Padilla had to say.

We knew that he had been arrested, and were surprised to learn that he would speak. I remember that UNEAC was under close surveillance by undercover cops; the only persons allowed to enter and hear Padilla were those whose names appeared on a carefully checked list. The night Padilla made his confession was sinister and unforgettable. That vital man, who had written beautiful poetry, apologized for everything he had done, for his entire previous work, throwing the blame upon himself, branding himself a despicable coward and traitor. He said that during his detention at State Security he had come to understand the beauty of the Revolution and he had written some poems to spring. Padilla not only retracted all he had said in his previous work but publicly denounced his friends, and even his wife, all of whom, he claimed, also held counterrevolutionary attitudes. Padilla named them all, one by one: José Yanes, Norberto Fuentes, Lezama Lima. Lezama had refused to participate in Padilla's apology. While Padilla was giving out names of counterrevolutionary writers, Virgilio Piñera started sliding down from his chair and sat on the floor, as if trying to become invisible. All those whom Padilla named, between sobs and chest beatings, had to come up to the microphone next to Padilla, accept the blame for their errors, and state that they were unworthy people and traitors to the regime. All of this, of course, was put on film by State Security, circulated in intellectual centers throughout the world, and shown especially to those writers who had signed a letter complaining of Padilla's wrongful arrest, such as Mario Vargas Llosa, Octavio Paz, Juan Rulfo, and even Gabriel García Márquez, now one of Fidel Castro's most important standard-bearers.

All the writers mentioned by Padilla filed past the microphones making their confessions. Pablo Armando Fernández's confession was long and sickening; he accused himself even more violently than Heberto Padilla had done. César López was also there, and he confessed all of his ideological errors. Norberto Fuentes did also, except that at the end, when the proceedings seemed to have concluded as planned by State Security, Fuentes asked for the floor and returned to the microphone. He said that he did not agree with what was going on, that Padilla was in a very difficult position and had no choice but to make his confession, and that he, Norberto, felt very differently because he worked hard and, for being a writer, had to starve. Moreover, he did not consider himself a counterrevolutionary for simply having written several books of short stories, imaginative or critical; and he ended by pounding the table with his fist. The State Security officers stood up and I saw some of them reach for their weapons. Norberto Fuentes was silenced by shouts and threats of violence.

While the shameful spectacle of Padilla's confession was taking place, Castro's government was organizing what was called the First Congress of Education and Culture, which significantly concerned everything that opposed what its title implied; it was evident that what he wanted was to put an end to all Cuban culture. Even positions concerning fashion were dictated there. Fashion was being identified as ideological diversionism and a subtle penetration by Yankee imperialism.

The cruelest attacks of that congress were unleashed against homosexuals. Paragraphs were read labeling homosexuals as pathological cases, and more important, it was decided that all homosexuals who held positions in cultural organizations should be immediately severed from their jobs. The system of *parametraje* [parameterization] was imposed; that is, every gay writer, every gay artist, every gay dramatist, received a telegram telling him that his behavior did not fall within the political and moral parameters necessary for his job, and that he was therefore either terminated or offered another job in the forced-labor camps.

Agricultural labor or gravedigger jobs were the kinds of work offered to the "parameterized" intellectuals. It was evident that a dark cloud had descended upon Cuban intellectuals. By then it had become impossible even to think of leaving the country. Since 1970 Fidel had been proclaiming that all those who wanted to leave had done so. Thus the Island became a maximum-security jail, where everybody, according to Castro, was happy to stay.

Every artist who had a homosexual past or who had slipped politically ran the risk of losing his job. I remember the case of the Camejos, who had created one of the most important Cuban artistic institutions, the Guiñol [Puppet] Theater. Along with most of the actors and puppeteers in that group, they were suddenly parameterized and their theater destroyed.

Agents of State Security, such as Héctor Quesada or Lieutenant Pavón, were now in charge of the witch-hunt. The raids had resumed and the splendid big boys of State Security again dressed up as obsequious faggots and went out to arrest anyone who dared look at them.

One of the hottest scandals of the moment was Roberto Blanco's arrest and public trial. He had been a very important theater director in Cuba during the sixties, but had recently made the mistake of admiring the erect phallus of one of those splendid big boys of State Security; handcuffed, his hair close-shorn, Blanco was escorted to a public trial held in the very theater of which he had been the director.

Public humiliation has always been one of Castro's favorite weapons: the degrading of people in front of a public always eager to make fun of any weakness in another, or of any person who had lost favor. It was not enough to be accused; you had to say you were sorry and beat your chest before an audience that would applaud and laugh. After that, shorn and handcuffed, you had to purify yourself of your weaknesses in a sugarcane field or by doing some other agricultural work.

One arrest followed another. Even a writer who had won national poetry awards, such as René Ariza, was suddenly sentenced to eight years in jail, accused of ideological diversionism. Another writer who had won awards, José Lorenzo Fuentes, was also sentenced, but to thirty years in jail. El Beny had also been detained, for corruption of minors or something like that, and was by then at a forced-labor camp. Others, of course, tried to get out of the country by any means available. Esteban Luis Cárdenas jumped from a building into the Argentine embassy; he did fall into the patio of the embassy, but Cuban authorities, not inclined to respect any diplomatic treaty, went in and dragged him off to jail.

How many young people have died, and are still dying, trying to cross the Florida Strait or simply gunned down by the coast guard of State Security? Others opted for a more foolproof way to escape, that is, suicide. The poet Martha Vignier chose this option; she jumped from the roof of her home and smashed herself to bits on the pavement.

Very few options were open to writers, or to anyone, for that matter. Cuba is a police state, and the most practical solution for many is to become policemen. Pepe Malas, Hiram Prado, Oscar Rodríguez—all of a sudden they became informers for Fidel Castro's regime. Others, who wanted to continue writing against all odds, gathered in small groups such as the one I and the Abreu brothers formed in Lenin Park.

On one occasion, my need to read a story to someone was such that we rented a boat at Patricio Lumumba Beach, when this was still permitted. We were not allowed to venture very far, but we rowed a little offshore and I did read my story to Reinaldo Gómez Ramos, Jorge Oliva, and the Abreu brothers.

Now it was no longer a question of preserving the manuscripts and getting them out whenever we could; the time had come to get ourselves out at all costs, to leave that place by swimming to the U.S. naval base at Guantánamo, or perhaps as a stowaway in an airplane, a feat that seemed totally out of reach.

It was said that someone had built a giant fan from one of the chairs at Coppelia and, using it as a helicopter, had soared over the fence of the base at Caimanera and landed in U.S. territory.

Some were lucky, such as Jorge Oliva and Ñica, who swam to the naval base at Guantánamo; by the time we found out, they were already in New York. According to gossip, Jorge Oliva sent a telegram to Guillén saying: "Didn't you call me a *pargo* [Cuba: red snapper/gay]? Well, I swam away."

I was fortunate during all those years in that my friendship with Jorge and Margarita Camacho was indestructible. Through some French tourist they always managed to send me a letter that would comfort me, and very often they would send a shirt, a pair of shoes, a handkerchief, or a bottle of cologne. These gifts became symbols of life to me, as I pictured them coming from a country that is free; they even smelled different. Wearing those clothes or shoes for the first time, we walked differently. This, to some extent, made us a little freer and connected us to a world in which people could still breathe. But the most impressive moment was when one of those tourists, to whom we had told our horror stories, returned to the West. That person became for us a magical being only because he or she could take a plane and leave the Island, leave that prison. How envious we were, watching Olga pass through the glass doors at the airport into the area reserved for those who had exit permits or for foreigners who had come for a visit. Olga would vanish behind those glass doors and we would run to the terrace from which we could see her walk up the stairway and disappear into the plane. There was great joy in imagining that we were the ones entering that plane, saying good-bye, and leaving that hell behind. And when the plane lifted off, we watched it vanish in the clouds, full of people who were able to leave, to hate the system, to say what they wanted, to buy themselves a pair of shoes whenever they wished to. But we had to stay behind, and had to stand in line then for a long time, waiting for a bus to return to Havana. We would look sadly at one another in our rustic clothes, our skin burned by the sun and our vitamin deficiencies.

A TRIP TO HOLGUÍN

One of my few escapes during this time was to visit my mother in Oriente. To get there was, needless to say, quite an odyssey. The ticket had to be purchased several months in advance, and there were long lines for the train, which was always overcrowded. And then, in Holguín, you saw so many shops shut down, and crowds of peasants who slept for days by the doors of the stores still in business, to see if they could get a pair of shoes.

Before getting to my mother's house, I would always think of her on the porch or even on the street, sweeping. She had a light way of sweeping, as if removing the dirt were not as important as moving the broom over the ground. Her way of sweeping was symbolic; so airy, so fragile, with a broom that swept nothing; it seemed that an ancestral habit forced her to repeat the motion. Perhaps with that broom she tried to sweep away all the horrors, all the loneliness, all the misery that had accompanied her all her life, and me, her only son, now a homosexual in disgrace and persecuted as a writer.

I see her even now, sad and resigned, passing that broom over the wooden porch, searching the horizon, perhaps still waiting for her lover, her fiancé, the man who seduced her one day and who never came back or wanted nothing more to do with her.

My mother's nightmare was that I would end up in jail. Every time I visited her in Oriente she asked me to get married. Her request was so sad and so absurd. I would finally let her persuade me. Why not give that woman, who had known so few joys in life, one last pleasure? She wanted me to have a son and to bring him to her so her old age would not be so lonely. And I would return to Havana sadder than when I left.

My aunt tried by every means to throw me out of her house and got me into all kinds of trouble with my neighbors. She told everybody that I brought men into my room, that I was a counterrevolutionary, and that if the block was full of thieves it was because of the friends I brought home. Incidentally, my aunt also often stole my few belongings, the clothes Margarita and Jorge had sent me from abroad. Her husband, a grotesque, fat man, was a member of the Communist Party. I felt he was a repressed queer and that was why he would always get so furious when he saw one of those beautiful recruits or students enter my room. My aunt deceived him with whoever was willing to go to bed with her, but there were not many: the grocer, the old man at the corner whose business had been taken over by the government, the husband of one of her best friends, Gloria, who also worked for State Security. While my aunt was making love with those men in the bedroom, my uncle Chucho would be doing the dishes in the kitchen.

Her two sons were young men already. The older one married and the other one, although homosexual, also wanted to get married, now that he had no other choice. Therefore, they needed to get me out of the little room I was occupying in their house.

My aunt was not only a wanton woman, a gossip, and a schemer; she could also be really cruel. She was a kind of picaresque character. For example, when she moved into the house in Miramar, which she had acquired through a high official of the Castro government, the first thing she did was to clean out all the neighboring homes. Their original owners and former occupants, the wealthy bourgeoisie, were now abroad. The area had been declared "frozen," and only the district director, Noelia Silvia Fonseca, was authorized to assign one of those homes. However, so many requirements had to be met to get one that for years most of them remained closed. My aunt, taking advantage of the situation, would enter the houses at night with her sons and steal whatever caught her fancy.

In Havana blackouts were common; the government would often shut off electric power during the evening to save energy. My aunt took advantage of the blackouts to invade those deserted residences and take everything she could. One night, while she was crossing the street with a cabinet full of fine dishes and crystal glasses, the lights came back on and my aunt fled, leaving it all in the middle of the street. The police were puzzled by that cabinet in the middle of Fifth Avenue, but they never found out that my aunt had been responsible.

My aunt's worst act of cruelty was not against me but against an old lady, a neighbor of hers. All of the woman's children were abroad; she had been left behind, together with a retarded daughter. My aunt, who was president of the Committee for the Defense in the area and, according to her own reports, an important informer for State Security, promised the woman that she would arrange an exit permit for her provided that the old lady gave her all her furniture in exchange. The old lady's home was emptied out. She was the mother of Alfonso Artime, who had been a famous political prisoner. Government officials thought that Artime would return by sea one day to visit his mother secretly, and they could arrest him; for that reason they would not allow the poor woman to leave. And my aunt, while promising the old lady that she would help her leave, was filing terrible reports on her with State Security, so that they would never permit her to go. The old lady died in Cuba in an absolutely empty house; all of her furniture had been moved to my aunt's home.

I was afraid not only of the police but also of my aunt's vigilance, which to me was much more dangerous. It meant that during my last years in her house, everything I wrote had to be hurriedly hidden in the roof that same day.

By then—that is, during 1972 and 1973—I was already known abroad for my novels *Fray Servando* and *Singing from the Well*, which had been translated into various languages, and also for a collection of short stories. Publishers frequently wrote me letters which I never received; my aunt, who was in charge of receiving the mail, would intercept them. At other times State Security did not give her the opportunity to perform this heroic, Revolutionary duty: my mail did not even reach her hands.

When Hiram Prado was sent to a concentration camp in Oriente, he wrote me incessantly, making references not only to his own erotic adventures but also to mine. One fine day, a lieutenant of Security, Vladimir Cid Arias, a cousin-in-law of mine and close friend of my aunt, came up to my room. He said, "Reinaldo, you have to leave this house because you are an immoral person; here is the proof." He produced a letter addressed to me by Hiram Prado; it was a letter I had not read because I never received it. My aunt had taken the liberty of opening it, reading it, and arranging for my cousin to kick me out of the room. This was too much. I was furious and told him it was an invasion of privacy. Although it was absurd, I told him I would call the police and accuse them all of violation of privacy. Finally, although he did not return my letter, he said he would rather not get involved in such a crooked deal.

My aunt also mounted a fierce watch on the young men who visited me. If one of them jumped over the wall to get to my room, she would come out with a broom and, screaming fiercely, threaten to call the police.

Among the poets who visited me behind my aunt's back

was Guillermo Rosales, then a handsome young man who had written a wonderful novel and had ideas for fifty more, with excellent plots. Guillermo would often sit on the balcony of my little room until I had finished typing some chapter of whatever novel I was then writing. Once, while Guillermo was waiting for me to finish my writing, Nelson Rodríguez and Jesús Castro Villalonga, both writers, came to see me.

After finishing my chapter, which I believe was part of *The Palace of the White Skunks*, I switched from the agonies of what I was writing to the agonies of my friends, who were desperate. Guillermo wanted to leave the Island even if it meant going up in a balloon; he always had incredible plans: to leave on a raft pulled by swift fish; to disguise himself as Nicolás Guillén and take a plane, since Guillén was the only Cuban writer allowed to travel out of the country. By the way, when Padilla was arrested, we planned to kidnap Nicolás Guillén and to demand, in exchange for his freedom, that Padilla be placed on a plane going to any free country in the West. The idea was mine, but it was totally out of the question, considering we were in a communist country. If they refused our demands, we would send Guillén's head to the administrator of UNEAC, the fearsome Bienvenido Suárez.

It was a crazy idea, but Padilla did not give us any time to carry it out. It should be pointed out here that Nicolás Guillén, undoubtedly aware of what was going to happen at that UNEAC meeting, at least spared himself the indignity of being the one to introduce Padilla to make his confession, a function which, as president of UNEAC, he was expected to perform. A month before the event he became suddenly "ill" and admitted himself into one of the hospitals that the Cuban government had established for its high officials. There Guillén sequestered himself and did not come out until after Padilla's unprecedented mea culpa.

The person in charge of those dirty theatrics was José

Antonio Portuondo who, together with Roberto Fernández Retamar, is one of the most sinister figures of Cuban culture.

NELSON RODRÍGUEZ

Guillermo Rosales's uneasiness that afternoon in my house came from his wish to read us a chapter of a novel he was writing inspired by the personality of Stalin. He read it frantically and left. Nelson and Jesús invited me for a walk on the beach. Nelson had been in one of the concentration camps in 1964 and now, in view of the renewed persecutions, was terrified; he did not feel strong enough to live through those horrors again. He said he needed my help because he wanted to leave the country, though he did not tell me how he intended to accomplish this. The help he wanted was of an intellectual nature; he needed me to write a letter recommending a book of stories that he had written; it was an extraordinary book of vignettes about the UMAP concentration camp where he had been held.

We returned home, I wrote the letter, and then we went to UNEAC, where I still had to sign a register in order to collect my salary. Needless to say, by then I was not allowed to write for UNEAC; I was not even allowed to check the work to be published in *La Gaceta de Cuba*, but since I had not yet been fired, I had to sign the register. When we were done at UNEAC, Nelson and Jesús invited me for ice cream at El Carmelo, on Calzada Street. We stood in line for a long time, and finally were able to get a table. There was not much to talk about in Cuban restaurants, where you did not know who would be sitting next to you listening in, but I noticed that Nelson tried to stretch out our stay there. At some point he said, "The only one who could have saved us from this situation was San Heberto." He often referred to Heberto Padilla this way while Padilla was in jail, but now Padilla was no longer a saint; in front of all those people he had become a traitor. As we were leaving, Nelson told me, "Now, there is only one choice: to escape from this country, and that is what I intend to do."

We walked through the streets of the Vedado, criticizing everything, even the sun, the heat; everything bothered us. Nelson was very grateful for the letter I had given him; it was a recommendation to my editor in France. Finally, late at night, we hugged and said good-bye. During the whole evening I had the impression that he wanted to tell me something else but did not dare.

Two days later, on the front page of *Granma*, I read the following news: "Two homosexual counterrevolutionaries, Nelson Rodríguez and Angel López Rabí, tried to hijack a Cubana de Aviación plane and divert it to the United States." The report said that everyone on the plane had reacted against those antisocial people and overpowered them quickly. It also said that one of the counterrevolutionaries had thrown a grenade, but luckily, the plane had been able to make an emergency landing at José Martí Airport, and that the counterrevolutionaries would be condemned by a military court. This is all *Granma* said; evidently they did not wish to publicize the fact that those involved in the incident were both writers.

I was terrified. Nelson must have boarded the plane with my letter of recommendation for his manuscript of UMAP stories. We later found out what had actually happened. Nelson, his friend Angel López (fifteen years old and a poet), and Jesús Castro had purchased tickets for a domestic flight to Cienfuegos. They planned to board the plane with all their luggage and old books with the idea of going to the United States. Jesús and Nelson, while in the army, had appropriated some grenades and hid them in their yard. Their plan was to threaten the pilots with the grenades if they refused to divert the plane. But Jesús Castro got cold feet at the last minute, and did not board. After takeoff,

Nelson pulled out a grenade and told the passengers that he would throw it if the plane was not diverted. Immediately the heavily armed official guard (one was assigned to every Cuban plane) and several Security agents rushed at Nelson, trying to kill him. One of the passengers on the plane, whom I am not going to name because he is still in Cuba, told me the story in detail. Nelson ran through the entire length of the plane holding his grenade behind the terrified passengers in a threatening manner, while his pursuers tried to get a straight shot at him. Nelson yelled to Angel to throw his grenade, but Angel did not dare, so Nelson tossed his. One of the Security chiefs threw himself on the grenade to smother the explosion, but to no avail. A large hole was blown in the plane, which had already gained some altitude. As soon as the plane was able to land, Nelson took advantage of the confusion and jumped through the hole blown out by the grenade, but he was hit by the plane's propeller. Seriously injured, he spent a year in the hospital. When the State Security doctors finally managed to patch him up, he was sentenced to death and executed, together with his friend Angel López, who was then only sixteen years old.

Jesús Castro Villalonga, who had not taken the plane but had known of the plans, was sentenced to thirty years in jail.

The other passengers, who had remained in their seats without helping Castro's police, were arrested on suspicion and had to submit to an investigation. I think they also wished the plane had been hijacked.

As to my letter, I presume it disappeared in the midst of the grenade explosion and the fire that ensued, or perhaps found its way into the files of State Security as further evidence against me. They knew I was in their hands.

While still in Cuba, I wrote a story about Nelson's experiences at the concentration camps, *Arturo, la estrella más brillante* [*The Brightest Star*, published together with *Old Rosa*, the title of the book]. It is dedicated, of course, to him: "To Nelson, in the air." Later, in exile, I wrote a poem in which I asked the gods to always keep Nelson in that defiant stance, grenade in hand, fleeing the island. I do not know if they have granted my wish.

My aunt, naturally, had learned about Nelson's intent to flee. Now, according to her, I was not only a counterrevolutionary faggot but was linked to terrorists who hijacked planes, grenades in hand. One way or another, I had to get out of her house, but I had no place to go.

In Cuba the State owns all housing; to get a simple apartment is a privilege enjoyed only by high-ranking officials. To get a television set or a refrigerator required many years of cutting sugarcane, of accumulating labor and political credits, and of demonstrating irreproachable behavior. I had none of those credits and my conduct was indeed far from irreproachable.

Nevertheless, there were many empty houses in my area, though a number of them were occupied by female scholarship students who, coming from remote towns in Cuba, were happy to live in a plush Miramar mansion, which they were slowly but relentlessly destroying. Once my aunt and I heard loud noises; the peasant girls were dismantling all the windows of the mansion and using the wooden frames to build a huge fire in the yard so they could boil and whiten their clothes. In this manner, many of the most elegant features of those homes, and also their furniture, ended up as firewood.

THE WEDDING Near my aunt's house there was an empty room in one of the abandoned homes. Whoever had once lived there had died years ago; no one was there now. I requested it through UNEAC, but Bienvenido Suárez, a crook who could at times be charming, told me that the room could only be given to a married couple. What Bienvenido Suárez was evidently trying to tell me was that the Revolution was not going to give the room to a homosexual for him to bring men there. I had to find a woman, get married, and submit a formal request for the room to Mrs. Noelia Fonseca, the district director.

Ingrávida Félix was a talented actress who had given an extraordinary performance in *La noche de los asesinos* [The Night of the Murderers], a theater piece written by José Triana and directed by Vicente Revuelta. She was also featured in one of the most famous Cuban movies of the time, *Lucía*, by Humberto Solás. Ingrávida liked men, she was certainly not a lesbian; she was divorced, and her private life could not be considered immoral just for having a lover now and then. However, Castro's puritanism also looked askance at single women who had a rather free sex life. For these reasons, Ingrávida was parameterized and fired from her job, in spite of her enormous acting talent. This parameterization even caught up with the famous singer Alba Marina because she had a lover twenty or thirty years her junior.

During that time, there were notorious arrests of women at trysting hotels. These hotels had been created by the Revolution so that heterosexuals could rent a room for a few hours to make love. The police, however, would raid them to find out which women were committing adultery, especially if any happened to be the wife of some Communist Party stalwart. The women were punished and even fired from their jobs, and their husbands were immediately informed in a public assembly.

The Castro regime, in other words, regarded women, along with homosexuals, as inferior beings. "Macho" men could have several women and it was seen as a sign of virility. This situation brought women and homosexuals together, at least for protection, and especially if the woman, like Ingrávida Félix, had suffered persecution for the same weakness: because she liked men. So when I spoke with Ingrávida about my predicament, she agreed to marry me, and I could then submit an application for that room. She had two kids and had to figure out a way to support them and herself; I helped her with my UNEAC salary. Virgilio Piñera also organized collections so that she and her children would not starve. With the purchase permits given in Cuba to people about to be married, we bought some clothes, and then got married.

The best man at the wedding was Miguel Figueroa, who wanted to go to bed with Ingrávida that same night, provided I did the same with Olga. Poor Miguel, always looking for gays to go to bed with his wife. I refused because I was eager to go to the beach. Another extraordinary privilege for newlyweds was that they could rent a house at the beach for four or five days.

Ingrávida finally agreed to go to a hotel with Miguel, or perhaps to the house where he lived with Olga, and she would meet me at the beach the following day. There was a group of young guys next to the beach house, and while I was waiting for Ingrávida I developed a relationship with one of them. I told him I was waiting for my wife and that I had just gotten married; this seemed to get him even more excited. We had a memorable encounter, although perhaps because I was the man who had just married, he decided to play the passive part. He was, all the same, really virile and this was quite unexpected.

When Ingrávida arrived, I already had a lover who began acting jealous because my wife was so beautiful; Ingrávida was then an extremely beautiful woman. She came with her kids, who had never had a chance to play at the beach. There was a park with a playground nearby, and we spent the whole day pushing the kids on the swings, always under the jealous eyes of my young lover.

At the beach we wrote the letter to Noelia Silva Fonseca requesting the room. The gossip of the town was that this woman was Celia Sánchez's lover. The text of the letter was pretty pathetic, making an appeal to Noelia's womanhood and to her Revolutionary spirit. But that room, like all our plans, was never to be anything else: just a plan.

The woman did not even bother to answer us. I had to stay in the maid's room at my aunt's house, with my aunt always threatening to throw me out into the street or send me to jail. To top it all, Ingrávida became pregnant, not even knowing herself by whom; she had no idea whether the baby she was expecting would be black, brown, or have Asian features. Her financial situation became desperate, and since we were married, I would be legally bound to take care of that baby.

I felt besieged and with good reason. Sometimes while I was writing, the patrol car came by and was parked under my window for hours; it was like a warning or a way of further intimidating me. Now Miguel Figueroa, Jorge Dávila, and I met only on the beach, where there would be no police to listen in on us. Olga had gone to Paris again, and Miguel had asked her to bring swim fins and diving equipment so he could escape, even if it meant he would have to swim out and, once on the open sea, hope that some ship would pick him up and take him no matter where.

At Lezama's home I heard the story of a woman who jumped into the water at the Malecón in the hope of swimming out to a Greek ship that was leaving port. The Greeks helped her aboard, and then called the Cuban police and turned her over to them. Those Greeks were a distant cry from the classic Greeks who fought in the battle of Troy.

At times people were arrested with no clear proof that they had intended to leave the country. They were arrested just because of some suspicious comment or plan they had made. This happened, for example, to Julián Portales, who had told some friends that he wanted to seek asylum in a Latin American embassy. His friends were State Security informers, and they encouraged him to go to the Argentine

embassy. He was arrested before he had even made it to the
~~embassy side of the street.~~

This was one of the most vicious acts perpetrated by Castroism: to break the bonds of friendship. To make us mistrust our best friends because the system was turning them into informers, into undercover agents. I already mistrusted many of my friends.

The most dramatic aspect of this situation was that such people were victims of blackmail as well as of the system itself, and they were on the point of becoming dehumanized.

Ingrávida finally gave birth to a white boy with sort of bluish eyes. Whose child could he be? Ingrávida said René de la Nuez was the father, but he was enraged and forced her to officially state in a letter that he was not the father of her son. This man was a member of the Communist Party, and worked as a cartoonist for *Granma*; he did not want to be involved with a woman of ill repute.

THE ARREST I thought that my predicament had reached its limit, but if there is a lesson to be learned under a totalitarian system, it is that calamities never seem to end. In the summer of 1973 Pepe Malas and I were bathing at Guanabo Beach. We had sex in the mangroves with some young guys and really enjoyed ourselves with them.

After making love, we left our beach bags in the sand and went back into the water. Within a half hour we realized we had been robbed; our recent lovers had taken our bags. Pepe called the police, and this should never have been done in our case. The patrol car drove us along the beach to see if we could find the thieves. We did indeed find them, as well as our beach bags, in a pine grove near the shore.

The police arrested them and the matter was clear-cut:

they were caught with the stolen property. We had to go to the police station, which was ill-advised in this situation. If you live in a country such as this, any contact with the police is best avoided. The young guys arrived in a very good mood and said, "These are a couple of queers who tried to fondle us; they touched our pricks. We took their bags because when we beat them up, they fled. We were on our way to the police station to return them." The story was not credible, but we were obviously homosexual, and the boys had an uncle who was a cop at the Guanabo police station. So, from accusers we had turned into the accused, and that night we were already under arrest and slept at the police station.

I was naive enough to think the boys had no proof against us, and if anything could be proven, it was that they had robbed us. But I had overlooked a Castroist article of law stating that in the case of a homosexual committing a sexual crime, anyone's accusation was enough grounds for prosecution. Not only were legal proceedings brought against us, but we were taken to the Guanabo jail.

The UNEAC report was very damaging for me. All of a sudden, everything positive had disappeared from my file, and I was nothing but a homosexual counterrevolutionary who had dared to publish books abroad.

We were released on bail. I remember that Tomasito La Goyesca took care of getting the cash, which would not have been easy for us because we had to pay four hundred pesos and neither of us had that kind of money. When we were out on the street we continued to hope we would be acquitted; the whole thing was completely absurd, and there was no evidence against us.

I still had to go to UNEAC, of course, to sign the register and collect my salary, though every day I was given dirty looks as if I had the plague; and now, as the final blow, I had a trial pending. Suddenly, it seemed I had become invisible; not even the door guards greeted me as I walked in;

it didn't make any difference that some of them were also gay.

I had appointed a lawyer to handle my case. He told me not to worry; there really was no proof against me, and there was no crime they could accuse me of. But one afternoon he called me, rather nervous, and asked me to see him at his home. He pulled out an intimidating dossier of evidence against me, including a list of titles and descriptions of all the novels I had published abroad. That lengthy report, in which I was accused of being a counterrevolutionary who had smuggled all his books out of Cuba without UNEAC's authorization, was signed by people who, apparently up to that moment, had been excellent friends of mine and only recently were patting me on the back, telling me not to worry, nothing would happen to me. Among those who signed it, accusing me of constant counterrevolutionary activities, were Nicolás Guillén, Otto Fernández, José Martínez Matos, and Bienvenido Suárez.

Evidently, I was no longer being accused of just a common crime, a public scandal, as the original arrest records showed. Now I was a counterrevolutionary engaged in incessant propaganda against the regime, which I published abroad. Everything had been set up in order to convict me. The district attorney, in his provisional conclusions, said that my crimes warranted eight years in jail.

Pepe Malas's case had been separated from mine in a strange way; he was accused only of causing a minor public disturbance. His name scarcely appeared in the proceedings.

My aunt, naturally, knew all about it. She had also submitted a long report for the courts, informing on my depraved life-style and my counterrevolutionary activities. There was no escape.

Olga, Miguel's wife, was returning to Paris shortly and perhaps for the last time, because she was also afraid that, at some point, they would no longer let her out of Cuba. I told her all about my problems. She said that once in Paris, she would contact my friends Jorge and Margarita Camacho, and my publisher. They would find some way to smuggle me out of the country. I told her that I was in immediate danger of being arrested before my trial, that it would be better for me to flee than to have to stand trial. I would hide somewhere and send Olga a telegram saying, "Send the flower book." They could send an inflatable boat, a false passport with my photograph in it, and diving gear—something I could use to escape from the country.

These, to be sure, were farfetched hopes, hopes born of despair, but hope is, after all, mostly for the desperate. I did not want to resign myself to imprisonment. Before Olga left, I quickly typed my poem "To Die in June, Gasping for Air"—I had given the draft to some friends who are still in Cuba—as well as "Leper Colony," which begins with my experience in the Guanabo jail. Olga smuggled these long poems out.

I knew a beautiful black guy with whom I frequently made love amid the shrubbery of Monte Barreto. I could no longer make love in my aunt's house because she had threatened to call the police. To be mounted by that man, naked and surrounded by nature, with the smell of fresh grass around us, was actually more exciting than it would have been in bed. I told him what was happening to me, and he asked me to meet him the next day at the beach; from there we would go to Guantánamo, and he would help me escape through the naval base.

That night I met Hiram Prado and Pepe Malas. I told Hiram about my decision to leave the country in a boat via the U.S. naval base at Guantánamo. Confiding my plans was, unquestionably, an act of extreme naïveté; in Cuba you cannot tell secrets to anybody. The next day I got up very early. I had already given my typewriter to the Abreu brothers, and they had provided me with some money for the trip to Guantánamo. The police, however, had gotten up even earlier.

I heard a knock at the door and went out on the balcony to take a look. Several cops had surrounded the house; they came in and arrested me at once. I was treated with unnecessary violence. They beat me, stripped me to see if I had any weapons, made me dress again, and escorted me to the patrol car. As I was getting into the car, my aunt opened the door; I saw her radiant face and expression of complicity as she looked at the cops who were arresting me.

They locked me up in a cell with twenty other people at the Miramar police station. Before being jailed, I was questioned briefly; major interrogations would come later. The questioner asked me why I had been arrested. I told him that I did not know, that I was free on bail and, therefore, my arrest was illegal. That was enough for the interrogator to beat me up.

THE FLIGHT There was no bathroom in the cell—it was outside—and the detainees were constantly asking for permission to go. The police officer stood by the cell door, padlock in hand, to watch the others. On one of those occasions, while the officer was waiting by the cell door, another officer arrived and announced that he had brought hot espresso, a privilege in Cuba, where coffee is rationed at three ounces a month per person. The announcement started a great commotion at the station; all the police officers rushed to the coveted Thermos bottle. The officer guarding the gate also went, leaving the open padlock on the gate. I quickly unbolted the lock and, crouching, escaped from prison.

I ran out through the back door, which led to the shore, freed myself of my clothes, and jumped into the water. I was a good swimmer then. I swam away from shore and to Patricio Lumumba Beach, near my aunt's house. Once there,

I saw a friend with whom I had had a few erotic adventures. I told him what had happened, and he managed to get me a pair of shorts from one of the lifeguards. Dressed that way, I immediately showed up at my aunt's house. She was absolutely flabbergasted to see me there; it was only a short time since I had been arrested and taken away in a patrol car. I told her it had all been a mistake that was cleared up right away and I only needed to pay a fine; I had come home to get the money. But my money was no longer there; my aunt had taken it. I demanded, somewhat violently, that she return it. A little intimidated, she gave me back only half of it.

I ran toward the beach to meet my black friend, but it was swarming with policemen. They were evidently searching for me. Luckily, it did not occur to them at first to look for me at home, which enabled me to pick up the money and destroy everything there that might compromise me. The friend who had gotten me the shorts hid me in one of the booths at the beach, then checked my house and confirmed that it was surrounded by policemen with guard dogs. He told me to jump into the water and hide behind a buoy, where the dogs would not be able to find me. I stayed there all day, and in the evening my friend signaled me to come out of the water. He bought me a pizza with his own money; mine was completely soaked. He then hid me in the lifeguard's booth. The following day the beach was crawling with policemen looking for me; I could not come out of my hiding place. My friend provided me with an inner tube, a can of beans, and a bottle of rum. In the evening we walked through the pines to La Concha Beach. He had also gotten me a pair of swim fins, and the only solution seemed to be that I leave the country on an inner tube. Before jumping in, I hid my money under some rocks near the shore. My friend and I said good-bye. "Good luck, my brother," he said. He was crying.

I tied the tube to my neck with a piece of rope. He had

fitted the tube with a gunnysack in such a way that I could sit on it. A small jute bag held the bottle of rum and the can of black beans. I stowed the bag securely, and got into the water. I had to make my escape from the very beach where I had spent the most beautiful years of my youth.

As I was swimming out, the ocean was turning increasingly rougher: it was the choppy November surf, announcing the arrival of winter. All night I swam out, but at the mercy of the waves my progress was slow. When I was about three or four miles away from shore, I realized it would be difficult to get anywhere. On the high seas I had no way of opening the bottle, and my legs and joints were almost frozen.

Suddenly a boat appeared in the darkness, heading straight at me. I jumped off and submerged so I could hide under the tube. The boat stopped about twenty yards from me and extended a huge claw—it looked like a giant crab—which plunged into the water. Apparently it was a sand hauler trying to dig up sand. I heard voices and laughter, but they did not see me.

Clearly there was no point in going on. Farther out I saw a line of lights: the coast guard, fishermen, or more sand haulers. They formed a sort of wall on the horizon. The waves were getting rougher and rougher. I had to try to get back.

I remember seeing something shiny in the deep and was afraid a shark might take a bite out of my legs, which, of course, I tried to keep out of the water. A few hours before dawn I realized that the whole thing was absurd, that even the tube was a hindrance; that I could almost get to the United States faster by swimming freely than by riding on that tube, without oars or direction. I got off the tube, and swam for more than three hours toward shore, the bag containing the bottle and can of beans tied to my waist. I was almost paralyzed and my greatest fear now was to get cramps and drown.

I reached the coast at Jaimanitas Beach and noticed some

empty buildings. I hid in one of them; never had I felt such intense cold or such deep loneliness. I had failed and would be arrested any minute now. There was only one way for me to escape: suicide. I smashed the bottle of rum and with the pieces of broken glass slashed my wrists. I thought it was the end, of course, and lay down in a corner of the empty house, slowly losing consciousness. I felt that this was death.

Around ten o'clock the following day I woke up thinking I was in another world. But I was in the same place where I had attempted, unsuccessfully, to end my life. Though I had bled profusely, at some point the bleeding had stopped. With the shards of the broken bottle I opened the can of beans; they restored my strength somewhat. Then I washed my cuts in the sea. The inner tube had also washed ashore, not too far away.

I started walking along the beach, without any clear sense of direction, and suddenly came upon a group of men, close-shorn, lying on the sand. They looked at me a little surprised but did not say a word. I realized they were forced laborers, prisoners at a farm in the Flores section. I had walked by them barefoot and with cuts on my arms; they could not have thought I was a mere bather. Finally I arrived at La Concha, and recovered the hidden money.

On my way to the place where I had hidden the money, I heard someone calling me: it was my black friend, who was signaling me to come. I quickly told him what had happened, and he said we could still go at once to Guantánamo; it was his hometown and he knew the area well. Lying under the pines, he traced a map of Caimanera in the sand and told me how I could reach the U.S. naval base.

It was imperative now to get clothes to wear. I saw one of my cousins at the beach, and told him I needed some. He warned me that the police were looking all over for me. The stupidity of the police was incredible; they were searching in vain for me in the very same area where I was. My cousin said he would try to get me something. He left the girl he was with and soon came back with a complete outfit. It was a voluntary, unexpected gesture of kindness I found quite surprising.

I dressed quickly and went with my black friend to his home in Santos Suárez. It was a huge house, full of glass cabinets. He cut my hair very short, almost to the skull; I looked like a different person. When I saw myself in the mirror, I was shocked. Instead of my long hair I now had short hair parted in the middle. He also exchanged the shirt that my cousin had given me for a rougher-looking one. According to him, this was the only way I could avoid being arrested before reaching Guantánamo.

With the money I had, and a little more that his grandmother gave him, we went to the train station. It was not easy to buy tickets for Santiago de Cuba or Guantánamo; you always had to reserve way ahead. But he managed to get them by talking to an employee and slipping him a few pesos.

Again I was in one of those slow, steamy trains to Santiago de Cuba. The black guy immediately made friends with everyone who shared our seat; he had bought a bottle of rum and started drinking. At some point he told me it was a good idea to socialize with everyone around to escape notice.

He spent the whole trip, which lasted three days, drinking and sharing with the others, laughing and telling jokes. He quickly made friends with other black men, some of whom were in fact very beautiful. I would have liked to get off the train and make love with him in any hotel, the way we used to at Monte Barreto; in moments of danger I have always felt the need to have someone close to me. He said it would be difficult to get a hotel room in Santiago, but that we could perhaps find accommodations in Guantánamo.

At Santiago we took a bus for Guantánamo, but first we ate some of those croquettes sold at cafeterias in Cuba and jokingly called "palatial" croquettes because they had a tendency to stick to your palate in such a way that it was almost impossible to dislodge them.

We arrived at Guantánamo, a town that seemed horrendous to me, flatter and more provincial even than Holguín. The black man took me to a tenement, which looked like a den of criminals. He told me to take off all my clothes because he had acquired another set even more rustic than mine. He also asked me to give him all my money; it made no sense for me to take that Cuban money with me if I was going to enter United States territory. I did not like the idea, but I had no choice. He took me to the terminal from which I could take the bus to Caimanera, and refused to accompany me on this trip. He had given me all the necessary instructions: to get off at the checkpoint, turn right toward the river, walk along the riverbank and when the lights of the airport became visible, hide in the bushes till nightfall, swim across the river and proceed on the other side until reaching the ocean; then stay hidden around there all day, and the following night, jump in and swim to the naval base.

It was not hard to remain unnoticed inside the bus; the black man had been right in disguising me the way he did. After I got off, to avoid being seen I walked almost on all fours for many hours. Around midnight, while I was crawling through those wild bushes, startled quail and other birds would fly off. I crawled on. Suddenly I heard a thunderous noise; it was the river. It was a great joy to look at the water. My black friend had not deceived me; the river was there. I continued walking along the riverbank; it was very swampy. I still had in my hand a piece of bread the black man had told me not to eat until I was ready to jump in. At dawn I finally saw the lights of the airport; they seemed like party lights to me. They would go on and off, as if they were beckoning me. It was time to get into the water.

While walking next to the river I kept hearing crackling sounds. I do not know why, but it seemed to me that the Moon was telling me not to go into those waters. I continued walking until I got to a place where I did not hear those crackling sounds anymore, and looked for a good spot to enter the river. Suddenly, strange green lights began appearing in the bushes. They looked like lightning, except they did not come down from the sky but sprang out of the ground, next to the tree trunks. I kept on walking and seeing green lights. A few seconds later I heard machine-gun fire; the bullets seemed to be grazing me. I later found out that those green lights were signals; they were infrared lights. The guards had discovered that someone was trying to cross the border; they were trying to locate and, of course, to exterminate the intruder. I ran to a tree with a dense canopy and climbed as high as I could, hugging the trunk. Cars came, full of soldiers with dogs, looking for me. All night they searched, at times rather close to my hiding place. At last, they left.

I spent the whole day and the following night up in the tree. It was hard to get down without being seen, especially since the area was already on alert. At dusk I finally climbed down. Tired, I had to gather all my strength to get back to Guantánamo, and from there plan a different, perhaps less hazardous, escape route that would get me to the naval base. I dragged myself through the mud and, once close to the highway, fell asleep in the shrubbery. Early the next day I washed my face and cleaned my clothes as best I could, returned to the number 1 checkpoint, and took the bus back to Guantánamo. I arrived in town with no idea where to look for my black friend, and wandered aimlessly through the streets, a dangerous proposition in my case. I had no money. At the Guantánamo train terminal I came across the black guy. He looked scared; evidently he thought I was either dead or at the naval base. He told me that it would be impossible to make another try, that the place he had directed me to was really the best one, and that every place was being watched much more closely now, according to his friends. He told me I had been very lucky after all, because some boxes that I mentioned having seen were mines, and if I had stepped on one, it would have blown me to bits. But I refused to give up; a return meant accepting failure. I decided to try again. The area was under closer surveillance, but I had nothing to lose. It had been absurd to listen to the Moon. This time I entered the water and by the light of the Moon I was able to see where the crackling sounds had come from: the river was infested with alligators. I have never seen so many sinister-looking animals in such a small expanse of water. They were just waiting there for me to get in so they could devour me. It was impossible to cross that river. Again I returned to Guantánamo covered with mud. No doubt the bus driver thought I was a coastguardman working for State Security who had been newly transferred to that region.

For three days I walked around Guantánamo, without any food. I didn't have a penny, and continued to sleep at the train terminal. I never saw the black man again. I met some young men at the terminal who were planning to go by train to Havana as stowaways. They told me all one had to do was to hide in the men's room when the conductor came by. I had no other choice, so I decided to make the trip that way.

We boarded the train and the three of us hid in the men's room when the conductor came. It was not long before they became sexually aroused, so I was able to enjoy those excited guys while the train moved slowly through the hills of Oriente. The train would stop at every town and I would get off. Then the train continued, and whenever the conductor passed by, about every four hours, we would hide in the men's room, they would get excited, and those beautiful legs would get entangled with mine. I told them I was a draft evader trying to return home to Havana. They were real draft evaders who wanted to go to Havana because they thought it would be easier to escape notice there than in Guantánamo, their hometown. At one of the stops where we got off, Adrián, one of the young men, gave me an ID. He told me he had another one, and that it might come in handy. The ID had his picture on it, but those photos are so unclear and impersonal that they could look like anyone. From then on I was Adrián Faustino Sotolongo. At Cacocún I left the train and started walking toward Holguín. It was a long stretch. I finally hitched a ride on a truck full of laborers who did not ask any questions. I arrived home at daybreak.

I was returning home alone, persecuted, defeated. My mother opened the door; she screamed at the sight of me, but I asked her to keep quiet. She began to cry silently, and my grandmother fell to her knees and started praying, asking God to please save me. My other aunts said that I should hide under the bed. My mother brought me a piece of chicken and said it pained her greatly to see me like this, under the bed like a dog, hiding to eat. All this distressed me so much I could not have a bite, even though for several days I had had no food at all.

My grandmother was still on her knees, asking God to help me. I had never felt so close to her; she knew that only a miracle could save me. At some point there was an opportunity for me to talk with her, but I did not know what to say. I had not seen her since my grandfather died; she had loved him very much even though he beat her quite often. When she came into the room for a moment, I crawled out from under the bed and hugged her. She told me she could not live without my grandfather Antonio, who had been such a good man. I cried with her; he had beaten her almost every week, but they had lived together for fifty years. Evidently, there had been a great love between them. My grandmother had suddenly aged.

The following day my mother and I left for Havana. Vidal, one of my uncles by marriage, walked us to the train station and lent us some money. I had hoped that perhaps Olga, to whom I had given the address of the Abreu brothers, had been able to make some contacts abroad on my behalf. I had already sent her the Mayday telegram we had agreed upon: "Send me the flower book." She knew that meant I was asking them to get me out by any means.

I was able to sleep on the train. I had never taken a train trip with my mother, and never traveled in a sleeper. She said, "How sad to take such a beautiful trip under these circumstances." My mother was always complaining about everything, but this time she was right. I thought about how beautiful it would have been to enjoy the scenery without the feeling of being persecuted. How pleasant it would have been to travel at my mother's side if I had not been in such a predicament. The simplest things now acquired extraordinary value for me. During the entire trip my mother tried to persuade me to give myself up; she said it would be best for me. She was telling me that one of her neighbors who had been sentenced to thirty years had been released after only ten, and now was free and walked by her house every day, singing. I could not see myself singing in front of my mother's house after ten years in jail; this was not a really promising future. I wanted to get out of that hellhole in any way possible.

When we arrived at the Havana train terminal I was arrested by two undercover cops. My mother was terrified. Her skinny body was shaking. I took her thin hands in mine and told her to wait for me, that everything would be all right. The policemen took me to a small room and asked a few questions. I told them that I had come from Oriente and that my name was Adrián Faustino Sotolongo, and showed them my train ticket and ID. They told me I resembled someone they were looking for who had escaped from a police station in Havana. I answered that it would not be logical for me to be the suspect because I had just arrived in Havana, and the person they were looking for would obviously try to get out of Havana, not come to the city. My reply made sense and I had produced proof of a different identity, so they let me go, after having taken God knows what measurements of my neck. My mother was out there trembling, looking more pathetic by the minute. I told her that we had to separate, that she should stay with my aunt Mercedita, who lived in East Havana. I would call and let the phone ring once. If she received that signal, it meant that she should return to the terminal, where we could meet to work out some plan.

I would try to hide in the home of a friend. I had hopes that if somebody talked with the French ambassador, perhaps he could arrange for me to be granted political asylum at the French embassy; perhaps the ambassador could hide me in his home and obtain an exit permit for me. After all, all my books had been published in France. I was hoping that my mother would go to the home of a French citizen who had been one of my professors, and with whom we had established a certain friendship; it would be easy for him to speak with the ambassador. We had left Holguín with a letter addressed to the ambassador; it was a crazy idea, but perhaps it might work.

I called on Ismael Lorenzo, who lived with his wife. He was very generous and told me I could stay with them. He and I had planned our escape many times, thinking of the Guantánamo naval base. He said it was a miracle that I did not get caught, because when the infrared rays send their signal, the army men do not stop until they have captured their man. He explained to me the real advantage of those infrared rays, that the signal is triggered by heat and the heat source can be any living creature near the detectors. The search team probably thought it had been an animal and therefore had given up.

Lorenzo's home was under surveillance because he had submitted an application for a permit to leave the country, and the Committee for the Defense paid him frequent "friendly" visits. I did not want to endanger his position. After spending a night there, I went to see Reinaldo Gómez

Ramos. He looked at me, terrified. He knew of my escape, of course, and told me it would be absolutely impossible for him to take me in, that I had to leave immediately.

I returned to the terminal and called my mother. We agreed to meet at a nearby park. My uncle Carlos had arrived from Oriente; he was aware of my situation. Carlos was a member of the Communist Party, but for him the family came first and he was good to me. He offered to go with my mother to see the French professor and show him my letter.

They returned a few hours later. They had seen the professor, who was very responsive and within a couple of hours had taken my mother and Carlos to the ambassador. But the ambassador's reply was absolutely negative; he said he could do nothing for me, though he kept my letter. That was the news they brought me.

I gave my mother and Carlos the address of the Abreu brothers. It was absurd for me to remain at the bus station; that was the center of police activity, where they asked for everyone's ID. At night, when I saw the patrol cars, I had the feeling that they were all looking for me. I decided to hide in Lenin Park; it was a park used for many official events and perhaps the last place where the police would look for a political fugitive. I wrote a short message to Juan Abreu. I gave him a date and time when we could meet on the left side of the amphitheater in the park. The amphitheater was surrounded by bushes where I could hide safely.

I did not have to explain much to Juan about my plans to escape with Olga's help. I told him that perhaps she would send someone over from France to get me out of the country. Abreu looked at me and replied, "That person is already here; he arrived three days ago. We were all desperately looking for you. I stopped by your aunt's and she almost had me put in jail." He added that he would see the person the following day; that he seemed to be a very intelligent Frenchman who spoke perfect Spanish.

The Abreu home was being watched closely; everybody

knew they were among my best friends. The Frenchman had shown up there with a bottle of perfume, and said that he had a message from Olga about the "flower book." He had managed to give the hotel police the slip and, without knowing Havana, after taking three or four different buses to confuse the police, had reached the home of the Abreus. Juan Abreu told him the truth, that I was a fugitive and my whereabouts were unknown. The Frenchman's entry permit allowed him to stay a few more days. I had reappeared at just the right time.

My friends in Paris, Jorge and Margarita, informed by Olga of my situation, had decided that it was necessary to immediately find someone unknown to the Castro regime who could go to Cuba and try to get me out. They had contacted Joris Lagarde, the young son of friends of theirs, who was an adventurer and spoke perfect Spanish. He had traveled all over South and Central America hunting for treasure supposedly buried by Spanish conquistadors or lying at the bottom of the sea. He theorized that certain galleons had gone down off the coast of Maracaibo and that there was plenty of gold and sunken treasure just waiting for an expert diver. He was an excellent swimmer and also knew a lot about sailing. Lagarde was the right person to come to my rescue. Jorge and Margarita had purchased a sailboat and a compass, and Olga added some hallucinogenic drugs to keep me high. They bought Lagarde tickets to Mexico, as a cover-up, with a stopover in Cuba. He was to explain to the authorities that he was going to take part in sailing races in Mexico, and that he would like to train along the Cuban shoreline. That plan would justify the boat. He had arrived in Havana at the same time I was attempting to escape through the Guantánamo naval base.

Around midnight Lagarde and Juan arrived at Lenin Park. He was really a fearless young man and did all he could to get the sailboat into Cuba, but the airport authorities told him that although he was allowed to visit Cuba, the sailboat had to remain in custody until the time of his departure for Mexico. A boat was, of course, a forbidden mode of transport in Cuba. Only high officials were allowed to use boats, and some of them had left in those boats for the United States.

Again my hopes to leave Cuba were dashed. Joris Lagarde gave me his own lighter and all the foreign cigarettes he had, as well as the compass and the boat's sail. He promised he would go to France and come back for me somehow. We talked all night. He felt bad about leaving me stranded and told me we would meet again in four days, before his departure.

The next day Juan brought me a razor, a small mirror, Homer's *Iliad*, and a small notebook so that I could write. I immediately wrote a communiqué that began: "Havana, Lenin Park, November 15, 1974." It was a desperate appeal, addressed to the International Red Cross, the UN, UNESCO, and the countries still privileged to hear the truth. I wanted to report all the persecution I was being subjected to, and began as follows: "For a long time I have been the victim of a sinister persecution by the Cuban regime." I went on to list the censorship and harsh treatment that we Cuban writers had suffered, and to name all the writers who had been executed; the case of Nelson Rodríguez, the imprisonment of René Ariza, the fact that the poet Manuel Ballagas was held incommunicado. In one paragraph I explained the desperate situation I was in and how, as persecution was escalating, I was writing those lines in hiding, while waiting for the most sinister and criminal state apparatus to put an end to my existence. And I stated: *I want now to affirm that what I am saying here is the truth, even though under torture I might later be forced to say the opposite.*

Lagarde arrived at the appointed day and hour to see me, and I gave him the communiqué with instructions to have it printed in every publication possible. I also gave him a letter to Margarita and Jorge, asking them to publish all the manuscripts I had sent them in which I openly denounced the Cuban regime. The Abreu brothers also took advantage of Lagarde's visit to get as much of their work as possible out of the country. We agreed that I would stay in hiding as long as feasible, until Lagarde could return and rescue me somehow.

He returned to France with the news of my situation, and all my friends mounted a campaign on my behalf. The document was published in Paris in *Le Figaro*, and also in Mexico City. I had conceived the idea that Margarita and Olga send telegrams with my signature to various government officials in Cuba, telling them that I had arrived safely. Thus, while I slept in the culverts at Lenin Park, Nicolás Guillén received a telegram reading: "Arrived OK. Thanks for your help. Reinaldo." The telegram was sent from Vienna.

All this confused them for a week, but then they realized that I had not escaped, and they tightened their surveillance of my friends. The Abreus' home was surrounded and the terror led them to unearth the manuscripts of all my novels and burn them, together with all the unpublished work they had written—approximately twelve books. Nicolás and José felt they were being so closely watched that they did not dare come to see me in the park.

Several of my friends who were now informers (Hiram Prado was one) had called on Nicolás Abreu where he worked as a movie projectionist, to inquire about me. The police not only were watching José; they threatened to put him in jail if he did not disclose my whereabouts. The person directing the group in charge of capturing me was a lieutenant by the name of Víctor.

Once an undercover cop sat next to José Abreu on the bus. The cop started to praise the United States and then added that Reinaldo Arenas was his favorite author. José just changed seats, without saying a word. When the surveillance intensified, Juan would go to the place where we had agreed to meet and instead of waiting for me, he would just leave me something to eat.

I started writing my memoirs in the notebooks that Juan had brought me. Under the title "Before Night Falls" I would write all day until dark, waiting for the other darkness that would come when the police eventually found me. I had to hurry to get my writing done before my world finally darkened, before I was thrown into jail. That manuscript, of course, was lost, as was almost everything I had written in Cuba that I had not been able to smuggle out, but at the time, writing it all down was a consolation; it was a way of being with my friends when I was no longer among them.

I knew what a prison was like. René Ariza had gone insane in one; Nelson Rodríguez had to confess everything he was ordered to and then he was executed; Jesús Castro was held in a sinister cell in La Cabaña; I knew that once there, I could write no more. I still had the compass Lagarde had given me and didn't want to part with it, although I realized the danger it posed; to me it was a kind of magic charm. The compass, always pointing north, was like a symbol: it was in that direction that I had to go, north; no matter how far away it might take me from the Island, I would always be fleeing to the north.

I also had some hallucinogenic drugs that Olga had sent me. They were wonderful; however depressed I was, if I took one of them, I would feel an intense urge to dance and sing. Sometimes at night, under the influence of those pills, I would run around among the trees, dance, sing, and climb the trees.

One night, as a result of the euphoria that those pills gave me, I dared to go as far as the park amphitheater, where none other than Alicia Alonso was dancing. I tied several branches to my body and saw Alonso dance the famous second act of *Giselle*. Afterward, as I reached the road, a car stopped all of a sudden in front of me and I realized that I had been discovered. I crossed near the improvised stage platform, which was on the water, dove in and came out on the other side of the park. A man with a gun was following me. I ran and climbed a tree, where I stayed for several days not daring to come down.

I remember that while all the cops and their dogs were searching for me in vain, one mutt stood under my tree, looking at me happily without barking, as if it did not want to let them know where I was. Three days later I came down from the tree. I was ravenously hungry; but it would have been difficult to contact Juan. Strangely enough, on the very tree in which I had been hiding there was a poster with my name, information about me, my picture, and in large letters the heading: WANTED. From the information supplied by the police, I learned that I had a birthmark under my left ear.

After those three days of hiding, I saw Juan walking among the trees. He had dared to come to the park. He told me my situation was desperate, that in order to mislead the police he had spent the day switching buses to get to the park, and that there appeared to be no way out. Moreover, he had not heard from anyone in France, and the international scandal caused by my escape was amazing; State Security had sounded the alarm. Fidel Castro had given the order to find me immediately; in a country with such a perfect surveillance system, it was inconceivable that I had escaped from the police two months before and was still on the loose, writing documents and sending them abroad.

In water up to my shoulders, I would fish with a hook and line that Juan had brought me. I would make a little fire to cook the fish near the dam, and try to stay in the water as much as possible. It was much harder to find me that way. And even in that situation of imminent danger I had my erotic adventures with young fishermen, those always ready to have a good time with anybody who cast a promising glance at their fly. One of them insisted on taking me home—he lived nearby—so that I could meet his parents. I first thought it was because of the wristwatch I had, another present from Lagarde, but I was wrong; he simply wanted to introduce me to his family. We had dinner, had a good time, and later returned to the park.

The hardest part was the nights. It was a cold December, and I had to sleep out in the open; occasionally I would wake up soaking wet. I never slept twice in the same place. I hid in ditches full of crickets, cockroaches, and mice. Juan and I had several meeting places because a single spot would have been too dangerous. Sometimes at night I would continue reading the *Iliad* with the help of my lighter.

In December the water behind the dam dried up completely and I sought protection against its great walls. I kept a sort of mobile library there; Juan had brought me a few more books: *From the Orinoco to the Amazon River*, *The Magic Mountain*, and *The Castle*. I dug a hole at the end of the dam and buried them there; I took care of those books as if they were a great treasure. I buried them in polyethylene bags, which could be found all over the country; I think they were the only item the system had produced in abundance.

While hiding in the park I got together now and then with the young fisherman I had met there; he was alarmed by the excessive surveillance of the place. He told me that, according to the police, a search was in progress for a CIA agent hiding there. He also told me that other fishermen and State Security were spreading various stories to alarm the people of the area so they would inform State Security if they saw any suspicious-looking character. They were saying that the person they were looking for had murdered an old lady, raped a little girl; in short, he was supposed to have committed such heinous crimes that anyone would inform on him. It was unbelievable that he had not been captured yet.

T H E   C A P T U R E Since I scarcely had eaten in the last ten days, I ventured down a path leading to a little store in the town of Calabazar with the *Iliad* under my arm. I think at that moment I felt suicidal. That, in any case, is what a friend whom I had met in the park had already told me. His name was Justo Luis, and he was a painter. He lived nearby and was aware of everything that was happening to me; the night I saw him he brought me something to eat, cigarettes, and some money, and said: "Here you are giving yourself away; you have to go somewhere else."

In Calabazar I bought ice cream and quickly returned to the park. I was finishing the *Iliad*. I was at the point when Achilles, deeply moved, finally delivers Hector's body to Priam, a unique moment in literature. I was so swept away by my reading that I did not notice that a man had approached me and was now holding a gun to my head: "What is your name?" he asked. I replied that my name was Adrián Faustino Sotolongo, and gave him my ID. "Don't try to fool me, you are Reinaldo Arenas, and we have been looking for you in this park for some time. Don't move, or I'll put a bullet in your head," he exclaimed, and started to jump for joy. "I'm going to be promoted, I'm going to be promoted, I've captured you," he was saying, and I almost wanted to share in the joy of that poor soldier. He immediately signaled other soldiers nearby and they surrounded me, grabbed me by the arms, and thus, running and jumping through the underbrush, I was led to the Calabazar police station.

The soldier who had captured me was so grateful that he selected a comfortable cell for me. Although my mind told me I was a prisoner, my body refused to believe it and wanted to continue to run and jump across the countryside.

There I was in a cell, the compass still in my pocket. The police had taken the *Iliad* and my autobiography.* Within a few hours the whole town was gathered in front of the police station. The word had spread that the CIA agent, the rapist, the murderer of the old lady, had been captured by the Revolutionary police. The people were demanding that

* It seems that R.A. was able to recover the *Iliad* later.

I be taken to the execution wall, as they had so loudly shouted for so many others at the beginning of the Revolution.

Those people actually wanted to storm the police station, and some of them climbed on the roof. The women were especially incensed, perhaps because of the rumored rape of the old lady; they threw rocks at me, and anything else they could find. The cop who arrested me yelled that Revolutionary justice would take care of me and succeeded in calming them down a little, although they still remained outside in the street. At that point it was dangerous to take me out of there, but the police finally managed to do so with a heavy escort of high-ranking officers. I then met Víctor, who had been interrogating all of my friends.

Víctor had received orders from the high command to transfer me immediately to the prison at Morro Castle. As we drove through the streets of Havana, I saw people walking normally, free to have an ice cream or go to the movies to watch a Russian film, and I felt deeply envious of them. I was the fugitive now captive, the prisoner on his way to serve his time.

P R I S O N Morro Castle is a colonial fortress built by the Spaniards to defend the Port of Havana against corsair and pirate attacks. It is a dank place, sitting atop a promontory. It had been converted into a prison. The building is of medieval construction, with a drawbridge that we had to cross to enter. We walked through a long, dark tunnel, then the portcullis, and finally entered the prison itself.

I was taken to the booking station, a cell where prisoners are classified according to crime, age, and sexual preference, before being taken inside to serve their time. Strangely enough, neither the officer of State Security who had apprehended me and who was expecting a promotion nor even the high official named Víctor was allowed through the portcullis. They may have been as shaken as I was and for that reason were not able to pull rank to get in; besides, they were in civilian clothes. So in all that confusion, I entered with my ID in the name of Adrián Faustino Sotolongo, the compass, my watch, and all my hallucinogenic pills.

In that cell there were about fifty prisoners; some were in for common crimes, others had been in traffic accidents, and still others were political prisoners. What struck me most in the prison was the noise: hundreds and hundreds of inmates were marching on their way to mess hall; they looked like strange monsters, yelling and greeting each other. It sounded like a unanimous roar. Ever since my childhood, noise has always been inflicted upon me; all my writing has been done against the background of other people's noise. I think that Cubans are defined by noise; it seems to be inherent in their nature, and also part of their exhibitionism. They need to bother others; they can neither enjoy nor suffer in silence.

That prison was perhaps the worst in all Havana. The toughest criminals were sent there; the prison held mostly common criminals, with only a small section reserved for political prisoners who were awaiting trial or sentencing.

I wanted very much to keep the watch and give it to my mother, so I hid it in my underwear. An older prisoner, whom I later befriended, and who had already been through various jails, advised me to hide the watch quickly. When I showed him the compass, he remarked how amazing it was for me to have entered the prison with that instrument. Eduardo—that was his name—told me that some prisoners had been sentenced to eight years simply for possessing a compass, and that I should flush it down the toilet immediately to remove all proof of ever having had it.

The hallucinogenic drugs that I still had could be lethal if taken in excessive doses. I was afraid of torture, and afraid of compromising my friends, some of whom had taken great risks on my account. I therefore took a number of those pills with a little water. After taking them, I lay down near a rough but good-looking trucker who had committed God knows what kind of transit violation. I did not expect to wake up again, but three days later I regained consciousness in the prison hospital: in a wing full of people with infectious diseases. The doctor told me it was a miracle that I was alive; they had expected me to remain in a coma and die of a heart attack.

From now on, all my old energy, with which I had enjoyed hundreds of youths, would remain locked up next to two hundred and fifty criminals.

The sea seemed to be very remote from the prison, inaccessible beyond a double set of bars. I was just a common prisoner, without the kind of influence that would allow me to get close to the bars and look at the sea, if only from afar. Besides, I did not want to look at it anymore, just as I rejected the sexual advances of the other prisoners. Making love with a free man was very different from making love with an enslaved body behind bars, someone who perhaps chose you as an erotic object because there was nothing better to be had or simply because he was bored to death.

I refused to make love with any prisoner, even though some, in spite of hunger and mistreatment, were quite desirable. There was no beauty in the act, it would have been a degradation. It was also very dangerous: those criminals, after mounting a prisoner, felt they owned him and his few possessions. In jail, sexual intercourse became something sordid, an act of submission and subjugation, of blackmail and violence, even of murder in many instances.

The beauty of a sexual relationship lies in the spontaneity of the conquest and in its secrecy. In jail everything is obvious and miserable; jail itself makes a prisoner feel like an animal, and any form of sex is humiliating.

When I arrived at El Morro I still had Homer's *Iliad* with

me. I had read all but the last song. I wanted to read it and
forget everything around me, but it was difficult; my body
refused to accept that it was locked up, that it could no
longer run free in the fields. Although my brain tried to
explain, my body could not understand that it had to remain
for months or years in a bunk full of fleas and in that sweltering heat. The body suffers more than the soul, because
the soul can always find something to hang on to, a memory,
a hope.

The stench and the heat were unbearable. Going to the
bathroom was an odyssey; the bathroom was just a hole in
which everybody defecated; it was impossible to get there
without having your feet and your ankles full of shit, and
there was no water to clean up. Poor body, the soul could
do nothing for it under those circumstances.

It seemed as if all the noises that had been torturing me
all my life had come together in that place and I was a
prisoner. There was no way out for me.

I arrived at El Morro with an infamous reputation not as
a political prisoner or a writer but as a rapist, a murderer,
and a CIA agent; all this gave me an aura of respectability,
even among the real murderers.

As a result, I slept on the floor only the first night after
my arrival at ward number 7, to which I had been assigned
and which was not, in fact, for gays but for prisoners con-
victed of various crimes. Homosexuals were confined to the
two worst wards of El Morro: these wards were below ground
at the lowest level, and water seeped into the cells at high
tide. It was a sweltering place without a bathroom. Gays
were not treated like human beings, they were treated like
beasts. They were the last ones to come out for meals, so
we saw them walk by, and the most insignificant incident
was an excuse to beat them mercilessly. The soldiers guarding us, who called themselves *combatientes*, were army recruits sent here as a sort of punishment; they found some
release for their rage by taking it out on the homosexuals.

Of course, nobody called them homosexuals; they were called fairies, faggots, queers, or at best, gays. The wards for fairies were really the last circle of hell. Admittedly, many of those homosexuals were wretched creatures whom discrimination and misery had turned into common criminals. Nevertheless, they had not lost their sense of humor. With their own sheets they made skirts, and with shoe wax obtained from relatives they shadowed their eyes; they even used lime from the wall whitewash as makeup. Sometimes when they were allowed on the roof of El Morro to get a bit of sun, they made it into a real show. The sun was a rationed privilege for prisoners; we would be taken out for about an hour once or twice a month. The fairies attended as if it were one of the most extraordinary events of their lives, which it almost was. From the roof we could see not only the sun but the sea as well, and we could also look at the city of Havana, the city of our suffering, but which from up there seemed like paradise. The fairies would dress up for this occasion in the most unusual ways and wear wigs made out of rope, which they obtained God knows how. They wore makeup and high heels fashioned from pieces of wood, which they called clogs. To be sure, they no longer had anything to lose; maybe they never had anything to lose and therefore could afford the luxury of being true to their nature, to act queer, to make jokes, and even to express admiration to a soldier. For this, of course, they could be punished by not being allowed out into the sun for three months, which is the worst that could happen to an inmate. In the sun one could kill the ticks, get rid of some of the fleas and lice, which lodge in the skin and burrow beneath it, making life miserable and sleep impossible.

My bunk was the last in a row, next to a skylight. It was pretty cold there and when it rained, water came in. The beam of the Morro Castle lighthouse would come in through the skylight; it was difficult to sleep with that intense light shining on my face every two or three minutes. Added to this were the noises the prisoners made, and the lights of the prison itself, which were never turned off.

I slept embracing the *Iliad*, smelling its pages. To keep busy, I organized French lessons. There were, of course, no books for the lessons, but little by little we managed to get some paper, pencils, and other items. I would give the lessons from my bunk. It was very difficult to pronounce clearly and make yourself understood in French in the midst of the clamor, but they did at least learn a few sentences, and at times we could even have a dialogue in French. The classes had a more or less set schedule, after meals, and on occasion lasted up to two hours. In a prison there are always people, young and old, interested in learning something, and even murderers could enjoy the French language.

On the other hand, not all the prisoners were murderers. There was, for example, an unfortunate father with all his sons, who had been sentenced to five years because they had killed one of their cows to feed the family, something Castro's laws did not allow. Still others were in jail for killing cows they did not own, to sell the meat on the black market. There is so much hunger in Cuba that people would quarrel desperately over those few pieces of meat on the black market, sold at sky-high prices.

Many inmates in my ward said they were in jail because they had committed "penicide." This was the name they had given to the rape of women or minors. But penicide included almost anything. For example, one of my fellow prisoners was there because some old ladies had seen him taking a shower, in the nude, in his own backyard and denounced him. There were some who had indeed committed forcible rape with face slashing. For those, the district attorney had requested the death sentence, and they had received thirty-year jail terms. Many prisoners did not know yet how many years they would have to serve; I was expected to get from eight to fifteen years; others, thirty years or death, depending on the district attorney's request.

Prisoners always managed to find out what crimes others were in for, even from the guards themselves. There was a young man who in full military uniform had entered a house and committed several robberies. This was a serious offense because he wore the uniform of Fidel Castro's army to commit a crime.

Once a month we had one hour to receive visitors. I had none because my mother was in Holguín; besides, I did not want any visits. I would spend the time watching how other prisoners received their relatives. The relatives of that young man were expecting he would be given a short sentence. Instead, he got thirty years. I will never forget how his family wailed: his mother, his sisters, his girlfriend. He tried to calm them down; his mother's screams pierced the air. Thirty years.

A prisoner who had been in jail several times for political reasons, and who was now serving time for a common crime, helped me a little to survive in those circumstances. His name was Antonio Cordero. This man knew all the tricks; the first thing one had to learn was how not to die of starvation. He advised me not to eat my bread during mealtime but to save it. Inmates ate the small amounts of food they received ravenously—a little rice, a little spaghetti without salt, and a piece of bread. Lunch was at ten in the morning and dinner not until six or seven in the evening; if you did not save your bread, you would get very hungry on the miserly rations we received. Sometimes, for reasons never explained, there was no dinner, and it was unbearable to be without food for such a long time; it was then that a piece of old bread was a treasure, not to be eaten all at once but in little bites, every three hours, followed by a little bit of water. To get some sugar was a real triumph; sometimes they would allow in a pound or two from a food bag that had been brought at visiting hours; a sip of sugar water was one of the greatest pleasures at El Morro. My friends, my students of French, formed a cooperative to which I had nothing to contribute, but they made me a member. All members would contribute whatever their relatives brought during visiting hours to a common pool to be shared by all as collective snacks.

Needless to say, it was not easy in that place to hold on to water or sugar, or even to pillows or blankets. The most dangerous criminals and the prisoners who ranked as ward "chiefs" would steal everything. Sometimes you had to go to mess hall carrying your few possessions—a piece of bread, a little bit of sugar, even your pillow. I did not let go of my *Iliad*, which I knew was much coveted by other prisoners, not for its literary value but because with its fine paper they could roll "cigarettes" by using the stuffing of bunk mattresses or pillows. Books were in great demand; prisoners used them as toilet paper, in those toilets full of shit and flies that fed on the shit, and then buzzed around us all the time. My ward was near the toilet and I had to bear not only the stench but also the noise of the bowel movements. Sometimes a special kind of herb was used in the food, on purpose I think, to cause diarrhea among the prisoners; it was horrible to have to listen from my bunk, surrounded by flies, to those furious discharges, those incessant farts, excrement falling on excrement, right next to my ward. Our bodies were so impregnated with the stench that it became part of us. Taking a bath was something almost theoretical. Every other week, on visiting days, the ward chiefs would fill some tanks with water and we would have to line up naked and walk by those tanks, where the chiefs would fill a jug with water and pour it over each of us. We would continue to walk, soaping up until we again passed by the chiefs, who would throw another jug of water at us. But even that sort of bath was a great comfort to us. The ward chiefs would stand on top of the tanks, sticks in hand, and if anyone tried to take a second bath, they would beat him up. Needless to say, within that group of men there were some queers who would check out the young men with good physiques and proposition them later; there was also an occasional faggot who had managed to be there with his lover. At the baths I once saw all the ward chiefs fucking an adolescent who was not even gay. One day the boy asked to be transferred out. He spoke with one of the guards and explained his predicament, but the soldier ignored him, so he had to keep on making his ass available, against his will, to all those people. Moreover, he had to wash all their clothes, take care of their things, and give them part of the food allotted to him. Like slaves, the poor fairies and defenseless adolescents had to shoo away the flies and fan those criminals.

Whenever new boys came in—"fresh meat," as they were called—they got raped by those thugs. The ward chiefs had sticks with metal spikes at the end, and whoever refused was jabbed on the legs with those spikes; it was difficult to say no. First they had to suck cock and then let themselves be fucked; if they refused, they got their legs pierced by the spikes. Some prisoners, unable to bear this torture, committed suicide. Inside the prison, suicide was difficult, but some took advantage of the occasion when they were taken out into the sun on the rooftop of the fortress. If you jumped off, you would smash yourself to pieces on the rocks at the base of El Morro. Many inmates did just that. One boy I knew did jump but miraculously survived; he broke both legs and became paralyzed. A month later I saw him back in the ward in a wheelchair.

When these boys complained to the prison authorities or to the guards about the abuses they were subject to, little or no attention was paid to them. There was also a cell with adolescents only, and that was the most infernal place in prison. Those kids were really vicious and ruthless.

The boys who were not homosexual but were raped repeatedly by the men would eventually declare themselves queer so that they would be transferred to the queer wards, where at least the fairies would not rape them. But they found no peace there either; for one reason or another, the fairies hated and envied those who came in for having been fucked by men, and always managed to cut up and mark their faces. Besides, the quarrels among the queers verged on the macabre; there was always a feeling of violence in the air and it was usually vented on the most wretched inmate.

The queers made themselves a very effective weapon which consisted of a stick studded with razor blades; no matter where someone got hit by one of them, he was wounded.

The inmates who were criminals but not queers used sticks with a nail at the end, switchblades and daggers, or any piece of iron sharpened on one edge. The queers favored the stick with razor blades because with this weapon it was difficult to kill a person, but the victim could be disfigured. Once someone got hit with it, he was covered with superficial cuts that left permanent scars. When two queers fought with these weapons, the goal was to pull the blades several times across each other's face. Their heads turned into balls of blood.

The soldiers took no part in those battles; they rather enjoyed watching the queers cut each other up. Such events usually occurred before meals and in the yard, perhaps because there was more room. Inside the cells, space was tight and you risked your life sometimes, climbing down from a bunk. Should you accidentally step on the hand or face of someone sleeping below, he could take offense and kill. To get out of my bunk I would jump down or slide down the post at the headboard without inconveniencing anybody too much. On reaching the floor you also had to be careful, because someone without a bunk could be sleeping there and you might step on him. I determined that most of those people, including the murderers, were mentally retarded; for that reason rampant violence was provoked by just about anything; the most insignificant argument could become explosive. But the government was not interested in taking them to a mental hospital.

There were queers who, in spite of all this, enjoyed themselves by having sex with everyone in the ward. They ran great risks, however, because prisoners eventually fell in love with the queer they fucked; they would get jealous and, to show their "manliness," would slash him or cut his face, merely because the queer had looked at someone else's fly, or because someone had offered him a sip of coffee, or because he said hello to one of the other "macho men" in the prison. Moreover, if you were seen with a real man, you would be subject to blackmail and had to let yourself be fucked by everyone in the jailhouse. An envious queer could attack you or initiate a whole series of intrigues against you, the worst one being to accuse you of acting as a stool pigeon for the guards.

I had no sexual relations while in prison, not only as a precaution but because it made no sense; love has to be free, and prison is a monstrosity where love turns into bestiality. In any case, I was also the hard-core criminal who had raped an old woman, murdered God knows how many people, and was a CIA agent. So I arrived with a great criminal aura and in a state of euphoria produced by the pills I had taken. The other inmates never thought that I had tried to kill myself, but that I had taken those pills to escape from the reality of imprisonment. I was called Pillhead because for weeks I staggered around; in mess hall, carrying the food tray, I would sometimes totter back and forth and drop the tray.

But in time everything becomes known; they found out that I was a writer. I do not know what the word *writer* meant to those common prisoners, but many came asking me to write love letters to their girlfriends for them or letters to their families. The fact is that I set up a sort of desk in my ward, and they would all come to have me write their letters. Some had two or three girlfriends show up at the same time on visiting days, and I then had to make up two or three different explanations, always apologizing to the women. I became the literary boyfriend or husband for all the prisoners at El Morro.

When those women came and hugged their husbands or boyfriends, I felt glad because I had made the reconciliations possible. Many prisoners wanted to pay me for writing their letters, but money had no meaning in prison and besides, it was not allowed; the best form of payment was with cigarettes; in jail a good cigarette was a special privilege. It was difficult to have cigarettes because we were allowed only one pack every two weeks and had a hard time obtaining from the outside anything not permitted by prison rules. Before and after visits we were all subjected, naked, to a rigorous inspection.

I had always wondered why so many soldiers wore dark glasses. It took me a while to figure it out: Some of them would get sexually aroused, and with dark glasses, they could look freely at the naked bodies of the inmates. It must have been a great pleasure for those men to see us walk by in the buff. Sometimes the inspection became meticulous and for no reason they made us go down on all fours, pull our buttocks apart, and lift our testicles and penises. Apparently they feared that we could be smuggling messages, pills, or other forbidden items into the ward, particularly money. It was usually the younger and better-looking prisoners who were subjected to such inspections. The guards wanted not only to look at them but to humiliate those masculine young men by making them pull their buttocks apart in such a fashion.

There was, however, a way to outwit such inspection; this was done by a group of highly skilled queers called "porterettes." The inmates would give the porterettes whatever their relatives had brought them: cigarettes, money, pills, crucifixes, rings, anything. A porterette would place all this in nylon bags, go to the bathroom, and stick the whole thing up "her" ass. Some of them had an astounding capacity, and were able to transport five or six packs of cigarettes, hundreds of pills, gold chains, and many other objects. Obviously, no matter how closely the porterette was inspected, it was impossible to determine what she had up her ass. They would shove it in deep and, as soon as they got to their ward, run to the bathroom and unload the merchandise. They naturally charged for this service—ten, twenty, sometimes up to fifty percent of the smuggled merchandise—but the transport was safe.

On one occasion a fairy called La Macantaya refused to give up a pack of cigarettes she had transported for some prisoners, and a big melee ensued. She was able to keep the prisoners at bay using one of those sticks with razor blades and another one with a nail at the end. There was such an uproar when La Macantaya slashed the face of one of those claiming his merchandise that she was sent to the penalty cell.

Common prisoners do not forgive those who have offended them, and they practice the ethics of vendetta. Those prisoners swore to get even with the queer; they set up a quarrel among themselves, stabbing each other lightly, and were sent to the penalty cell with La Macantaya. That same night they cut her head off; that is, they guillotined her. The headless body of the queer was discovered three days later because of the stench. The soldiers did not enter penalty cells, and from a distance the body of La Macantaya could be seen and she seemed to be asleep. All the culprits were taken to the prison at La Cabaña and later executed; executions no longer took place at El Morro. As a result, whenever someone was taken to the penalty cell, it was feared that he would be transferred to La Cabaña to be shot.

Accounts were constantly being settled at El Morro on matters of honor. Those criminals, many of whom had committed a number of serious crimes, were possessed by a sort of exaggerated puritanism. If someone touched their behind or insulted their mother, they swore to kill the offender, and

BEFORE NIGHT FALLS

usually carried out their threat. Naturally, in case a prisoner requested and obtained a transfer to another ward, the inmate who had sworn vengeance would manage to watch for his victim until he came across him somewhere—during visiting hours, in the mess hall, or on the roof on sun day —and would kill him at the first opportunity by stabbing him with a sharpened metal rod or a knife.

Once during visiting hours I was in a line and had exchanged a few words with a prisoner. Everything then happened so fast that I barely had time to realize what had actually occurred. Another prisoner came up, pulled out a large sharpened metal rod, and stabbed the inmate beside me in the chest. He raised his hand toward his chest, doubled over, and died. What amazed me most was the face of the murderer, and his attitude once he had carried out his vengeance. He stood there, motionless, pale, with the metal rod in his hand. When a guard came to disarm him, he made no effort to resist, as if in a trance. Probably he was later executed.

Sometimes prisoners would direct their violence against themselves. I woke up one morning to find that a young man had hanged himself. They said he had political problems and had gone mad, which was not difficult in that jail; I thought I was half crazy myself. It was strange that he could string himself up in a ward of two hundred people. I really think he was executed by a group of inmates who were his enemies, perhaps because of sexual problems; he was a very good-looking young man. Perhaps they first killed him and then strung him up to make it look like suicide.

Even in cases of apparent suicide, the long arm of the State was sometimes involved. In our own ward, full of common criminals, officers of State Security had been planted; it was difficult to identify them because sometimes they lived for a year surrounded by excrement, beaten like the rest of us, but they were undercover agents for State Security whose job was to inform on any political activity that we prisoners might engage in. Often they were after a particular prisoner who had been placed in the ward of common criminals but was actually a political prisoner, such as myself. Later, when I was in the workers' ward, I found out who a few of those agents were. Strangely enough, some prisoners did not sleep in the ward and the guards did not seem upset, which made me realize that they had been given permission to visit their families. These were frightening creatures; they could stab anyone and nobody would know that they were officers of State Security; they appeared to be no different from other prisoners who would stab one another. Once an inmate was murdered, the culprit would, of course, be removed from the ward, supposedly to be executed, and we never saw him again. He had been promoted from lieutenant to captain or something like that.

But there were also genuine suicides, such as the one of La Maléfica [the Evil One], a black queer who would straighten his kinky hair right there in prison; he had a horrible face. He was said to have killed a few people. He made fun of everybody, did not even respect the guards, and was therefore treated accordingly, with kicks and bayonet beatings. One day at mess hall La Maléfica pulled out an iron bar that he had been sharpening against the cement floor for months. Everybody thought he was going to kill another inmate, but warning everyone not to get close, he swung the sharpened bar round and round and then, turning it with a fast sweep, cut his own throat. A self-beheading. One witnesses such a scene once in a lifetime. The other queers caused an enormous uproar. While bleeding profusely, La Maléfica kept on brandishing the bar still in his hands and yelling for everybody to stay away, until he collapsed and died. The soldiers laughed and had a lot of fun with all of this. Then they pulled the bloody body of La Maléfica away, presumably to bury him.

The guards were sadistic types, perhaps chosen for their jobs because they possessed that particular virtue; on the other hand, it's possible they had become sadistic in that environment. They enjoyed torturing us. There was an Asian man about twenty years old who would get sexually aroused by beating the prisoners, and he made this obvious by even grabbing his huge penis. It was impressive to behold the erection of that enormous penis under his pants while a prisoner was being beaten.

If, for example, a weapon was found in the ward, the soldiers tried to get the inmates to tell them whom it belonged to. Obviously no prisoner would say a word, because it could cost him his life. Punishment was then collective, and really draconian. We were taken to the yard and made to lower our pants; then a guard would thrash us on the back or buttocks with a stick until he was tired out. The men controlled themselves and kept silent, but the fairies screamed wildly as they were being beaten. The Asian guy with the big prick would get really excited watching all this.

The only time one could sleep in that ward was after one of those beatings. Nobody was in the mood for talking, we were so beaten up.

A prisoner by the name of Camagüey improved his chances for survival by getting hold of a fish hook; he baited it with bread balls, and then, through the skylight next to my bed, he would fish for sparrows, which apparently were as hungry as we were. Sometimes he would catch a totí [a small black bird] or a swallow; he was a fisherman of birds who fished in the air instead of in the sea. Camagüey had a special gift for getting along with everyone and for being respected, perhaps because he had tried to leave Cuba on about five different occasions and had been caught every time. So he was able to prepare his sparrow soup and no one bothered him, not even the ward chiefs. He had developed a knack for survival and had a sense of humor. I enjoyed his sparrow soups; they helped me through.

Although I did not have any sex while in jail, as I already mentioned, I did have a platonic love affair with Sixto, a black man from Oriente who was our cook. Some said that he was a murderer, but others said that all he had done was to kill a few cows illegally. Sixto took a liking to me, and after he finished his work in the kitchen, he would invite me to eat. I think that he probably was a murderer, because those jobs were not given to people unless they had a strong character; a murderer who had killed a few was the ideal person to dish out food in the kitchen. He was implacable but honest, and would not give an extra grain of rice to anybody, even if threatened with death. Sixto would sit on my bunk and talk about any minor matter; we developed an affection for each other, but he never propositioned me, never even proposed a "shot," which was a sort of telepathic sexual act, very common in prison. The shot was something mysterious, almost impossible to detect. Two people would agree to do a shot; the passive partner would lower his pants while in his bunk, and the active partner, who could be at a considerable distance, would masturbate. When the active partner ejaculated, the passive one would cover his buttocks. Sixto never asked me to do this. After I left El Morro, I learned that he had been killed with a huge kitchen knife in an argument; I think it was with another man who had also been a cook and to whom Sixto had refused an extra spoonful of soup.

Though I did not witness Sixto's death, I did see that of Cara de Buey [Ox Face], who was a famous El Morro faggot; I think he was there because he had raped some boys. It was even said that after raping the kids, he had stuck them into a tank filled with lime so that they would not complain to their parents.

Cara de Buey was apparently expecting a death sentence, but Cuban courts sometimes take a long time before granting death. Since he was one of the prisoners who commanded respect, he was in charge of the kitchen and of the baths. When the prisoners were on their way to take a bath, he would position himself behind a low wall and get a kick out of watching them. Some prisoners complained, saying that Cara de Buey was jerking off behind the wall while they were taking a bath. This was true, I saw him once; he was old but had a large prick. His only pleasure was to watch the men and masturbate. This cost him his life; another prisoner caught Cara de Buey masturbating while watching him and killed him in the kitchen by stabbing him in the back.

Cara de Buey was always nice to me. He never talked about murders or crimes of any kind; he talked to me about his wife, but nobody ever came to visit him. He was not a violent man; his only moment of joy was at the baths when he jerked off looking at the buttocks of other men. He paid dearly for his sin, but sexual pleasure often exacts a high price; sooner or later we pay with years of sorrow for every moment of pleasure. It is not God's vengeance but that of the Devil, the enemy of everything beautiful. Beauty has always been dangerous. Martí said that everyone who is the bearer of light remains alone; I would say that anyone who takes part in certain acts of beauty is eventually destroyed. Humanity in general does not tolerate beauty, perhaps because we cannot live without it; the horror of ugliness advances day by day at an ever-increasing pace.

Speaking of beauty, I remember a boy at El Morro who was beauty personified. He was about eighteen and said he was serving time for military desertion. Others said he had been a drug dealer or had raped his girlfriend, which was absurd because that boy had no need to rape anybody; if anything, he was the one likely to incite rape in others. He was called El Niño [the Kid], perhaps because of his smooth skin, wavy hair, and a face where terror had not yet left its mark. He did not take part in any sexual activity; he remained aloof and, at the same time, friendly. But the prisoners could not tolerate so much beauty in the midst of all that horror. The ward chiefs tried to seduce him without success; that in itself was already dangerous.

El Niño's bunk was in the row opposite mine. I found great pleasure in being able to look at his body, his perfectly shaped legs. I imagine he was aware of the dangers of being so beautiful in that place; when he lay down to sleep he looked like a god. One day at roll call El Niño did not get up; while he was sleeping, someone had shoved a metal rod into his back and it came out through his stomach. Those metal rods were made by the prisoners from thick wires. Someone had gone under his bunk—all of them were made of canvas—and rammed the rod through him. No one heard any scream, so he evidently died instantly.

Prisoners feared this kind of death the most, a treacherous death while you slept, an attack behind your back. A death like this was the result of some vendetta, but the only crime that boy had committed was knowing how to smile, with such a perfect mouth, and having both a wonderful body and an almost innocent look.

Summer came and the unbearable heat exploded. Heat in Cuba is always unbearable: humid and sticky. But if one happens to be in a prison by the sea, with walls more than a yard thick, no ventilation, and two hundred and fifty people in one room, the heat becomes really intolerable. The bed ticks and lice of course reproduced at alarming rates; there were clouds of flies in the air, and the stench of shit became even more pungent.

Outside in the city, and along the Malecón Shore Drive, the 1974 carnival festivities were taking place; this was the festival Fidel had made into a party in his own honor around the 26th of July. The prisoners all wanted to get out and be able to drink beer and dance to the beat of the drums; it was the greatest happiness those men could dream of, and yet many of them would never again be able to experience such joys.

The fairies organized their own little carnival in their ward, with drums made from pieces of wood or iron. They

would dance the rumba in that hot ward; the highlight was
when someone sang *Cecilia Valdés*. He sang very well and
his soprano voice echoed through the prison to the words:
"*Si . . . Yo soy . . . Cecilia Valdés*" [Yes . . . I am . . . Cecilia
Valdés]. He could have been the star of any zarzuela or musical comedy.

The inmates were impressed listening to that queer, who
said his name was Yma Sumac. Gonzalo Roig would have
been proud to have such an accomplished interpreter. The
carnival would last until daybreak, when the soldiers entered the gay ward and beat them into silence, thus ending
the celebration. On one occasion, Yma Sumac was dragged
out all covered with blood; it was said that another queen,
who also wanted to do *Cecilia* but did not have the voice
for it, had stabbed him. We never saw "her" again.

After six months at El Morro I still had not been brought
to trial; others had been waiting for more than a year. One
day a guard called me to the gate. I walked out with no idea
why they would be calling me. I was then escorted to a
small room where I saw my mother; she had managed to
get in to visit me. When my mother came close to me and
hugged me, she was weeping. Feeling my prisoner's uniform
with her hands, she said, "Such heavy material . . . how you
must be suffering from the heat." Those words moved me
more than any other remark; mothers always have that enchanting way of treating us as if we were children. We
hugged each other and cried; I took advantage of the opportunity to ask her to see my friends and warn them to be
careful with those manuscripts of mine they were keeping
for me; she promised to visit them. I could not explain to
her what that place was like, but told her that I felt good,
that I would probably be out soon, and that she should not
come to see me again but wait for my release. When she
stood up, I realized how old she had become in those six
months; her body was bent and her skin had lost its
smoothness.

I always thought that, in my case, it was best for me to live far away from my mother so that I would not make her suffer; perhaps every son should leave his mother and live his own life. To be sure, we have here two conflicting selfish concepts: our mothers who want to mold us according to their wishes, and our desire to fulfill our own aspirations. My whole life had been a constant running away from my mother: from the country to Holguín, from Holguín to Havana; then, trying to run away from Havana to another country. I did not want to see the expression of disappointment on my mother's face because of the life I was leading, though her advice, practical and basic, was always unquestionably wise. But I had to leave my mother or become like her— that is, a poor, resigned creature full of frustrations with no urge for rebellion. Above all, I would have had to smother my own being's innermost desires.

That day, when my mother left, I felt lonelier than ever in my life; when I returned to the ward, the prisoners began asking me for cigarettes but realized that I was so disturbed that even the hardened criminals fell silent. When I got back to my bunk I noticed that someone had stolen my copy of the *Iliad*; it would have been useless to try to look for it; most likely, Homer had already gone up in smoke.

The next morning someone shouted my name at the gate and said that I had five minutes to get ready with all my belongings. The prisoners crowded around my bunk, making all kinds of conjectures. Some said I would be set free, others yelled that I would be taken to the mountains to work on a farm; still others said I would be sent to an open prison or to La Cabaña. What they really wanted was for me to distribute among them whatever little I had, the pillow, the cup, the water bottle. Camagüey came up and told me that no one was called to be set free at that hour, and besides, my case had not yet gone to trial. He also did not think I would be taken to the mountains, because when that happened they always called several prisoners at the same time;

he thought I would be taken to State Security. He was a wise man. I said good-bye to the people I knew and distributed my belongings. In such moments the mood in jail was always a mixture of euphoria and sadness, because the person who was leaving would probably never be seen again.

With no explanation I was taken to a penalty cell, and once there, the officer escorting me pushed me in, locked me up, and left. It was the worst place in the whole jailhouse, a way station for the most intractable criminals soon to be executed; the men consigned to those cells were awaiting the "little stick," meaning the post to which prisoners were tied at the execution wall. The cell was a sordid place with a dirt floor; I could not stand because it was only one meter high; there was no bunk, only a metal bedspring and no mattress. You had to relieve yourself in a hole in the ground, and there was not even a cup for drinking water. The place seemed to be the warehouse and supply center for fleas and lice; those insects leaped on me in happy welcome.

In *The Ill-Fated Peregrinations of Fray Servando* I had written about a monk who had been in several sordid prisons, including El Morro. Once there I decided that in the future I would be more careful about what I wrote, because I seemed destined to live through whatever I had written.

The first day no one came to see me or bring food; since most of the prisoners there were about to be executed, there was no great interest in feeding them. You could not even complain to anyone; it was utter isolation and despair. Two days later they brought me some food and had a roll call, which was absurd because from those maximum-security cells no escape was possible.

There was a prisoner who sang day and night, imitating the voice of Roberto Carlos to perfection. Those sad songs had been like hymns for the Cuban people; in some way they had become everyman's private screams. And the prisoner sang the songs with more authenticity and more pain than even Roberto Carlos himself.

A week later, the same officer who had brought me to the penalty cell opened the gate and ordered me to follow him. We retraced the route taken the week before, and he led me to an office in which Lieutenant Víctor awaited me; he stood up and shook my hand. He said he regretted that I had been confined to that cell, but they had isolated me because they wanted to ask me all kinds of questions and thought it would be best to hold me incommunicado so as not to attract the attention of the other prisoners.

I realized immediately that all this business of taking me to El Morro had been nothing but a scam; that State Security wanted to confuse foreign public opinion by labeling me a common criminal, but at the same time they actually wanted to question me. From friends who had been in the hands of State Security I knew what this meant: torture, every kind of humiliation, and incessant questioning until one ended up informing on one's friends. No way was I going to do that.

The officer continued talking, always in a friendly manner. He told me he was there to help me and that the length of my stay in the penalty cell would depend on my behavior. He got up, walked around the office, and scratched his testicles. I imagine he knew I was gay, and for him to scratch his testicles in my presence was like a proof of his manliness, like stating that he was the only man there. Víctor was thirty-something, tall, and good-looking. It was a pleasure for me to watch him walk while he grabbed his balls; it was a real joy, especially considering that I had not had any sex for six months. Back in my cell, I was able to masturbate, despite my weakness, with a pleasant fantasy: Víctor, with his hand on his crotch, would approach me and open his fly; I would go down on him. That night I slept peacefully.

Víctor came to El Morro every day for a week to question me, and continued rubbing his testicles. State Security wanted to know how I had smuggled out my manuscripts and the communiqué to the International Red Cross, the

UN, and UNESCO. My friends Margarita and Jorge Camacho had stirred up an enormous campaign with the French press concerning my situation. *Le Figaro* reported that I had disappeared five months ago. Now Security wanted to know who had been in contact with that newspaper, who my friends were in and out of Cuba. In my room at home I had a few automobile tires and also some inner tubes; my aunt had informed the police of this when my room was searched. Merely to own a floating object was proof enough that one wanted to leave Cuba, and this could mean eight years in jail. My case was complicated. Víctor told me that one night, while I was a fugitive, a mine had exploded and a young man had been blown to bits; they thought I was responsible. They knew of my trip to Guantánamo and wanted to know who had helped me get there. In short, if I confessed, I would have to inform on more than fifteen or twenty friends who had made sacrifices for me. I could not do that. Therefore, after a week of interrogations, I tried suicide again, which was not easy in those penalty wards; there were no knives, not even shoelaces. I stopped eating, but the body resists fiercely and often prevails.

One night I tore my uniform, made a sort of rope with it, and, crouching on the bed board, hanged myself. I hung there for four or five hours and finally lost consciousness, but apparently I was not very good at hanging myself, because I did not succeed in dying. I was found by the guards, who opened the cell and took me down, throwing me on the ground. The same prison doctor who had taken care of me six months earlier when I swallowed all those pills told me, "You're out of luck, you failed again."

They came for me with a stretcher. I was naked and the soldiers made fun of my buttocks; they were good for a fuck, they said. Those soldiers were not bad-looking; they were all buggers, and they were touching my bottom while the prisoners on death row laughed. For about two hours I was on the floor, in full view of those prisoners in death row.

They were euphoric; someone was showing his ass, someone was lying there naked, in front of them.

I was finally taken to the hospital, given IVs and medication. The next day the doctor came to see me. He was a rather cruel man, and said to me that he did not think I would be in El Morro much longer because State Security did not want any suicides before confessions. In fact, on the third day, Víctor returned with two other officers; they ordered me to get up and follow them. They took me out of El Morro, put me in a squad car, and, escorted by armed soldiers, quickly drove me through Havana.

VILLA MARISTA We arrived at Villa Marista, headquarters of State Security. Once inside, they brought me to an office, removed all my clothes, and gave me yellow overalls. They took off my slippers and gave me another pair, and then sat me down on what looked like an electric chair, full of straps for the arms and legs. Yes, it was a sort of tropical electric chair. There I was photographed and fingerprinted. Then I was taken to the second floor; in passing I saw the small cells with a single bulb that stayed lit day and night above the prisoner's head; I realized, without a doubt, that this was worse than being in the hands of the Inquisition.

I was assigned to cell number 21, and shoved inside. The small hatch through which one could look out on the hallway remained shut. In that place you could not tell day from night; the bulb remained on at all times. The toilet was a hole in the floor. For four days I stayed there without seeing anybody. On the fourth day I was taken out and led to the interrogation room.

A lieutenant who said his name was Gamboa started the interrogation by asking me if I knew where I was. I answered that I knew I was at State Security. Then he asked, "Do you know what that means? It means that here we can make you disappear, we can wipe you out, and nobody will know; everybody thinks you are at El Morro, and there are many ways you could die there, you could easily get stabbed." Of course I understood what he said: I understood why I had not been taken directly to State Security but to El Morro; to all my friends I was at El Morro, even to my mother, whom they had intentionally given a pass so that she would see me there. Now, if they murdered me, people would think I had died at the hands of some killer at El Morro and that I had never been at State Security.

It was difficult for me not to be confused by the thousands of questions that were thrown at me. Sometimes the interrogators started at dawn and would continue all day; then I would not be questioned for a week and it seemed as if I had been forgotten, only to be taken again to the same officer. That man did not believe a word I said. Sometimes he would leave in a rage, and I would remain alone in that interrogation chamber; sometimes another officer would continue the questioning.

There were many Russians at State Security, which was under the absolute control of the KGB, like a branch office. The Soviet officers were more respected and feared than the Cubans, everyone saluting them as if they were generals; perhaps they were.

Lieutenant Gamboa stressed again and again how isolated I was, saying that all my friends had abandoned me and no one would do anything for me. He also dwelt on my sexual relations with Rafael Arnés. He started out by asking me how my lover was doing, and I had no idea whom he meant because there had really been so many. He then told me that he was referring to Arnés and asked me various questions about him, some very intimate. Security always wanted to know as much as possible about any individual, even though he might have close ties to the agency, in the event he should lose favor or they might want to get rid of him. At that point, I had nothing to say about Arnés.

"And what about the Brontë sisters?" the officer asked me one afternoon. I realized then that one of the people who had been informing on me for many years was Hiram Prado; the Brontë sisters were the Abreu brothers, and only Hiram Prado knew that I called them affectionately by that name. The lieutenant knew of our meetings at Lenin Park and about our friendship. I was not too surprised to learn that Hiram Prado was an informer; after living so many years under that regime, I had come to understand how humanity disappears bit by bit in everyone, and how human beings break down in order to survive. Informing on others is something most Cubans do every day.

After my release from jail I learned that Hiram Prado, under pressure from State Security, had visited most of my friends to find out where I was hiding while I was a fugitive. He even went to see my mother.

The night I knew for certain that Hiram Prado was an informer, I returned to my cell rather depressed.

One day a strange noise came from the cell next to mine; it sounded as if a piston were releasing steam. An hour later I heard bloodcurdling screams; the man had an Uruguayan accent and he was yelling that he could not bear it anymore, that he was going to die, that they should stop the steam. I then understood the purpose of the pipe sticking out near the toilet hole in my own cell; its function had been a mystery to me. It was a tube through which steam could be released into the prison cell, which, being tightly shut, would become a steam room. To release steam was a method of torture similar to fire; the closed cell full of steam could almost suffocate a person. Every now and then a doctor would come in, take the prisoner's blood pressure, check his heart, and say: "You can give him a little more." The steam would continue to build up, and when he was about to die from a heart attack, he would be removed from his cell and taken to the interrogation chamber.

My neighbor was subjected to this torture for over a month. I would knock on his wall and he would knock right back. In all truth, he was being murdered. Nobody could resist those incessant steam baths in that state of semistarvation. After a while the baths stopped. I thought maybe he had confessed or perhaps died.

I was switched to a cell that was even worse than the one before. I felt that this was in punishment for my lack of sincerity with the lieutenant who was questioning me. However, the accusations made against the government by my foreign friends were having an effect; although my keepers continued to threaten me, they also feared foreign public opinion. Of course, they did not let me out of the cell. They wanted me to make a confession stating that I was a counterrevolutionary, that I regretted the ideological weakness I had shown in my published writings, and that the Revolution had been extraordinarily fair with me. In other words, a confession that sounded like a conversion, and of course, a commitment that I would work for them and write optimistic books. They gave me a week to think it over. I did not want to recant anything, I did not think I had to recant anything; but after three months at State Security, I signed the confession.

Needless to say, this only proves my cowardice, my weakness, the certainty that I am not the stuff of which heroes are made, and that fear, in my case, had won over moral principles. But I was comforted by the fact that in the communiqué I had written in Lenin Park to the International Red Cross, the UN, UNESCO, and many other organizations that never published it, I stated that my accusations against the regime of Fidel Castro were absolutely true to fact, even if at some point I denied them. I did know the moment might come when I would have to recant.

When I told the officer that I agreed to write a confession, he himself gave me pencil and paper. My confession was a long one; I talked about my life and my homosexuality, which I detested, about having become a counterrevolutionary, about my ideological weaknesses and my accursed books, the likes of which I would never write again. I actually recanted all I had done in my life, my only hope for redemption being the possibility that in the future I could join and become part of the Revolution and work day and night on its behalf. Needless to say, I was requesting rehabilitation, that is, to be sent to a labor camp; and I committed myself to work for the government and write optimistic novels. I also praised the henchmen who had informed on me, stating that they were wonderful people whose advice I should have always heeded: Portuondo, Guillén, Pavón; they were heroes. I took advantage of the occasion to state all the worst I knew about Hiram Prado, but they paid little attention to me because his work as an informer among the intellectuals and in Havana's underworld was so important to them.

After I had finished writing my confession, the lieutenant took his time reading it. Three days later he came to my cell to congratulate me. He seemed euphoric, and it was evident that he had been pressured by his superiors to have me sign the confession and get me out of there. I later learned that the foreign press had reported my disappearance and that I was not registered as an inmate in any of Havana's prisons; it was time for State Security to move me back to El Morro. Four months of isolation had gone by.

My confession, of course, did not mention anyone still in Cuba who could have been harmed, or the names of any of my friends in other countries. It all amounted to my admitting that I had been a counterrevolutionary who smuggled his manuscripts out of Cuba and had them published, and to my promising, now repentant, that I would never again have any contact with the rest of the Western world or write a single line against the Cuban Revolution. I also promised to reform my sexual behavior.

Once my confession was signed, I was returned to my cell. I have seldom felt more miserable. About fifteen days later I was transferred back to El Morro and had another interview with Lieutenant Gamboa. Lieutenant Víctor was also present and he seemed to waver between being infuriated and being friendly. Neither man could really have thought that my confession was sincere, but then, they could never have expected any truthful declaration to come out of a torture chamber.

While I was writing my confession they insisted I include that I had corrupted two minors, the two hoodlums who had stolen our clothes—mine and Pepe Malas's—at the beach. By the way, Pepe Malas never went to jail, because he was an informer for State Security. He was released as soon as he identified himself at the police station, while I was sent to jail.

I would be tried for a serious common crime, corruption of minors. There was even talk of rape. By convicting me of a common crime, they would avoid an international scandal. Keeping me in jail for at least eight years, the system would manage to obliterate me and separate me from the literary world.

During the days following my confession, one of the soldiers on guard in the hallway would sometimes stop to talk with me; I imagine he had been so instructed by Lieutenant Gamboa. That good-looking mulatto would open the hatch and at times talk with me for over an hour; he would scratch his testicles and I would get sexually excited; I would often masturbate while he was walking by my door.

One night while I was asleep, he came in and asked me for a match. Of course I was not allowed to have matches in jail. We talked for about five minutes and he left. Perhaps he wanted to make me feel uneasy and test my signed resolution. From that night on, I dreamed that he would enter my cell and we would make love. Perhaps he knew that I masturbated watching him, and maybe it amused him. Anyway, our conversations kept getting longer until I was transferred out.

Before my confession I had a great companion, my pride. After the confession I had nothing; I had lost my dignity and my rebellious spirit. On the other hand, I had made a commitment to the lieutenant to collaborate in any possible way, and they could ask me to make a public appearance to read my whole confession. Moreover, after my confession they could also obliterate me physically.

Now I was alone in my misery; no one could witness my misfortune in that cell. The worst misfortune was to continue living after all that, after having betrayed myself and after having been betrayed by almost everybody else.

AGAIN AT EL MORRO

I was finally taken back to El Morro; I was sent to ward number 10, which held murderers over forty or fifty years old who had committed a number of crimes. There was very little humanity left in those hardened criminals. The sparrow catcher was also there. One day while we were on our way to the visitors' area, a guard came to him and kicked him viciously; the sparrow catcher was old and walked slowly, but from that day on he was paralyzed. There were no wheelchairs, so he had to lie down all day or pull himself on a low, little bench in order to drag himself to the bathroom. I do not know what happened to him; when I left he was still there.

Since those prisoners had nothing to hope for, sex was more open. I remember a black fairy saying: "We have to start fucking here." And with a bed sheet over her bunk, she made a sort of tent and opened a great fucking place; men would line up to fuck the fairy. Sometimes she would rent that "apartment" made out of sheets for a few cigarettes.

Marijuana and cocaine also found their way easily into the ward. Apparently the prisoners had long-standing connections with the guards and knew how to negotiate with them; there were dealings going on between the guards and the prisoners, paid for in cash at visiting time.

Since I had promised to rehabilitate myself, one fine day they took me out of the ward and brought me to the workers' ward, that is, to ward number 6. This ward had very poor ventilation and held hundreds of prisoners, but they had one privilege: they could work in the yard or up on the roof at El Morro. Life was at least less boring and there was perhaps less danger of being murdered.

In this ward there were people who, like me, had signed confessions or who still belonged to Fidel Castro's army but had committed crimes. For example, there was a man who had been a lieutenant, sentenced to twenty-four years for having murdered his wife and her lover; he was later released.

The atmosphere in the workers' ward was not one of camaraderie but of snitching; most people there were informers and could report you for almost anything. They had no scruples about snitching on anyone just to obtain some privilege.

I was put to work as a laundryman together with ten or twelve others under the direction of a guard by the name of Rafael, who was implacable. We had to go to the terrace at El Morro and wash in huge tanks of water all the clothes of officers and soldiers. The prisoners' clothes, of course, were never washed, but when Rafael looked the other way we would, in our underwear, do our washing.

From there we could at least see Havana and its port. At first, I would look at the city with resentment, telling myself that, in the end, Havana was merely another prison; but later I began to feel a great yearning for that other prison where you could at least walk and see people with unshorn heads and not wearing dark blue.

One day, while on the roof, we saw a prisoner tie a rope to the barbed-wire fence and plunge down the slope into the void in an effort to escape. He lowered himself on the rope, and when he reached its end, he was still about a hundred yards above the shore. He jumped anyway and broke both of his legs. Even in that condition he kept crawling toward the sea. The guards, in a clear display of sadism since the man did not have the slightest possibility of escaping, shot him dead. This happened during visiting time, and all the relatives had to stay for hours until the guards discovered who had brought the rope.

There were several escape attempts from El Morro; of course, every prisoner's dream is to break out of jail. One day one of them succeeded, and we were all punished for a month. For the guards an escaped prisoner was a terrible affront. We later learned that the man had been captured, which was to be expected; it is not easy to remain a fugitive in Cuba with the checks and control systems that have been set up all over the country.

The man was brought back badly beaten and was paraded by our cells while the guards kicked and hit him; they were giving us an example of what could happen to us if we tried to escape. Needless to say, an escaped prisoner gets additional time. But we all continued dreaming of escape; sometimes our dreams were really wild.

One prisoner dreamed of his family bringing him a balloon, which he would inflate immediately and then head north for the United States. Others thought of escaping disguised in civilian clothes, which was of course utterly impossible.

When my trial came up, the first fact that surprised the jury was that the boys supposedly sexually abused by me were not minors. They were strong, and over six feet tall. The district attorney and the presiding judge evidently wanted a conviction. They questioned one of the youths whom I had supposedly raped; he came dressed as a schoolkid with his hair parted on one side, looking like an angel. But when asked whether he had had sex with me, he said no. The court repeated the question; the young man looked at me and his answer was again no. This young man was the most important witness for the prosecution. At one point the presiding judge stood up in a fury and asked: "Well, did he suck your cock or didn't he?" The youth said no.

I don't know what made him do this. State Security supposedly had worked him over to ensure that he would state that I was guilty, but the fact is he did not do so. Perhaps in the last moment he felt a sense either of dignity or of compassion, or was afraid; perhaps it was his machismo, his not wanting such information in his record. The youth limited his declaration to stating that there had been a proposition to spend some time together at a house. The judge asked him who had made the proposition and, strangely enough, he turned and pointed to Pepe Malas. The judge looked at him angrily and repeated his question. The youth again pointed to Pepe Malas. The judge then looked at me with a hatred such as I had never seen in anyone's eyes.

Still to come was the statement of the second witness, a younger boy with whom both Pepe Malas and I did have sex. His declaration was even shorter. He said he knew nothing, that his friend had called him and reported that two queers had propositioned him, but he had told him to forget about it, and had not gone anywhere. This enraged the court even more; the young men were called liars and threatened with punishment for perjury, but they did not waver.

The court, nevertheless, gave a long harangue contending that I was a counterrevolutionary and an immoral person, and that I should be sentenced for corruption of minors. The lawyer for the defense, cowed by State Security threats, hardly said a word. The trial ended with sentence to be pronounced at a later date; Pepe Malas was released and I was taken back to the Morro Castle prison.

The same wardens who had escorted me to the trial told everyone in prison that I had been accused of corruption of minors and of sucking the cocks of those boys; after that I got a new nickname: "the Calf." From then on I had many offers in the workers' ward, but needless to say, I refused them all as a matter of precaution.

One day, on the sun roof of El Morro, a young man of about twenty took out his penis and started to masturbate looking at the sea; he beckoned me, but I did not dare; I only looked at him and he looked at me, and he ejaculated, releasing his vitality to the sea.

The study circles also took place on the roof. They consisted in a monotonous reading of Fidel Castro's speeches and in agreeing with everything that he said. Generally this went smoothly without any mishaps. It did, that is, until the day they took to the roof a group of Jehovah's Witnesses who were in jail because they had refused compulsory military service. The officer gave the copy of *Granma* with a speech of Fidel's to one of the young men to read, but he refused, stating that his religion did not permit him to do so. The officer struck him with the butt of his rifle, threw him on the ground, and kicked him while beating him on the head, stomach, and ribs with the rifle. He beat him so hard that other officers came running, asking him to stop because he was going to kill the boy. The officer then gave the newspaper to another young man and ordered him to read; the young man trembled and cried the whole time he was reading. This was fifteen years ago, and I have not been able to forget this young man.

In addition to the Jehovah's Witnesses there were others who also spoke out against injustice. I remember a young black man in the prison yard who kept yelling for a whole week: "Down with Fidel Castro! Fidel Castro, murderer! Son of a bitch! Traitor!" The guards would come and kick and beat him. They had tied him up but he kept on yelling every possible kind of insult against Fidel Castro, with that hateful invective so typically Cuban which begins by insulting the mother of the offender and ends with calling him a faggot. I never saw anyone so infuriated against the dictator. Besides beating him, the soldiers did not know what to do.

It took State Security a week to determine their treatment for that black man. Then they tied him to a stretcher, gave him an injection, declared him absolutely crazy, and sent him to an insane asylum. Yes, bravery is crazy, but there is nobility in it.

One day I was called to the portcullis, that is, to the gate of Morro Castle; once again the prisoners, with great enthusiasm, assured me that I would probably be released, and that I should leave them everything I owned because I was going to be on the street. But what I got was my sentence: I was given a two-year jail term for lascivious abuses; the prosecutors could not convict me for corruption of minors. Even in a country like Cuba, henchmen had to obey the laws they themselves had made; for that reason, they could not give me twenty or thirty years. It was a victory for me.

I returned to my cell with the sentence document. When the prisoners noticed the thin paper on which it was printed, they jumped for joy and asked, "Come on, give us that paper to make cigarettes." I took the sentence, threw it to them through the cell bars, and that afternoon they smoked cigarettes made with official Justice Department paper.

The next day State Security came to take me to Villa Marista. Lieutenants Gamboa and Víctor were already there waiting for me, and Víctor was furious. He asked me if I knew my sentence yet, and almost laughing, I replied that I did, that I had been given two years. Víctor's rage mounted, and Gamboa tried to calm him down by saying that it was not the real sentence but only a provisional one. I told him, to cut him short, that it was, indeed, my sentence.

Now, if they refused to accept my sentence, all they could do was accuse me of political crimes.

Back in my cell I again saw, through the hatch, the mulatto from Oriente province who so often used to talk with me. He greeted me in a very friendly manner and chatted for a while, perhaps to give me time to masturbate while watching his beautiful legs.

This time I did not stay long at State Security; after three days I was summoned again by Víctor and Gamboa. Now their demeanor was very different; they greeted me with open smiles, saying they were really happy that I had been sentenced to only two years, and that I was to take part in the rehabilitation plan and would be working with them.

First, I had to give them a list of people who were enemies of the Revolution; I told them that I would be delighted. They gave me paper and I wrote down the names of all the agents of State Security who had informed on me; I had seen their names on a list that the lawyer had shown me: Bienvenido Suárez, José Martínez Matos, Otto Fernández, and many others who were informers out of sheer meanness, such as the lieutenant on my block and the woman president of my CDR. Of course, I could have added the names of Pepe Malas, Hiram Prado, and of my aunt, but I did not do so; after all, one had to recognize that they were also victims of the system. When I was finished with the list, Víctor and Gamboa sent me back to El Morro with the promise that I would soon be taken to a farm for my rehabilitation.

Upon my return to El Morro, I was again sent to ward number 10, which I considered to be a bad omen. Evidently the agents of State Security were neither convinced of my conversion nor persuaded by the list of counterrevolutionaries I had concocted for them.

The inmates in that ward were starving. One of the cooks slept there, and he had a bag filled with hard rolls. Sometimes I would dream about those rolls. Once when I had the chance, I stole one, and bit into it with such force that I broke my two false teeth. It was for me one of the most desolate moments in that prison because, although I did not have sexual relations with any inmate, I tried at least to keep a pleasant appearance and, of course, to smile; now, with my two front teeth gone, I could no longer smile. I spent the day trying to stick them back in. I could do it, but as soon as I began talking, they would fall out again.

So now, without those teeth, my reputation declined even further; I was no longer the Calf: I had become "the Toothless Calf."

In the midst of this situation I met an inmate by the name of Rogelio Martínez who wrote poetry; he had discovered that I was a writer, and developed a certain admiration for me. He had to keep an updated list of the prisoners in the wards, what crimes they had committed and what they had been tried for. He would take me out with him in the evening on the pretext of needing my help to organize a card file in his makeshift office. He was allowed use of the prison yard, and wore a nurse's smock although he was not a nurse.

What he really wanted was to read me his poems, which, unfortunately, were pretty bad, romantic and hackneyed; they always were about captivating women who would later betray him. A mix of eroticism and corny rhymes, they were totally worthless. But it was great to be able to get out of the ward and spend time with that poor young man who needed someone to listen to his poems. On occasion he managed to bring a bit of food and we would eat together while holding our literary sessions.

We amused ourselves watching the rats that would congregate near the gate of his improvised office. I never saw so many rats in one place, nor had I ever seen bigger ones; some were bigger than a *jutía* [a Cuban rodent]. The hundreds of rats would fight and bite one another, making such a racket that the poet would stop reading to watch the animals' antics.

Lieutenant Víctor visited me sporadically; through him I found out—and he was in a rage about this—that my novel *The Palace of the White Skunks* had been published in

France and in Germany; he showed me one copy but did not allow me to touch it. It was my book, and I could not even touch it.

The publication of this book was proof of my existence, and that infuriated them. My friends in Europe had been very wise in organizing a campaign against the isolation to which I was subjected. Víctor made me write a letter to my publisher in France stating that I was in perfect health and that I would probably be home soon.

On several occasions I had to go through a strange procedure. I was called to the gate, and they made me gather my belongings. I lined up with a lot of other prisoners, but at the last moment they checked who knows what card and determined that apparently I could not leave El Morro but had to be sent back to ward number 10, to join two or three confirmed criminals still remaining there. Of course, two or three days later the ward was again filled with new arrivals.

From my ward I could see how, after roll call, some prisoners would abandon their various cells: they were the undercover agents of State Security posing as prisoners.

One day all of us in ward 10 were called up; we were led directly through the portcullis and transferred to ward number 1, which was underground, just above the penalty cells. I do not know why this was done, but the fact is that now we were in the most humid part of El Morro; at high tide the water would come up to our feet.

From there, a group of prisoners was transferred to work at the Combinado del Este, a modern, maximum-security prison. But I was left behind, all but cut off from any possible incentive to continue living.

Unexpectedly Norberto Fuentes came to visit me; this was odd because only class-one relatives were allowed to visit us: mothers, sons, brothers. Norberto told me that he had obtained a permit through a relative who worked at El Morro. He brought a bagful of wheat meal and a novel by

Lisandro Otero. I knew, of course, that he worked for State Security and that his visit was nothing but a contact arranged by Security; perhaps they thought I would confess to Norberto that I wanted to leave the country, in itself a crime. But I told him just the opposite of what I felt and again reasserted my wish to join the Revolutionary "bandwagon." Norberto hugged me, and said that I would probably be free soon, that there would be great changes in Cuban cultural politics.

I stayed a few more months at El Morro, though. Now we were shown Soviet films once in a while; they were really terrible. The cell in which the films were shown was a sordid place where the prisoners peed on the floor; one had to sit on the urine of the other prisoners. At those times I felt the greatest loneliness ever.

One evening the soldier on duty told me to go to the portcullis with my belongings; this had happened so many times before that I did it almost mechanically, without any expectations, although anything seemed preferable to staying in that dungeon. At the portcullis I was met by Lieutenant Torres, a potbellied, pimple-faced mulatto, a real criminal who loved to humiliate prisoners; his maliciousness was notorious. He looked at me with his snake's eyes and told me that he personally was taking me to a rehabilitation farm.

My bag was full of clothes from the prison that I had accumulated while working in the laundry. Torres said, ironically: "Well, you have done well for yourself; you came here with nothing and now you're leaving with a lot of luggage." We walked to Torres's car; I was heading for the back seat, but he told me that I could sit in front with him. He started the car and we drove through Havana. For me everything seemed to shine after I had been locked up in those cells at El Morro; the city no longer looked run-down but clean and bright.

We reached Fifth Avenue and Twentieth Street in Miramar. In between the large tree trunks I saw Heberto Padilla walking down the sidewalk; he looked wan, puffy, and lost, the very image of defeat. They had also managed to "rehabilitate" him. Now he walked like a ghost among those trees.

AN "OPEN" JAIL

We arrived at a so-called open prison in Flores, next to Miramar. Torres signaled and whispered something to the guard. We entered, and they gave me a new mattress and uniform. The jailhouse was by the ocean and there was even a small seawall where one could walk and sit; it was a considerable improvement.

I was able to take a shower on a wooden platform above the sea. I opened my mouth to let the water run in and purify me, and my false teeth ended up in the sea, beneath the platform.

The next day they got us up at dawn and, after roll call, took us to work, which amounted to building houses for Soviet advisers. We worked from dawn until eight or nine at night. I was put to work as assistant to a mason named Rodolfo; he was a man of about forty who had helped the rebels fighting against Castro at the beginning of the Revolution, and had been sentenced to death; later his sentence had been commuted to thirty years.

Many of the men in that prison had been sentenced to thirty years and had already served almost fifteen; the forced labor had aged them. Their whole lives had been destroyed by the system; they had gone to jail when they were eighteen and many were now almost forty and had served only half of their sentences.

Sunday afternoon was the only free time, and visitors were allowed every other week. On one of those visiting days, Juan Abreu came to see me; he could not hold back his tears when he saw me in prison uniform and with my head shaved. I tried to comfort him, and asked him to bring me a copy of the *Iliad* on his next visit so that I could continue my reading. When Abreu was leaving, Norberto Fuentes arrived. Full of optimism, he told me that I looked good and would probably be out of there in a few months. Naturally, I again made myself sound optimistic for his benefit, and promised that once out I would write nothing but praise for Fidel Castro's Revolution.

Juan Abreu brought the *Iliad* on his next visit. As soon as he left, I started reading the last song, which I had not been able to finish after being captured in Lenin Park. After I finished it, I cried as I had not done since my imprisonment. Rodolfo, whose bunk was next to mine, could not understand why I would cry just because I had finished a book, and tried to comfort me. He told me not to worry, my mother would probably come on the next visiting day, and not to cry, because I would soon be released.

Every day at shower time I searched for my teeth in the water beneath the platform, but it was hopeless.

One afternoon one of the prisoners who served as liaison between us and the prison officials called me. He told me there was someone important waiting for me at the prison office. I came in and met Víctor, who stood up and greeted me with enthusiasm. He congratulated me and said that he was aware of my good behavior in jail, and that it was a pity I had to push so many wheelbarrows full of dirt; therefore he was going to try to transfer me to a bureaucratic job in the same prison. Everything was going well and, no doubt, I would soon be released. He also asked me to write a letter to my publishers in France, stating that I was practically free already and was spending my weekends at home. I wrote the letter and Víctor left quite satisfied; he had gained another victory. What he did not know was that through Juan Abreu I had sent secret notes to my friends in France, apprising them of my real situation and begging them to do all they could to get me out of the country.

Víctor came frequently and asked who had visited me. I knew that I was being watched and told Juan on his next visit not to come anymore because it was too risky for him. This was the last time I saw Juan at that jail. Norberto, however, visited me frequently, but I had no need to protect his name from State Security.

It was possible for prisoners to lock themselves up in a room of the house they were building for the Russians and have erotic encounters. Generally, the chief mason would select someone as his assistant, and that person eventually became his lover; in that way encounters could take place with greater ease, since chief and assistant had to work together and it would not seem so odd for them to be in one of those buildings or to continue on voluntary overtime during the evening, which earned them merits.

When Rodolfo chose me as his assistant, he had his erotic expectations. Men with thirty-year sentences had very few opportunities to have sex with a woman. It is true that many of the Russian women, wives of Soviet advisers, would sit around crossing their legs, wearing no panties, in order to provoke us as we walked by. I learned later that some of the prisoners sneaked out during the night and had sex with those Russian women. This was punished harshly, not only because the escapade was against the rules but because it was political treason. Even so, the women enjoyed the visits, and whenever we went by, they managed to lift their legs so that the prisoners could admire them. They were taking advantage of our situation for their own fun, we used to say.

Rodolfo would tell me how the Russian women excited him, especially a blonde with huge thighs and enormous breasts; he said he could not stand it any longer, and from my bunk I would see him getting an erection while he was talking to me. I never ventured to reach over and touch that exciting bulge, never dared to play the part of the Russian woman.

I remember another young prisoner whom I knew from

my time at El Morro, who propositioned me. He was an assistant as well, and while we were preparing the mix for our master masons he would say, "Look, if you are going to wait until you are released, your ass is going to rust." I paid no attention to him, and we continued working as friends.

Our place of work was next to the yard of a woman who had been a famous Cuban performer and later lost political favor. Xiomara Fernández was the perfect example of the type of woman that drove Cuban men wild. Every day she would come out and cut some of the roses growing in her yard, and she would intentionally bend over in such a way as to expose her bottom to the prisoners. Every day at ten in the morning, the rose ceremony would take place. The prisoners who were ready for the moment masturbated; it was a beautiful way of paying homage to her, which she accepted with great pleasure.

My best friend during that time was again the cook. He was called Sancocho [Slop Stew] because according to the inmates, the food that he prepared was mush fit for pigs. He weighed about three hundred pounds, he was a sort of human balloon; his greatest concern in life was the preparation of that food, which he concocted with such passion that he became the soul of the mess hall. His real obsession was not gluttony but the very act of preparing the food.

From the time I arrived he took a liking to me and always managed to bring me some of the leftover food. He had been sentenced to fifteen years, also for political reasons, and he knew the story of almost every inmate. He warned me about people I had to watch out for, and people I should not speak to at all. He was definitely gay but never said a word about it. Our friendship was platonic, a tacit brotherhood. While all the other prisoners called him Sancocho in a derogatory way, I always called him Gustavo, his real name. He was perhaps the kindest person I came to know in that prison. He had the peculiar intelligence that makes some people able to survive under any circumstances, and the special wisdom prisoners develop that enables them to forget the world outside, beyond the prison walls, that allows them to survive, hanging on to their small daily obligations and the ever-present petty quarrels and inconsequential gossip. With help from Sancocho, who provided me with a skimmer, I was able at last to fish my false teeth out of the water below the showers.

At noon Sancocho and the other cooks would take our lunch to wherever we were working; he distributed the food evenly; if he gave me a little more it was because there was some left over. One day, a big trailer truck pulled in to unload its cargo of reinforcing bars next to the building where we were working. Sancocho was standing by, watching, when the driver backed up suddenly and one of the steel bars pierced Sancocho's huge body, killing him instantly. I do not know whether this was a simple accident; perhaps the driver did not bear him any ill will personally but just wanted to have some fun. Many prisoners laughed and thought it was funny to see how the steel rod had ripped through that huge body. No one ever mentioned Sancocho again.

Luckily for me, there was a general mobilization at the time and all of us were transferred to the countryside to build a school, one of the many basic secondary schools being built in Cuba with slave labor—that is, by prison inmates.

We arrived at a huge banana plantation where in two weeks we had to build a school. The students would come and keep the plantation clean, working for free for the government. The change of location was almost pleasant; I was in the country and I enjoyed the smell of fresh vegetation. There was a brook where we could swim during our few free moments. We worked day and night; many of those schools were built so quickly and with such meager building materials that they collapsed a month or two later. But by then it would be somebody else's problem; ours was to finish the school as soon as possible.

In spite of working constantly, we prisoners were happier there; we could have our meals outdoors, and in the evening some men would make music, using a stool for a drum, and dance to it. It was not difficult to catch glimpses of bodies disappearing among the banana plants in search of erotic adventures.

One night someone sat down on my bunk; I thought he had made a mistake. In the darkness I felt hands on my chest as a voice said, "It's me, Rodolfo." He then lay down on my bunk, scarcely big enough for one person, and, trying to make as little noise as possible, pulled down his pants. Right there in the barracks, surrounded by more than five hundred prisoners, I masturbated Rodolfo who, at the end, could not help but groan with pleasure.

The next day we continued working without a word about what had happened, and we never did it again. He kept on talking to me about his hypothetical girlfriend and the fun he would have with her once he got his leave pass.

I had one major worry; I did not know whether I still had syphilis. The first thing I had told the doctor at El Morro after I recovered consciousness was that I had had syphilis around 1973. To get rid of it had been a major ordeal because the government controlled everything and the required medications were in the hands of the State. Another fear came from a doctor who had told me that syphilis could induce a flare-up of the meningitis I had had in my childhood.

Through my foreign friends I had been able to get penicillin, and checkups had shown that the syphilis was practically gone. Anyway, after I was released from State Security the doctor gave me another clandestine penicillin treatment, although he said I was cured.

Upon our return to Flores, while I was taking a shower, an imposing mulatto came in. As soon as he got in the shower he had an impressive erection; I have always been sensitive to that type of man. He approached me with his erect penis, and with my soapy hand I was fortunately able to rub him a few times until he ejaculated. I never saw anyone so happy after an ejaculation; he jumped up and down on the platform and said he was very glad to have met me. He told me we had to get together after twelve the next day, and I assented although I had no intention of meeting him. In any case, the next day the mulatto was mysteriously transferred. In my paranoia I thought he had been sent to me to determine if I was persisting in my sexual behavior, since in my recantation I had promised not to have further homosexual contacts.

Some Sundays we managed to swim in the ocean; it was a great joy to be able to jump into the sea and swim at least fifteen or twenty feet away from shore. This, of course, we did without the guards' permission, and one of us had to stand watch in case a guard came. Naturally, when an inmate is transferred to an open jail, he does not try to escape because he knows that he will then be sent back to a maximum-security prison, and because he is convinced that no escape is possible. It was a privilege to be in a place like ours; some prisoners were even permitted to visit their families at times. I was eligible for a pass but did not take it because I had no place to go. Norberto Fuentes told me I could stay with him, but I preferred to remain in the prison until I was released.

Theoretically, no homosexuals were allowed where I was; they had to stay at El Morro or were sent to special concentration camps. But some homosexuals always managed to slip through into those jails for men. Besides myself, there was a very obvious fairy who was called La Condesa; his real name was Héctor, and he received "visitors" every night in the prison yard. I do not know how he managed, but he made tea and talked about ballet, poetry, and other topics of an artistic nature. We could read books there and always had something to talk about. Héctor's predicament was that he was notoriously gay. One day the men told him he could no longer stay there because he was a faggot, which meant he would have to return to El Morro. He asked me for advice and I told him to make a list of all the men he had had relations with in that prison, and to threaten to inform on them. His list was endless. When the men found out, they had second thoughts on the matter of expulsion: "Hey, guys, drop it; there are married men here and you are going to get us in trouble," they were saying. In short, the threat of exposing the prison as nothing but a queers' den prevented Héctor from being expelled by the very men who had fucked him. He was able to complete his reeducation there, and at the same time, he was reeducating men in the bathrooms on his own while the rest were asleep.

Toward the end of 1975 there were already rumors among political prisoners about talks between Fidel Castro's officials and those of the United States concerning amnesty for political prisoners and the possibility of their being able to leave for the United States. Naturally, that presented a huge dilemma. A few U.S. senators came to Cuba, and State Security handpicked the prisoners who would talk with them; in this way Cuban prisons did not make too bad an impression on these gentlemen.

Víctor came to see me one day and said that I was almost at the point of being released, and that they could perhaps find a job for me. I had no idea what to do with my freedom, or where I would live. My real friends were few in number; there are never many when one is out of favor with the system. The others, the police agents, were not to be trusted.

OUT ON THE STREET

I was released in early 1976 and stayed with Norberto Fuentes for two or three days. He read me the book he was writing: a horrible, bulky work on Hemingway dedicated to none other than Lieutenant Luis Pavón, one of the most sinister apparatchiks in Fidel Castro's inquisitorial machine, a real homophobe who had persecuted writers and destroyed the Cuban theater.

Norberto, of course, took me in on orders from State Security; my stay at his house was a subtle form of interrogation. He showed me a book by Cabrera Infante that had just been published in Europe, *Vista del amanecer en el trópico* [View of Dawn in the Tropics]. He gave it to me to read in order to see what my opinion would be. Of course I told him that, although excellent, it was counterrevolutionary. Then he offered me all kinds of literature unavailable to anyone in Cuba except officials in Fidel Castro's government.

I had to get out of Norberto's apartment but did not know where to go. My first objective was to retrieve the manuscript of *Farewell to the Sea*, which was in my room, under the roof tiles in my aunt's house. Not surprisingly, I could not get in; there was a padlock on the door. My second goal was to make sure my syphilis had been cured, and the third was to go to the shore, by the sea, where I had spent the happiest moments of my youth. Then I wanted to see my mother in Oriente, and to go to a dentist to have my two broken teeth cemented back in place.

One night I arranged with the Abreu brothers to see if we could rescue the manuscript of my novel from the roof. Toward dawn, while they waited at the corner, I climbed up and lifted the tiles: there was nothing. That terrified me: the police had been really efficient.

Now I had to rewrite my novel once more, but I had no typewriter, no paper, and no place where I could work. Someone at UNEAC made a collection, thanks to which I was able to live for a few days at the Colina Hotel, facing the University of Havana. Norberto Fuentes was aware of my every step.

Víctor showed up at the Colina Hotel carrying an envelope under his arm. He told me I had not been completely honest with him. I showed surprise, and in response he took the novel I had hidden under the roof tiles out of the envelope. All I could say was that I did not even remember where I had left it, that it was worthless as far as I was concerned, and that I had no interest in it whatsoever.

To have to leave that manuscript in the hands of State Security enraged me so completely that I promised myself to write the novel again, no matter how.

Castro Palomino was the famous doctor I consulted to treat my syphilis. He was a man of another era, who had miraculously held on to his practice. He sat behind a huge desk and, after a test, told me not to worry because I was easy to cure and not contagious. He himself was able to obtain some injectable penicillin and gave it to me at no charge. I asked how I could repay what he had done for me, and this man, who was over eighty years old, said to me: "The only thing I want is for you to tell Rodríguez Feo to bring me the *Playboy* magazine he promised me some months ago." Rodríguez Feo was the person who had referred me to this doctor.

I walked around Havana with six vials of penicillin, trying to find someone to inject me; Amando García did; and also Oscar Rodríguez, as well as Mrs. Abreu, the mother of the Abreu brothers.

Amando García took me in for the night. He lived in a house belonging to a lady by the name of Elia del Calvo, and his room was next to the kitchen. This lady was the widow of a commander in Castro's Revolutionary Army who had been murdered in one of Castro's many foreign guerrilla ventures. His nickname was Pichilingo. She spent the whole day talking about Pichilingo, and now, living alone in that big house, she had twenty-seven cats.

Most of the other rooms in the house were empty. One of them was occupied by Julie Amado, a Frenchwoman with an uncontrollable sexual appetite, even more unrestrained than Amando's or mine. Elia did not sleep, and cats were all over her bed. She would sit on a chair and put her feet on the bed, and all the cats would sleep at her feet among dishes of half-rotten fish.

In order to get to the Frenchwoman's or to Amando's quarters, one first had to walk through Elia's room. I remember that Amando would watch and wait until Elia fell asleep so he could sneak a man in. Then I would either go to sleep in the living room or wait outside the house. One night, as Amando was walking past Elia's bed with one of those hoodlums, the man stepped on a cat; when Elia saw him by her bed, she let out a scream and caused a great commotion. She wanted Amando García out of her house right away. I interceded, telling her that we were going to have a reading; she loved literature, and Amando was thus able to spend the night with his lover of the moment. The Frenchwoman also had problems bringing in the men she took to her room; I think that Elia envied all of them.

I was sort of Elia's confessor; she spent the day making disparaging remarks about the men, telling me they were lazy bums. She finally agreed to let me live at her house on condition that I, in exchange, would get fish for her twenty-seven cats and would write her memoirs; she used to walk behind me, all through the house, telling me the story of her life, and I, notebook in hand, wrote everything down. I do not know which was harder for me: to write down the corny, crazy story of Elia's life or to stand in those unending lines to get fish for her cats.

Luckily Elia had a typewriter, and while I typed her memoirs I also wrote my novel *Farewell to the Sea* for the third time. I had to be very careful because Elia was an inveterate Stalinist, and according to her, even Fidel Castro was too generous and suffered from ideological weaknesses. One day she showed me a long report detailing the depraved, antisocial behavior of Amando García; she was going to give it to one of her friends at State Security. I was able to dissuade her, telling her that perhaps Amando was an important agent of State Security. I was quite possibly telling her the truth. So many agents inform on other agents that I imagine at times reports are filed and no further investigation is made.

The situation in that house was really unbearable. It was an absolute madhouse. You opened a drawer to take out a towel, and instead, you would find a screaming cat. Some of the cats jumped off the balcony, perhaps trying to kill themselves, but Elia would not let them die; she would run down, cause a great ruckus, and bring the cat back up with her. Elia picked up all sorts of stray cats and brought them home; she ended up with more than fifty. The one good thing about the house was that you could see the ocean; I mean see it, because by then swimming in it was forbidden. By government order, only authorized workers who had paid their monthly union dues were allowed on the beaches. Even so, those workers could not go to the beach of their choice but had to go to the one allocated to their union. To divide one beach from the other, huge walls had been put up all the way down to the water; bureaucracy had even reached the sea. Without a job, I could not get near one of those beaches. The closest I could get to the sea was to sit on the Malecón.

Swimming at the Malecón was also prohibited; anyone caught in the act would be arrested. How could you live on an island and have no access to the sea? I always thought that in Cuba the only thing that saved us from absolute insanity was that, being surrounded by water, we had the chance to go to the shore and swim.

To get to the beach you had to stand in an endless line for a bus to Guanabo. Then you had to change in the bushes and carry your clothes around with you; there was no shelter and surveillance was everywhere. It was, moreover, almost impossible to get from Havana to Guanabo. The lines started at daybreak, you would get to the beach after midday, and by then you could not even find a place to drink a glass of water. To return, you had to wait in another line for hours and get home at daybreak. Rather than a fun outing, it became an ordeal; the joy of life had been lost; it was no longer possible to do anything without enormous sacrifice. The whole trip was like doing penance.

In the middle of summer I went to see my mother in Holguín. When I arrived in my neighborhood, it seemed that nothing had changed since the fifties, and there, in front of my grandfather's house, was my mother, sweeping as usual. When I asked her about my grandmother, my mother said she was in the hospital, and very ill. She said the whole family had gathered in the house except Aunt Agata, and she would be arriving shortly; my grandmother's death was expected at any moment.

A whole universe died for me when my grandmother died; her death was an end to the possibility of counting on someone who could stop in the middle of a simple conversation to call upon God; a kind of wisdom disappeared, a completely different way of looking at life. I wanted to cry, seeing that face with which a whole era of witches, ghosts, and spirits would disappear, with which all my childhood, the best part of my life, would disappear. But I could not cry.

A few days later I returned to Havana and called Lezama; I had not spoken with him since before going to jail. He greeted me warmly and invited me over that same night. During my visit he did not ask about my time in jail, but talked about literature right from the beginning. My grandmother's death affected him greatly, but he told me that because of their grandchildren, grandmothers never die; when I wrote, she would be by my side.

Virgilio Piñera also visited that night and read us his poem "The Photograph," dedicated to Olga Andreu. Lezama livened up and also read a few poems from the book he was working on, while María Luisa prepared tea. Virgilio mentioned that he was translating some African poems but that at times he could not be given any credit and his name would not appear. He had been told, however, that there was some hope that people would be permitted to leave the country.

Lezama had received an invitation through UNESCO to travel outside Cuba but had rejected it at the last moment. He had a fear of cold weather and also of being in a foreign country; he felt tired. Although the government had not authorized the trip, María Luisa was really eager to go; she had secret hopes of not returning to Cuba. Almost her entire family was in the United States, and Lezama's novel *Paradiso* had received international recognition; perhaps they could even live comfortably. Lezama ended the conversation saying, "To go to Paris and stay is depressing, but to return would be impossible." Upset, María Luisa went to her room, and the three of us started gossiping about local matters and about the meanness of some of the UNEAC writers. Lezama said that he had forbidden Rafael Arnés and Pablo Armando Fernández to visit him because they were nothing but undercover policemen. As regards Padilla, Lezama would only exclaim with rage: "That scoundrel, that scoundrel." After Padilla's confession, Lezama and María Luisa reduced their circle of friends. Lezama said Eliseo Diego, Cintio Vitier, and Fina were miserable people, and told the story about how Cintio and Fina went to Puerto Rico for a conference and said wonderful things about Castro, and then traveled through the country buying shoes to resell on the black market in Havana. At midnight we parted and Lezama said to me: "Remember that our only salvation lies in words: Write!" And he told me enthusiastically that he was expecting shortly the arrival of his complete works, published in Spain by Aguilar.

He was never to see those volumes, however. While I was feeding Elia's cats one day, Amando García came in and said: "We lost Joseíto." "Who? Which Joseíto?" I asked, and he said, "Haven't you heard? Lezama Lima died yesterday." He then showed me a short newspaper report in which, among other insignificant news, one could read: "José Lezama Lima buried."

There was no announcement of his death, but of his burial. This was done to prevent his many admirers from getting together at the funeral home.

That evening I went to Julio Gómez's house, where beautiful youths usually gathered. This man was quite a character and somewhat misshapen, he looked like a turtle that had gotten up on its hind legs. Amando García arranged to bring him all kinds of young men, mostly hoodlums who eventually stole something from him. This openly gay man had never been purged in spite of all the purges carried out in the theater, apparently because he worked for State Security. That evening, the day Lezama was buried, I went to visit Julio and his houseful of adolescents in bathing suits, every one ready to go to bed with any of us. I went out on the porch and at some point started to scream. Amando and Julio came out to find out what was going on. I kept yelling, "Today they buried Lezama Lima! Today they buried Lezama Lima!"

The death of Lezama and that of my grandmother, both in the same year, plunged me into the deepest feeling of despair imaginable. From then on, reality loomed, ever more evident. How could I explain to Amando and to Julio, and to all those boys cavorting half naked around me, that after those deaths I would never be the same person again.

Elia del Calvo insisted that I could sue my aunt inasmuch as I had lived in that house for over fifteen years and, by law, had a right to the room. She was a woman who still believed in the law. She made me go to a judge to initiate a suit against my aunt Agata in order to get my room back.

My aunt was alarmed by all this; after all, I really had the right to live in that room. Even though I had the right, my uncle had a fairly high political position, and the suit remained pending and was given several postponements. My aunt was afraid that I would regain the room, which, in spite of being sixty years old, she was using for her sexual encounters with her grocer or with the man who took care of her garden.

But she was out of luck. In spite of all the friends from State Security whom my aunt brought to court, the president of our CDR, who knew about her erotic activities and dirty dealings, and about the thefts her sons committed in the neighborhood, testified in my favor. She did so not because she liked me but to harm my aunt. The judge once more declared that the trial could not be completed, and added that it should be moved to another jurisdiction for its conclusion. My aunt saw she was in serious danger of losing the room.

One day I was out buying food for Elia's cats, when the doors of a bus opened and Hiram Prado got off. He seemed glad to see me. I was about to insult him, but what came out of my mouth at that moment were my two false teeth, which landed in Hiram Prado's face. He started roaring with laughter, I had to laugh too, and we hugged. I knew I was hugging a policeman, an informer, but also an excellent poet with whom I had shared some wonderful times.

We agreed to meet the next day in Lenin Park, where we had had so many erotic adventures. We walked through the entire park and stood in line to buy cream cheese and chocolates. Then we went to the dam, full of water now, where I had been in hiding. When we were on the bridge above the dam, I started yelling again that I could not accept that Lezama was dead. Hiram picked up some long-stemmed mariposa lilies and started flogging me with them. I took all my clothes off, and Hiram kept whipping me while more and more people gathered around us. Then, with a final scream, I dove into the water to the very bottom, and swam to shore. That act of exorcism brought me back to reality. Hiram handed me my clothes, and less than five minutes later, we made arrangements with a bunch of adolescents to have sex in some nearby bushes. The whole little army fucked us but when they were done, they turned on us and started pelting us with stones. We ran desperately through the bushes and then climbed over a fence that was more than three meters high. The boys did likewise and followed us through the entire park. We ran off in different directions and I got back home at daybreak, my hands still bleeding from the cuts and bruises I suffered while climbing the barbed-wire fence.

The next day Hiram came to visit me at Elia's house. He was in a deplorable state, but I introduced him to Elia anyway and we told her we had been assaulted by a gang of young toughs. Elia let him in, and Amando García took care of his cuts and bruises. While we bandaged him, Amando said that he wanted me to meet, that same evening, a crazy ruffian who admired my work immensely; perhaps I could arrange with him for a place to stay.

That evening, at the Radiocentro cafeteria, I met this character; he was skinny, with bulging eyes, and the face of a mafioso. His name was Rubén Díaz. He said that he had read all the books I had published outside Cuba; his mother and father lived abroad. This man had two rooms in what used to be the Monserrate Hotel; he told me that he was selling one of them, and that I could move in now and pay him later.

We went to see the rooms that same night. They were unfurnished except for a folding iron cot with springs so overstretched that we hit the floor when we sat on it. The cockroaches reigned supreme in that place and there was a huge pile of garbage in one corner. To prove that he was the owner of the rooms, Rubén went through the enormous heap of papers looking for his ration booklet, which he finally found. In order to move in, all I had to do was add my name to the ration booklet and thus form part of the family nucleus. There were several glasses full of urine, and no bathroom because Rubén had sold the toilet; all that remained was a hole. After his family left the country, the man had sunk into progressively deeper poverty. He was an inveterate marijuana smoker, and also had a great weakness for literature; he showed me a long poem of his. Instead of electric light, he used candles because he had no money to pay for electricity, which had been cut off more than a year before though his monthly bill was only one or two pesos. The place looked ghastly, but I figured that living in one of the rooms would be better than staying with Elia and her cats. That night I slept there on the floor, and Hiram, who was also living on the move, stayed with me. He confessed that his latest erotic adventures, the most fulfilling ones, were with his grandfather, an old man of about eighty who also lived in Havana with one of Hiram's aunts. The house was very small, and Hiram slept with his grandfather. One night, he said, while they were sleeping, he sensed that his grandfather was masturbating next to him. Hiram went down on his grandfather's penis and started to suck it, until the old man came around and fucked him. After that his grandfather fucked him every night and Hiram could only have a real orgasm when this happened. I told him that his love was not lasting because his grandfather would not live much longer. That is exactly what happened; the unrestrained erotic life that Hiram started with the old man killed him that very year. This time I was the one who flogged Hiram with mariposa lilies at Lenin Park while he howled.

Hiram decided that Elia had to meet Rubén as soon as possible. He said: "That old lady has money; she could sell any old thing from her house and get you the thousand pesos that Rubén wants for the room." So we introduced him as a serious young man who wanted to help me but needed the thousand pesos to get out of his financial difficulties. The man, in fact, was a shrewd crook who had sold the room several times already; he would collect the money, then throw the owner out of the room and sell it to someone else. This was easy; since in Cuba the sale of a house was illegal, you had to trust that the seller was acting in good faith, because the buyer's name would never appear on the deed. Rubén had done this several times; the last time, he had sold the room to another hoodlum, whom he threw out with the help of the police after collecting his thousand pesos. But now that man was prowling around the house and demanding his money, threatening to shoot Rubén at any moment.

Rubén was very scared and eager to get my money. He put on his best clothes to meet Elia del Calvo, but the interview did not last long. Elia was having a drink and Rubén said to her: "Lady, could you sell me a shot of rum?" When she replied, "I am no bartender to be selling drinks," Rubén then asked her to please give him a swig. Elia got up and went all the way to the kitchen for a glass. Rubén took the bottle and drank directly from it; when Elia returned he had drunk too much. Hiram had also taken a drink from the bottle. Elia was crimson with fury; she called us thieves and told us to get out of her home immediately.

I had already been living in the room for three days, when someone knocked at the door. It was Elia del Calvo walking with two canes. She greeted me as if nothing had happened and said: "I have a plan for you to get this room. Go see your aunt and tell her that you are willing to give up the room in her house, which is already yours since you have won the suit, if she gives you a thousand pesos. But, oh yes, you also have to finish my memoirs." I think she herself sent some people to see my aunt; she had many connections too with members of the Communist Party, and she played all sorts of tricks. For her purposes, she would send old ladies dressed in black and carrying walking sticks, commanding great respect; she would have other people, feigning deep voices, make telephone calls pretending to be my lawyers. At the time, my uncle had another suit pending and my aunt had problems with the president of the CDR; in other words, in those days they were out of favor. For that reason, when I arrived at her house to make my proposal, my aunt hugged me and, crying, told me that she had always loved me a lot and wanted the best for me; and that since I had had so many problems in that room, it would be best if I did not return to it. Needless to say, she had been the cause of all my problems there, although I did not tell her so. My aunt declared she would do all she could to get the money within two weeks.

Meanwhile, I stayed at Elia's. My situation was precarious because I did not have a job. The sinister Víctor had obtained Elia del Calvo's telephone number and kept calling to offer me a job if, in return, I would begin to write revolutionary and socialist literature. Once they took me to a house in the Vedado where many agents of State Security used to meet; the idea was to get me to write novels, stories, and articles in praise of the Revolution and of Fidel Castro. And that was not enough; they also wanted me to give up my homosexual life. A woman there, who had a high-ranking position at State Security, said to me: "Listen, kid, women are much more attractive than men." I felt that she was referring to her own personal preference.

I promised to reform completely and to write the great epic novel of the Castro Revolution. In the meantime I continued to stay at Elia's, rewriting *Farewell to the Sea*. Amando García told me I had the right to reclaim my job at UNEAC, and he wrote a letter stating that on a certain date and time I would be there to sign the register. I sent the letter and on the appointed day went to UNEAC. I had a hard time getting in but at last managed to speak to Bienvenido Suárez. The people at UNEAC looked at me as if I had come from another planet or had the plague. Terrified, Rafael Arnés turned his back when he saw me; Nicolás Guillén closed his doors. Bienvenido Suárez received me with his hypocritical smile, and told me he was sorry but he could not give me back my job since anyone who had been in jail for over a year could not return to his former position, and furthermore, according to the latest socialist legislation, anyone away from his job for over six months and a day could not return to it.

I had to continue getting fish for the cats; that same fish was frequently my own dinner as well.

It was so difficult to sleep at Elia's house that I sometimes stayed with Ismael Lorenzo, a writer who had never published anything in Cuba but who wrote novels with meticulous discipline. He lived in a huge house in Old Havana; I could sometimes sleep in the back room and find some peace. He was a friend and we could speak openly about our fears and plan once more how to get out of the country. His wife had already left Cuba but he had not been able to do so. He wanted to leave secretly; he knew a family named Hidalgo who had plans to obtain a boat, and of course I was included in the group. For years Ismael dreamed of that imaginary boat which never materialized.

Ismael's attitude was completely different from that of almost all UNEAC writers and of my former friends. The UNEAC people were particularly despicable; not one of them would even greet me. I had suddenly become invisible. Antonio Benítez Rojo, an official from La Casa de las Américas, stopped saying hello to me and would not see me if I walked by; most of them acted that way. Others, perhaps out of mere cowardice, forgot I existed, although we had shared long friendships. This is what happened with Reinaldo Gómez Ramos. He approached me one day to say that he did not want to keep my manuscripts anymore, that he had to destroy them or return them to me. I arranged to meet him at a street corner near his home to pick them up, although by now I trusted no one and considered the possibility that he might be an informer for State Security. Reinaldo approached me, obviously terrified, and handed me the manuscripts; I took them and threw them into the sewer. There was nothing else I could do in that situation, because if he was an informer, he would no longer be able to betray me since he had no proof. Even if he was not an informer, he was prone to gossip, and he might have told his friends, perhaps Pepe Malas, that he had returned the manuscripts to me. This could have terrible consequences for me. The attitude of many of the friends I had trusted was very distressing; I did not have a place to live now, and they could not even keep the manuscripts for me.

Fed up with all those who would not be friends at a time when friendship really mattered, I wrote up a somewhat ironic document that I called the Termination of Friendship Notice. It read as follows:

Mr. _____:

In accordance with the balance sheet of termination of friendships I prepare at the end of each year, based on meticulously exact data, I hereby inform you that your name has been added to the list of those terminated.

Yours very truly,

Reinaldo Arenas

I typed many copies of this mock notice and sent them to everyone who, in my opinion, had not dealt openly with me. The first person I sent it to was Nicolás Guillén; others were, of course, Reinaldo Gómez, Rafael Arnés, Otto Fernández, and Roberto Fernández Retamar.

Hiram Prado, as diabolical as ever, made more than a hundred copies of it and, forging my signature, sent them to almost all of my real friends. This caused dreadful confusion because people like Ismael Lorenzo, Amando García, and even Elia del Calvo received the communication. It did not take me long to figure out that this was the work of Hiram Prado, and I then sent a Termination of Friendship Notice to him. For a long time we did not talk to each other, and he took advantage of the situation by sending out more notices to everyone who had helped me. To get even, I wrote a few tongue twisters making fun of him; this was another of the weapons I used against those who had harmed me.

In 1977 those tongue twisters became famous throughout Havana; in them I ridiculed over thirty well-known people in the city's theater and literary worlds.

One of the most nefarious characteristics of tyrannies is that they take everything too seriously and destroy all sense of humor. Historically, Cubans have found escape from reality through satire and mockery, but with the coming of Fidel Castro the sense of humor gradually disappeared until it became illegal. With it the Cuban people lost one of their few means of survival; by taking away their laughter, the Revolution took away from them their deepest sense of the nature of things. Yes, dictatorships are prudish, pompous, and utterly dreary.

THE MONSERRATE
HOTEL My aunt, at last, scraped together the thousand pesos and I was able to move to Rubén's room. We entered into a sort of illegal contract, with my aunt and her two delinquent sons as witnesses, stating that he, Rubén, was giving up forever any rights over the room he was selling to me for the sum of one thousand pesos. That document, however, could not be shown to the Cuban authorities except in a desperate situation because the sale of real estate is prohibited by law. But it was a way to tie Rubén down; if he tried to eject me from the room, I could produce the document, even if both of us landed in jail.

Though by now it was nothing but a fifth-rate building, the Monserrate Hotel had once been a pretty good place, inhabited exclusively by prostitutes. Prostitutes had been using the hotel for their business, and with Castro's Revolution, they became owners of the rooms in which they lived, I imagine through their contacts with the new officers of the Rebel Army. This, of course, occurred at the beginning of the Revolution. When I moved in, only a few of those women, retired or semiretired, remained; old age had rehabilitated some of the others, who now lived in the rooms with two or three of their children.

It was a real jungle on the far side of the law. If the cops came, they would just have to put bars on the entrance to the building, the only way in or out, to turn the whole place into a jail.

Bebita and her friend lived on the first floor; these two women played drums and beat each other up every day because of jealousies. While her friend slept, Bebita would take other girlfriends to her room, and when her friend woke up, the ensuing ruckus would shake the entire building; cups and dishes would fly during the commotion.

"Snow White and the seven dwarfs" lived next to Bebita; it was a family of siblings, a woman and seven dwarfs who lived off the black market and the numbers game.

Across from Snow White and the seven dwarfs lived Muhammad, a fairy about sixty years old and weighing three hundred pounds. He had decorated his room with waxed-paper flowers and covered his walls with shiny paper and foreign magazine covers. His room was a strange combination of simulated and secret doors hidden behind the paper covering the walls; there he kept his money and his liquor. Muhammad spent his time making huge bouquets of awfully tacky flowers, which he sold in the building and all over Havana. He made some money selling those horrible flowers which had, however, a certain Versaillesque flair. The huge flower bouquets had a brilliance and outrageous splendor impossible then in Cuba, where even the most basic materials to make artificial flowers were unavailable. That man always had his room full of tough queers who ended up beating him and stealing his money, and then escaped through the balcony while Muhammad yelled at them. He lived with his mother, an old lady of about ninety, who would unburden her troubles to me or to Bebita and her friend, telling us that none of the men her son brought home was any good, they were not trustworthy people.

One day, one of those men, who was Muhammad's lover but lived with wife and son in our building, burst into the fairy's room and started beating him on the head with a stick; the room was splattered with blood and everyone rushed in to try to rescue him. The man fled, and it took Muhammad a week in the hospital to recover. His mother, who had received a blow in the scuffle, died a few weeks later.

There were also constant battles on the second floor, where I lived, and where Teresa lived. She apparently shared her husband with her sister, and the two sisters beat each other all over the building in the most outlandish manner.

Water for the building was collected in some old tanks that I had cleaned. One had to be on the lookout in order to fill them because water would come every other day. Rubén was literally starving to death, but he had no energy to work nor did he want to. He was bisexual, and when I moved in, it took some effort to keep him away; once in a while he would slip into my bed. I finally had to block off the door between our rooms with bricks. The work was done by a mason named Ludgardo, who had the most unusual imagination: In Guanabacoa, where he lived, he had constructed aerial channels made of zinc over the roofs of several houses, which allowed him to collect as much rainwater as possible in his own tanks and never be short of water. With tin drums punched with holes, he had also built a Ferris wheel, airplanes, and other equipment—a complete amusement park for his children. And when there were no shoes, he could make a pair of Swedish clogs out of any piece of wood; his whole family clattered around in those enormous artifacts.

Rubén was a lost cause; his life's dream was to buy himself a pair of jeans, and now that he had the thousand pesos that I paid him, he was shown a brand-new pair. He was told that for two hundred pesos he could have a pair just like it. Naturally, he took the money, paid the agreed amount, and was given his package. When he came to my room and opened it, he found nothing but old newspapers: he had been swindled. I tried to prevent him from spending that money, which he owed the other crook, but he paid no attention to me; he was very generous with his friends and was always inviting them to dinner. He even invited me once to the Moscow Restaurant, one of Havana's most exclusive places in those days.

Víctor, needless to say, quickly found out where I lived and came to visit; he asked me about my new friends and again promised me a job. To spare my real friends any complications, I hung a sign on my door reading VISITORS ARE APPRECIATED BUT NOT RECEIVED. I also painted the word NO in red ink on the wall. That NO sign was my way of protesting against any cops who, disguised as friends, might try to visit me.

Sometimes, at three in the morning Rubén would write a poem and knock on my door to read it to me; I had no choice but to listen.

Pepe Malas lived on the third floor of the building. The owner of the room was a French prostitute, and there was a big fuss when the men she brought in did not want to pay her or when she tried to steal their wallets. One day the woman decided to return to France, fed up with all the misery, and Pepe held on to the room.

Pepe and I kept tabs on each other, though we were not on speaking terms and in general tried to make each other's lives even more impossible.

One late evening Pepe and a group of his friends, among whom was Hiram Prado, pooled some money to pay a young man who charged twenty pesos to fuck them. When he entered the building, I happened to be in the elevator. All the fairies had gathered on Pepe Malas's balcony waiting for him. Since he did not know how to operate the elevator, I showed him, going up and down several times between the first and fifth floors. Pepe Malas and his coterie saw the elevator go up and down—it was a sort of hanging cage—without stopping on the floor where they, all excited, were waiting for him. We finally stopped at my floor. The youth had brought a pineapple, and I suggested that we eat it in my room. We ate the pineapple and then made love.

Pepe, enraged, went from floor to floor calling out for him, while we lay naked in my room, bursting with laughter. Pepe never forgave me for this. From then on, all kinds of things commonly used in witchcraft began to appear outside my door: chicken feet, pigeon heads, and the like.

In the meantime, I had again finished *Farewell to the Sea* and had stored it in a drawer in Elia's home, a very dangerous proposition because of her strong Revolutionary convictions. But it would have been even more dangerous to keep the manuscript in my room since I could be searched at any minute; Pepe could inform on me, or else any of the former prostitutes who were now Communist Party militants.

There was a "loft craze" in those days; that is, in any room where it was possible, people would build platforms that could be reached by small attached ladders. This was done to gain a little more living space. Many times the lofts were so close to the ceiling that you had to crawl, not walk, on them. The government prohibited the construction of lofts and so they had to be built in secret. Even Snow White and the seven dwarfs had one.

Not to be outdone, I managed to get some wood on the black market to build my own. One day, as I was carrying a large board, I came upon Alejo Carpentier, who was giving a lecture from a stand set up in the street. I interrupted his lecture by crossing between the writer and his audience, with the huge board on my shoulder. I stopped to comment to someone in the audience that the man could not even speak Spanish anymore, that all he could do was produce a guttural sound with such a heavy French accent that he sounded like a frog. This person burst out laughing and so did I, and the end of my board struck Alejo's makeshift lectern.

During my stay in Oriente to visit my mother I had met a beautiful recruit from Palma Soriano with whom I had a sort of flirtation. Since I did not have any address in Oriente to give him, we agreed to meet in three months at the Havana bus terminal. On the appointed day, I went to the terminal without the slightest hope that the recruit would be there; however, there he was. His name was Antonio Téllez, but he preferred to be called Tony. We went to my room, and strangely enough, the boy had never had any homosexual experience. When I began touching him, he laughed; it was evident that he was a novice; he was nervous and had trouble getting excited. We finally ended up being good friends.

Tony and Ludgardo were the ones who built my loft; it was not easy. Huge holes had to be opened in the walls with sledgehammers and chunks of iron, and we had to work without making noise so that the president of my CDR would not notice anything unusual. We had to wrap the hammers in rags to muffle the blows. It was a real ordeal to find boards and then to sneak them, late at night, into the building. Bebita, her friend, Muhammad, and I kept scavenging through garbage cans in Old Havana for pieces of wood and old boards.

Later Nicolás Abreu brought a huge quantity of small boards that he had found in garbage piles around his neighborhood in Arroyo Apolo; with these we paneled the loft. In the spaces between beams and flooring I was able to hide the manuscript of *Farewell to the Sea*, together with the document signed by Rubén Díaz stating he had sold me the room for one thousand pesos.

There was a bus stop near my building jokingly called the Stop for Success or the Last Hope. Facing the Manzana de Gómez, a landmark block, it was the preferred pickup place for gays. The area was so congested that it was difficult not to make a contact. Once more I came across Hiram Prado, who at that time was Pepe Malas's archenemy. We greeted each other and he asked me where I lived; I told him I lived with Pepe Malas. He was flabbergasted because he knew that Pepe was a cop, and that I had gone to jail thanks to him; he could not believe that we were living together. Hiram then started to spread the rumor all over Havana that I was living with Pepe Malas, and one night he came with a number of his hoodlum friends to Pepe's room, banging on the door and yelling vile insults directed at me. Pepe came out and tried to hit Hiram with a broomstick, but the thugs Hiram had brought along gave Pepe a monumental beating.

For months Pepe lived in a state of permanent rage because my mail would come to him and many visitors who wanted to see me would knock on his door.

On the same floor as Pepe, Marta Carriles lived with her family, as well as a "slave" they called La Gallega. I met La Gallega when she tried to flee with one of her lovers; through my window I saw an enormous suitcase being lowered on a rope. Later I heard loud noises on the third floor; Marta was chasing La Gallega to prevent her from escaping.

Marta Carriles's husband was a truck driver who brought home tubers and vegetables that Marta later sold in the neighborhood. Marta also practiced *santería* and many people came to her home for consultations. She had two beautiful sons, one of whom had had sexual relations with Rubén; he was an adolescent about fifteen years old. I frequently saw the other one, who was also very handsome, in the elevator with a woman. As far as I was concerned, I had no illusions without my front teeth. Besides, getting my teeth fixed was practically impossible because I needed a doctor's certificate, a worker's ID, a clinic's recommendation; I had none of those and perhaps never would.

I did, nevertheless, recover my smile thanks to Alderete, a man of about sixty who worked as a transvestite, sometimes at Tropicana or at other lesser cabarets. He had been very famous in the forties and owned a large collection of wigs in all shades; he impersonated most of the well-known Cuban performers and his best act was an impression of Rosita Fornés, displaying a more powerful voice than the artist herself. The tale was told that on one occasion he had taken home a juvenile delinquent who tried to rob him at knifepoint. Alderete asked him to wait a moment so he could get the money, and went into the closet. Soon he reappeared disguised as a beautiful woman, and the hoodlum was fascinated by that woman who sucked his prick and who, unnoticed, took his wallet. The youth did not realize that the beautiful woman was the same old queer he had tried to mug. Later, that hoodlum fell in love with Alderete's impersonation and Alderete used to wear his best attire when the youth came to visit.

Eventually the ruffian realized that behind all those clothes and all that makeup there was nothing but an old fairy; perhaps he had suspected it before, but the fact is that one day he got mad and took revenge by stealing everything Alderete owned, including his huge wig collection.

I met him while he was in the depths of a depressive crisis caused by "the great theft," as he referred to it. Totally bald and wrapped in a blanket, he actually looked as ghastly as Pepe Malas himself. But shortly afterward he recovered all his clothes and wigs, and was again impersonating Rosita Fornés.

It was through him that I was able to have my teeth fixed. Alderete knew a dentist who was an admirer of his, and who did not charge me a penny for cementing the two teeth I so badly needed back into the bridge. Now, whenever I opened my mouth, my teeth would no longer keep falling out.

Being able to smile again probably encouraged me to exercise, and I started to jump up and down on my loft, which, not being very secure, came down and I with it. I spent a week pulling nails with a hammer to take the loft apart so that I could rebuild it on new beams. I was working at this when two French citizens knocked on my door: a young man and a girl who had been sent by Jorge and Margarita Camacho. They were staying in Jibacoa Beach as tourists and had come to Havana for a week. With them, of course, my third version of *Farewell to the Sea* left the country.

That French couple were much surprised at my state when they met me; I was wearing shorts made from old pants cut off with a knife, no shirt, and was pulling nails from boards strewn all about the room. They could not conceive of a writer living under such conditions, much less after they had read my books in France. They invited me to have dinner at a restaurant and go with them to Jibacoa, but the authorities would not allow me to enter the beach town.

The French tourists left and I was terrified for a week, awaiting a visit from State Security. I did not know whether they had been able to get the manuscript out or if it had landed in Víctor's hands. Fortunately, they got it out.

I was still surrounded by boards and other junk when I heard Hiram Prado in the hallway; by then he had found out that I was not living with Pepe Malas. I stuck my head out the door and asked him to wait outside. Quickly I wrote another mock notice or bureaucratic document, like a pardon, stating that the penalty of two years' withdrawal of friendship had been reduced to six months and he should come and see me after that period had elapsed. Then I would give him the conditions on which our future friendship would be based. I handed him the document and he left.

Rubén decided to impose on me a fifty-cent charge every

time I had to share his bathroom; it was blackmail, but it was his bathroom. My situation was getting worse all the time, and I was at my wits' end when one day a beautiful young man showed up at my door, barefoot, with no shirt, and asked me for a cigarette. I didn't have any, but I asked him in and closed the door. He told me he knew I was a writer, but I was not in the least interested in discussing literature; I wanted him. I learned that he was the older son of Marta Carriles and that his name was Lázaro. Muhammad told me he was a great young man, but the elevator operator said that he was insane, and a delinquent.

His mother, Marta, was a witch who quarreled with her female neighbors and even had fistfights with them, as well as with her children. Lázaro himself told me how horrible things really were at his home and I soon found out that he was different from the rest of his family; he obviously had some psychological problems but he was not vulgar and sleazy like them. Lázaro longed for peace and wanted to be able to read good literature.

We made several trips outside the city; we went to Guanabo, swam out from the Malecón although it was illegal, and also swam near La Concha Beach. One day I noticed that there was a dangerous violent streak in him. We were horsing around and he hit me so hard in the face that I was afraid he had broken my teeth. Enraged, I ran after him with a stick. I think that after that emotional incident our friendship became deeper; he realized that he had to be a little more careful with me, and I learned that he had been committed to the Mazorra Psychiatric Hospital; this caused my affection for him to grow.

I found out that in order to have one mouth less to feed, his family had taken him to that insane asylum, the worst in Havana. At the hospital he had been given a number of electroshock treatments. He told me that on one occasion, when he returned home at night, his parents would not let him in; a farmer had given his mother a piece of pork and his parents had locked themselves in to eat it so they would not have to share it with him, their own son. He had to sleep outside the door that night. After hearing his story, I told him that he could sleep in my room anytime, and gave him a key. Our greatest pleasure was to walk all over the city; sometimes we would jump over fences and swim at the off-limits beaches.

Through Rubén we met another fascinating person who was always inventing the most unusual ways to escape from the Island. He believed we could leave on a plastic raft, provided we first caught some large fishes—sharks even— tied them to the raft, and pointed them north; he said that in this way we could arrive in Miami in about three days. He claimed his name was Raúl, but one never knew which were the real names of Rubén's friends.

At the Payret Theater there were always long lines because they showed French and U.S. films. Raúl figured out that the daily box office receipts would amount to some ten thousand pesos, and he thought of a weird plan to steal the money. He would approach the box office attendant with a huge balloon of compressed gas, open it, and, under cover of the gas cloud, steal the money and disappear in the crowd. Or he might approach the attendant with a bottle of chloroform, which she would smell and then faint, while we took the money.

Rubén and his cronies did manage to invent a machine to make counterfeit money, and one night they were all arrested. The printing press was in Julio Gómez's home, and he and Pepe Malas were close friends. The strange thing about this was that, while Raúl disappeared for good, Julio and Rubén remained free. One day I discovered the reason: I saw Lieutenant Víctor leave Rubén's apartment.

One of Rubén's visitors was a painter by the name of Blanca Romero, who apparently had fallen out of favor with the system. Her husband had been Sigmundo Bonheur, once in charge of some diplomatic service in Africa but later sent by Castro to a concentration camp in Camagüey. One day Rubén came into my room complaining that while he was in the bathroom Blanca had put on all his clothes and walked away with them. Rubén, Lázaro, and I went to Blanca's; it was sort of a hovel in a tenement on Monserrate Street, a cave with no windows, only a small door. Blanca had many children of many fathers: black, Arabian, and Chinese. She practiced a certain sexual internationalism. After her husband was jailed, she became a prostitute and that was how she made a living, because nobody wanted to buy the pictures she painted, even though they were extraordinary.

In those days she and her current husband, Theodosio Tapiez, would visit well-known painters such as Raúl Martínez, Carmelo González, and others, and while her husband praised the paintings, Blanca would steal some brushes and oils she needed to be able to paint. Under the counter, she would buy flour bags from grocers and pick up pieces of cloth from garbage cans. Thus she would paint the huge canvases that covered entire walls in her apartment.

When we arrived, Blanca proudly showed us one of her masterpieces, and we forgot to ask for the clothes. From then on I visited Blanca regularly; she always managed to have tea and a hard-boiled egg. This was the usual fare for most of us; eggs were not rationed and Russian tea could be purchased at the market, although with some difficulty.

One day Blanca summoned all her friends and children to her little room, where we almost suffocated. She said: "I have called you because I have terrible news for you: my tits have collapsed," and lowering her blouse, she showed us two small black breasts hanging over her stomach. This was a tragedy because she could no longer work as a prostitute, which was how she supported her children, her mother, and Theodosio, who was studying at the university and could not work. I remember her children surrounding her, crying because of the tragedy. We all tried to comfort her, including her mother, who said: "Don't worry, we'll find a way to help you. But now go and wash your feet, they are filthy." Blanca's feet were so dirty that her mother took a knife and started to scrape them.

The heat was oppressive and Blanca complained that her room did not even have a window. We immediately started to open a hole in the wall to make a window with what had once been a machete. The wall was over three feet thick, and when we got to the other side we realized that it did not lead to the street but to a huge convent, the Convent of Santa Clara, which had been abandoned by the nuns after Castro came to power. Practically intact, the convent was full of furniture, trunks, stained-glass windows, and all sorts of objects.

With a discipline worthy of ants we started to dismantle the convent and sell everything we found inside. Suddenly, out of Blanca's little room, with scarcely enough space for a few chairs, twenty or thirty rocking chairs would emerge, or four or five chests, which we would immediately sell all over Havana; on one occasion we filled a whole truck.

One day the president of the CDR in her block knocked on Blanca's door and said she could not understand how Blanca could have so many things in her small room; the opening to the convent was covered with one of Blanca's paintings. There was only one thing to do, to bribe the president of the CDR; she was told to take whatever she pleased. The woman took all she could, and did not inform on us.

I built a cedar loft in my room, installed a toilet and a marble kitchen, and completed my small living room with eighteenth-century furniture.

Next, Lázaro and I removed all the fine woodwork from the ceiling of the convent; in my loft I had a collection of samples of the wood for sale. Blanca, of course, collected a percentage of everything we made. Slabs of red marble were especially successful; even Elia and Pepe bought some.

One night, while we were hauling a great number of crucifixes, silver chalices, and other valuable objects, a cop stopped us and asked us what that "shit" was all about. We told him we had found everything in a demolished building in Old Havana and wanted to use the objects to decorate our homes. He thought that none of the stuff had any value and allowed us to continue with our load.

Ludgardo set up a Swedish clog factory, thanks to Blanca's hole. For us that hole constituted a true treasure trove; we even sold the floor tiles all over Havana.

Finally Bebita had the idea of building balconies and more lofts in our building, and this we did with the wood and the tiles from Blanca's hole. My room was suddenly an apartment complete with balcony with medieval iron railings. Even the very president of the CDR in our building had her loft.

When Rubén realized what my room had become, he told me that since I did not own it, he would reclaim possession any day now. I looked at him calmly and told him that I, indeed, had ownership of that place. He said I could not prove it and I went to my small kitchen, fetched a huge knife I had taken from the convent, and, showing it to him, said: "Here is my ownership of the room." After that, he never mentioned the matter again.

Blanca decided to throw a party in the hole after almost everything had been sold. We bought candles on the black market and decorated the whole convent with them. The party started at midnight. All we had was hard-boiled eggs and tea, but Blanca had invited all her old friends—that is, retired prostitutes, elegant pimps, queens who only ventured out at night. Hiram Prado was also there. That night Blanca and I drew up a document stating that, in view of the diabolic nature of Hiram Prado, we could only meet in places like that hole, on treetops, or at the bottom of the sea, but that we had definitely pardoned him. Hiram was writing his autobiography and that night he read some passages to us. He had included Blanca as one of the most cultured women and one of the greatest painters of this century, and he said that I was the José Martí of my generation. Later I learned that Hiram changed the text of his autobiography depending on where he was going to read it. In other versions I was a hoodlum, and Blanca a cheap hooker.

Another guest in that hole was Bruno García Leiva, an odd character who was always impersonating someone else, perhaps because he himself did not exist. That night he was disguised as a priest with a scapular and a black robe; he really looked like a monk, and many of the retired prostitutes asked him to hear their confessions, which he did with great solemnity.

Sometimes he disguised himself as a doctor and we would go to the Calixto García Hospital. While I wailed pitifully, Bruno would take me to one of the emergency wards of the hospital and pilfer medical certificates, rubber stamps, and prescription pads; these were real treasures. Bruno sold the certificates at the price of gold to people who did not want to work on the farms. Alcoholics bought the prescriptions so they could purchase alcohol at the pharmacy. Hiram Prado, a chronic alcoholic, would give anything for one of those prescriptions.

Also at the party in the hole that night were Amando García, Ludgardo, and Sekuntala. Ludgardo was a tall and strong mulatto whose penis and balls were clearly outlined under his pants. I remember that everyone at the party had to perform a skit, and Amando threw himself on the floor, covered himself with one of Blanca's canvases, and, voicing an increasingly passionate yearning, began to sing a song in praise of Ludgardo with lyrics—a silly tongue twister really—which ran more or less like this: "Oh, Ludgardo, calm my ardor; don't be laggard, don't be tardy, or I'll bite hard. Give me your dart, give me your dart, oh, my Ludgard." Ludgardo was not even gay, but he had a lot of fun.

I also recited some of my own doggerel, such as: "I feel as happy as Minerva, who did voluntary work all day, and received as her heavenly pay, from the Party an ice-cold Materva."

Alderete had brought his wig collection, and the voice of Rosita Fornés rang out among the candles. Finally Ludgardo declared that there should be some buried treasure in the convent and we had to find it. Blanca then made us sign a document stating that if treasure was found she would be entitled to fifty percent. So our party became a sort of treasure hunt. We started digging and did not find any gold, but we did discover a cistern of water, which in Old Havana was almost a treasure. It was fully operational.

From then on we sold up to two hundred cans of water daily; long lines formed in front of Blanca's hole.

Blanca and Amando García decided to hold Hiram Prado prisoner in the hole. When I inquired as to their reasons, they said they had found out what Hiram had indeed written about Blanca in his autobiography. Blanca had then taken possession of the autobiography, in which she was actually described as a seventy-year-old witch who had spread syphilis all over Havana and had been fucked by all the Greek sailors; it also said that she was a lesbian who had sexual relations with her own daughters, and that she was an informer for State Security. Blanca decided that Hiram would remain tied up in that hole until he had written a new autobiography and that, needless to say, she would never return the original. Three days later, Lázaro and I untied him.

By then there was nothing left in the convent to be sold but the walls, and that is precisely what Lázaro and I set out to do: tear down the inner walls of the convent, then clean each brick and sell them all over the city, which was good business because nobody in Cuba could ever get hold of a brick.

Not surprisingly, we received an "anonymous" letter from Hiram saying that he would report all the orgies and crimes being committed in Blanca Romero's hole to the higher authorities.

One day the president of the CDR summoned Blanca and told her that some cops had asked her whether it was true that Blanca was engaged in the illegal sale of wood and water. The woman suggested to Blanca that she stop all sales.

The only way to erase all our tracks was to tear down the convent, but before we did that, I wanted to strip the rest of the roof and sell the remaining boards. We enjoyed the wonderful view of Old Havana from up there.

While tearing down a wall, we suddenly discovered an enclosure hitherto unknown to us, with four safes, all of them locked. Apparently the nuns had built a false wall to hide the real treasure. Since we could not find the combinations to unlock the safes, we battered them with sledge-hammers for a whole week until we managed to open them. They were empty. This was evidently the reason the convent had been boarded up: Castro's officials had been there, emptied out the safes, and tried to cover up the theft. If we were accused of that theft, we could get thirty years for misappropriation. We quickly destroyed the wall that supported what little remained of the inner structure of the convent; then, when it was near the point of collapsing, Ludgardo tied a rope to it and we pulled hard from Blanca's room until, in the midst of a deafening rumble, everything came down.

A few days later a serious typhus epidemic swept over Old Havana. Fidel Castro walked through the neighborhood and said the disease was caused by the huge amount of garbage in the city. In fact, garbage had not been collected for over three years in that section of the city; buildings were caving in and it was a veritable paradise for rats and all kinds of vermin and disease-bearing animals.

Caravans of military trucks converged on the city in a "cleaning offensive," and in twenty-four hours everything that had remained of the Santa Clara Convent had disappeared.

A few weeks later Lázaro again had a nervous breakdown, which happened to him frequently. He would sit on the stairway, talk to himself, swear at the ceiling, and speak incoherently. In that state he knew no one, not even me.

He wanted to write but could not do so; after two or three lines, he would let go of the paper and cry in impotent rage. I told him he was a writer even if he never wrote a single page, and that gave him some comfort. He wanted me to teach him to write, but writing is not a profession, it is a curse; his terrible fate was to be touched by the curse while his mental condition actually prevented him from writing. I never loved him as much as on the day I saw him facing that piece of white paper, and crying because he could not write.

I lent him books that I thought would help him in his literary development; it was amazing how those books awakened his sensibilities to an even greater extent and enabled him to discover what many critics in many instances had not noticed. Sometimes he would call me from his bathroom window and read paragraphs of *Don Quixote* to me; occasionally those readings ended when our neighbors began throwing stones at us because we were not letting them sleep.

In our get-togethers we were joined by a wacky character named Turcio, a former boat skipper and a lover of literature who had been driven mad by his wife. Turcio talked nonstop and if, for example, he heard two women arguing, he would repeat incessantly during the whole day whatever those two women had said to each other. So when Lázaro and I had our literary meetings, Turcio would spend the day repeating over and over the passages he had heard, a sort of relay public-address system. Other times he would go into the hallway and yell out all the local news he heard: "This year there will be no meat"; "Chickens were received, but only for children under six"; "The thirty-two bus will no longer come this way"; and things like that. He would repeat everything his crazed ear took in.

One day the recruit from Palma Soriano, who was still my friend, came to visit with one of his cousins, a cop in full uniform, gun and all. The recruit said to me, "Don't worry, I brought him with me because I know that in this way you will gain prestige in the building, and nobody will bother you." The cop was a queer of Asian descent who, five minutes after arrival, had removed his gun and cartridge belt, and while I showed him my loft, he unzipped his pants and took out his beautiful Oriental penis. The recruit stayed below, smoldering. After an hour, though, we parted company on friendly terms. All this time Turcio had been yelling that the police were in my home; what none of the neighbors could imagine was the formidable weapon the cop was aiming at me.

Sometimes when the recruits or the cop came, Lázaro would have attacks of jealousy. I always told him the truth; he was the person I really loved, and the others were just pastimes. I have always thought that love is one thing and sexual relations are another; real love involves a deep understanding and intimacy that are absent in mere sexual intercourse.

Lázaro had sexual relationships with women, and I never demanded that he break them off; on the contrary, I encouraged him to continue; I thought this would lead us to a better understanding. I preferred to have relations with a man who had sex with women; I wanted to be his friend but not the woman who cooked for him and took care of his daily needs. Thus, when he made love to me, he would do it for the love of a friend and not because of any obligation.

So I was happy at the news that Lázaro wanted to marry Mayra, a very nice young woman who had been his fiancée for several years. They thought that by getting married they could be assigned a house, since her stepfather had pretty good government connections. The wedding took place at the official Wedding Palace and I was best man.

For their honeymoon they went to Santa María del Mar Beach, and Lázaro insisted that I go with them. One night Mayra knocked on my door and told me Lázaro was ill; it was his nerves again, and he wanted me in his room. He was having one of his breakdowns. I have never understood madness too well but feel that in a way insane people are angels who, unable to bear the realities around them, must somehow take refuge in another world. When I went up to him he asked me to stay, and laid his head on my hands; Mayra was intelligent and understanding. The next day he was feeling much better and the three of us went down to the beach.

Mayra's stepfather could not manage to get them an apartment and they had to move in with Marta Carriles. We built a loft over the kitchen; Marta already had one in the living room. Lázaro's loft was so low that they could not stand up in it. One day their pressure cooker exploded, hitting the ceiling; it sounded like a bomb. All the neighbors in the building ran out, thinking it was a real explosion, while the two of them continued making love in their loft, laughing. Lázaro called me through their small window, and I leaned out over the improvised balcony to wave at him; I knew what was going on and it also gave me pleasure.

Lázaro and I went to Pinar del Río together, and we swam nude in the rivers, rode horseback, and enjoyed nature. At night the iron folding bed that we were given creaked furiously.

While we were in one of those country shacks I learned the story of La Gallega. She had had a boyfriend who took her away from home, got her pregnant, and a few months later abandoned her. She was then rejected by her family and Marta Carriles took her in, but on condition that she be her maid. Actually she was more like her slave and worked nonstop, like my mother. La Gallega had a daughter being raised by her in-laws in the country, and she was not allowed to go see her.

On my return to the old Monserrate Hotel, one of the most notorious scandals in its history took place between Hiram Prado and Pepe Malas.

Hiram Prado had a lover in Holguín called Nonito, whom he apparently cared for very much. Again on friendly terms with Pepe, Hiram told him about the physical endowments of this young man, and Pepe, without further ado, took a train to Holguín and brought Nonito to Havana, enticing him with promises of shirts and jeans. One fine day, when Hiram knocked on Pepe's door, it was Nonito who opened it, and in the buff. Hiram went berserk; he came to my room asking for a sledgehammer and other construction tools, and armed with all those weapons he went back to Pepe's room and smashed his glass door. (All the doors at the Monserrate had glass panels, although I had backed mine with a metal plate.) Pepe and Nonito came out with a broom, and the commotion was such that Hiram, besides breaking Pepe's door, also smashed Marta Carriles's as well as that of a large family who were all Jehovah's Witnesses. When all those people went after Hiram, he took refuge in my room; I was afraid they would knock my door down and, at the top of my voice, called Bebita. She showed up with a knife, followed by her friend Victoria. "Civil war has broken out at the Monserrate Hotel!" proclaimed Turcio. In the midst of that madness everyone came out to settle old quarrels; Muhammad was attacked by Snow White and the seven dwarfs; Teresa and her sister again started pulling each other's hair; Caridad González, the president of the CDR, got slapped by Marta Carriles; the elevator operator was kicked by one of the Jehovah's Witnesses. In the meantime, hidden in my room, Hiram and I were listening to the din of battle, while Bebita and Victoria, with strong masculine voices, tried to restore order.

So great was the scandal that the next day Hiram Prado

and I left for Holguín; from there, after waiting in line for a long time, we took a bus to Gibara. Again I was face-to-face with the sea, the sea of my childhood, but by then the city was already a ghost town, and the port itself had been extensively reclaimed by the sand.

Back in Holguín we went to Hiram's home and had dinner with his mother, a poor peasant woman, discreet but aware of almost all of Hiram's erotic adventures. He seized this occasion to introduce me to a number of pretty well known, notorious characters in town, among them Gioconda Carrelero, whose husband was extremely gay. She loved her man above everything else, but he went crazy over adolescents. While we were there one youth called the woman's husband from the street, yelling: "Armando, you faggot, give me the pair of shoes you promised me! Do you think I stuck my cock in you for fun?" He was making such a racket that Gioconda came out of the house and gave him a pair of Armando's shoes.

I also met Beby Urbino, who had always been a repressed gay. He lived in an enormous house which was being invaded by wild vegetation. His philosophy was that love and sex were nothing but a source of sorrow. I, for one, have never been able to live in abstinence, and so I told Urbino: "I'll take my chances."

Hiram and I cruised around Calixto García Park, and it was easy for us to connect with a group of teenagers we met. To bid farewell to the city of Holguín, we took them to Loma de la Cruz. There, near the cross on the hilltop, we were fucked by a dozen adolescents and then, triumphant and rejuvenated, we took the train back to Havana.

Lázaro now had a job as a lathe operator in a factory. He had to get up early and on weekends do "voluntary" guard duty; this had again affected his mental state. He often left Mayra in the loft and came to sleep in my room. Later, when the harvest started, Lázaro had to go to Camagüey to cut sugarcane. A few days after he left I received a letter from him wanting to know how I was doing and asking me to come see him.

His brother Pepe and I took one of those infernal trains, and a week later arrived at a place called Manga Larga; from there we went to the labor camp, where we found Lázaro, who had one of his breakdowns and had been unable to work in the cane fields. The next day we went to work with him; the moment we arrived at the cane field, I felt as if I were entering Hell. We stayed with him for a week, but when he realized that we were about to leave, he became desperate and started yelling.

When he returned a month later, he had lost over thirty pounds; he was ill, his nervous disorder had intensified, and his mother wanted to get hold of the little money he had earned in the sugarcane harvest. I remember that Lázaro once got up at midnight, climbed down from the loft, and picked up a machete he had brought with him. I saw him swinging it around close to his stomach. I leaped down, and when I attempted to grab the machete, he attacked me. I ran out naked to call Lázaro's parents; they came at once and when we opened the door, he dropped to the floor, unconscious. He went through a terrible crisis for about a week.

His mother knocked on my door carrying a bucket with two turtles. She said Saint Lazarus had communicated with her and told her that these would bring me and her son good fortune, and we should keep them. I kept the turtles, although I was sorry to see them confined in that bucket and it was hard to get food for them because they ate only meat or fish.

Some time before, Hiram Prado had introduced me to a strange character who claimed he had been a political prisoner and was doing all he could to leave the country in a boat; his name was Samuel Toca, and he lived in a cell in the Episcopal cathedral in the Vedado. Samuel had actually already tried, together with some friends, to escape in a motorboat from the southern shore of the country, with the idea of making it to Grand Cayman Island. Samuel had a wild passion for England and thought that if he could reach Grand Cayman, he would be taken immediately to England to see Queen Elizabeth, for whom he felt a compulsive adoration. Way out at sea the boat's motor broke down and there was no way of repairing it because they could not find the wrench needed to open it. Since under the circumstances the motor was a hindrance, they threw it overboard to continue their trip by rowing to Grand Cayman. Then they discovered that the wrench had been underneath the motor. They drifted some more until they saw land and started to hail the Queen. They were quickly arrested by Cuban militiamen and later sentenced to eight years in prison. Samuel was "rehabilitated" and had to serve only two and a half years. When I met him he had been released from jail, and was living in the Episcopal church, though his mother was still alive, ill with cancer, in her home in Trinidad [Cuba]. When he later invited me to visit him in Trinidad, I noticed a large photograph of Queen Elizabeth in the living room. Below the photograph there was a small table at which Samuel sat religiously every day at five, dressed completely in black, with top hat and black gloves, to have tea with some of his friends.

Samuel used to walk around Trinidad in that attire, top hat and all, even though the temperature might be over a hundred degrees. It was not only his strange way of dressing, but that he looked as bizarre as humanly possible: he was tall and ungainly, with his straight hair streaking over his forehead, bulging eyes, a protruding, curved nose, large mouth, huge teeth and pimply face, long and bony hands. He looked like one of the witches from *Macbeth* or from Disney's animated films.

Although his love life was pretty open, he still had some of the customs of a seminarian; he had been studying for a religious career in Matanzas and was later transferred to the Episcopal church in Havana. Samuel's cell was more a center for literary gatherings than a place for religious meditations; every night more than fifteen people would meet there. One had to jump a high fence, walk through several hallways, and climb a long staircase before finally reaching Samuel's room. Héctor Angulo, Roberto Valero, Amando García, I, and other friends would meet there daily.

When we were alone, Samuel and I talked about the possibilities for leaving the country in secret. He said he knew someone in Matanzas who for a large sum of money could get us out of Cuba.

Every night around midnight Samuel's room was pelted with a shower of stones. He said the CDR people threw those stones to protest his religious activities. All the jalousies had to be closed. The attacks would last about half an hour, and then peace reigned again. At that time Samuel would ceremoniously serve tea, always in honor of Her Britannic Majesty, and he would read us some of his awful poems.

We finally went to Matanzas and actually saw a woman who told us she could get us out of the country. She asked for the names of those who would be in the boat; I did not want to give her my name or Lázaro's. Samuel was very open and talked to her as if he had known her for a long time. We then stayed at Roberto Valero's home and walked all over Matanzas with him. We went swimming in the bay and I'll never forget the image of Samuel Toca in shorts: with such a bony body, he looked perfectly frightful; some kids bathing nearby even threw stones at him. It was awful to be near such a ghastly-looking individual. I jumped in and swam underwater; when I came up, horrors! I was next to a Russian ship which, however, steamed away quickly.

On my return to Havana Víctor visited me and said, "Well, what happened to your secret escape boat?" I didn't know what to say; he already knew the full story. From then on I feared everyone, especially Samuel Toca. Víctor told me that I was a counterrevolutionary; I did not deserve the good treatment I had received from the Revolution, and anytime now I would land back in jail.

It was a time when what could be called the War of the Anonymous Letters started; everybody received insulting anonymous communications. Several of them were sent to me, or to others referring to me, in which I was described as a terrible person who had even murdered an adolescent. I am sure Pepe was responsible for that one. But I did not lag behind; in every rest room in Havana I left graffiti with lengthy slogans against Pepe Malas, stating that he was the most faggoty faggot of them all, and that he was an informer for State Security. Even Pepe was terrified, because whenever he went to a rest room in search of adventure, he would see those messages and run away.

The anonymous letter that really shook up Pepe was the one written about Samuel Toca.

Pepe Malas had told Samuel Toca that his poems were really dreadful, and thereafter Toca refused to talk to him. Hiram and I wrote a communiqué and sent it all over Havana; it was a moral and patriotic appeal to all decent and respectable people of the city to condemn the orgies taking place at the Episcopal church. The communiqué was really not too far from the truth because Samuel would bring anyone he met into the church, including a cop who happened to be a closet queen.

I had met that cop before Samuel did. I remember his telling me that when he and his partner were driving around in their patrol car and saw a good-looking young man, they would ask for his ID and then order him to come with them to the police station. Then, instead of going to the station, they would take him into the bushes, lower his pants, and suck his member.

Samuel's gatherings were not only literary but also erotic. Sometimes the bishop himself would come out of his residence in the church gardens to find ten or twelve young men in Samuel's cell. Samuel would tell him they were studying the *Book of Common Prayer*, used to teach catechism in that church. The communiqué we prepared covered the orgies and described them in even more sinister terms, including this: "At midnight you could hear the most extraordinary moans through the sacred halls, coming from the strangest of copulations." Then we listed the names of the participants in these orgies, a sort of Black Mass that took place after midnight at the Episcopal church. Each of the participants was described with an appropriate epithet, as for example, Rafael Arnés: antisocial, lecherous matron; Urania Bicha: wanton wench; Aristóteles Pumariega: inveterate satyr; Manuel Baldín: driveling queen; Cristina Fernández: a.k.a. the Hercules from Trinidad; Nancy Padregón: foul-mouthed cross-dresser who parodies "Sóngoro Cosongo"* in the cathedral; Reinaldo Arenas: ex-fugitive and outlaw; Hiram Prado: transvestite.

We included ourselves in that list as a cover-up, and Hiram, who then pretended to be an intimate friend of Samuel, told him that Pepe was preparing an anonymous missive against him that would be spread all around. The anonymous letter ended by stating that Samuel Toca, dressed in full religious garb, would stand at the door and hand out to each participant a copy of the *Book of Common Prayer*.

This letter circulated throughout Havana, and one of the first persons to receive it was the Episcopal bishop. As if that were not enough, one day when mass was to be celebrated, the letter was posted at the church door for all to read. Most of those who read it added their own contributions, making it something like a novel. Samuel was furious, and the bishop called him and asked for an explanation.

The letter mentioned another Dantesque individual

* Famous poem by Nicolás Guillén—D.M.K.

known as Marisol Lagunos, who was also an assistant or altar boy at the church, and whose name was listed with the comment "illegal streetwalker." One day the bishop got up at dawn and found Marisol completely naked and being fucked behind the main altar by a huge Negro. The bishop expelled him from the church and told Samuel Toca that he had only thirty days to vacate his room.

Samuel showed up at Pepe Malas's home with his black umbrella and accompanied by Cristina, who started punching Pepe while the latter threatened to call the police, swearing he had not written that letter. Marta Carriles came out in Pepe's defense and started a fistfight with Cristina.

Pepe had several of his teeth broken by the blows, but Samuel also took some slaps from Marta Carriles. In any case, no one took the letter seriously, and Samuel continued living in the church.

Amando García had moved to a room in the house of the painter Eduardo Michelson; the place was like a queers' den. When Amando moved in, he asked me to stay with him for a few days to help him fix it up.

One night Michelson handed out all kinds of weapons to his tenants: hammers, machetes, knives. He was expecting a lover that evening who was a real thug; if Michelson yelled, we were to take the weapons and run to his aid. Fortunately, he did not have to yell.

During the International Youth and Student Festival, Michelson decided to hold a mini-festival of his own; it was, of course, a clandestine event to which only trustworthy people were invited. I took Muhammad and Hiram Prado as my special guests.

We all had to present a little skit, and with the help of Muhammad and Hiram Prado who acted as my chorus, I gave my impressions of the four major categories of gays in Cuba.

The party continued into the next day; we were starving,

but no one dared go out in the street. The Defense Committees were watching every block so that no antisocial elements would be seen by the foreigners who had come to the Festival. Finally Pedro Juan, one of Michelson's tenants, decided to dress as a man and he went out disguised as a militiaman, stood in a long line, and bought a few packages of spaghetti. We cooked the whole thing in the tub. Michelson had a gallon of booze stashed away, but when he went for it he discovered that there was actually a gallon of water instead; he began to rant and rave and finally threw everybody out of his house, including those who lived there and paid rent to him.

At that moment stones rained on the house, smashing the few unbroken windowpanes left. Michelson told us not to worry, because that rock storm was a daily occurrence; it was the way some of his neighbors expressed their disapproval.

Fearing that the police would burst into the house at any moment, I decided to go to Matanzas, to Roberto Valero's home, until the Festival was over. Since the closing of Blanca's hole I had a friendly as well as business relationship with Valero; I would take clothes purchased on the black market or sent by Margarita and Jorge, and sell them in Matanzas with the help of Roberto, who would act as middleman. In Matanzas we also picked lemons and all kinds of fruit, which I would then sell in Havana.

When I arrived in Matanzas, Valero had been arrested by State Security, and his wife was terrified. For two days we had no news of him; they had searched his house but fortunately had not found anything really incriminating. The night of his release we went to Carilda's house; she was holding one of her secret gatherings at her home in Matanzas. Carilda, like Elia del Calvo, had a houseful of cats. At those gatherings she would read long poems, some loaded with marvelous tackiness but beautiful nonetheless; she had no limits, and for that reason frequently reached the point of being ridiculous. While she was reading, her cats did not just jump but almost flew around her.

Carilda's lover, much younger than she was and completely nuts, would parody her verses with a heavy baritone voice. A former singer of the lyric theater, he had had to give up his profession because of a nervous disorder.

Carilda whispered to us that she was very worried because her husband had drunk thirty-five glasses of water that night; he had some kind of prostate problem and was constantly drinking water. In addition to this passion for water, he had another weakness; he collected sabers. He had a room full of them, and assured us that one of the sabers had belonged to General Martínez Campos.

Dawn came and Carilda was still reading her endless poems. She saved the most erotic ones for last, like the one reading: "When I touch you with the tip of my tits, it addles my wits, my love. It addles my wits."

After she finished reading everything she had recently written, she announced that those poems were a world-premiere event on that early morning in Matanzas. One of the poems had a markedly pornographic theme, and Carilda's husband interrupted her all of a sudden with the saber of Martínez Campos in his hands, yelling: "I told you, bitch, not to read that poem!" Carilda, unflappable, continued reading. He swung the saber around in the air several times, and hit one of the cats. It was then that Carilda lost patience and said: "I'll let you do anything except abuse my cats; this is my house and here I do as I please." And to prove it, she took off her robe and stood there in her panties. Her husband brandished the saber ever closer to Carilda until he hit her on the back. She screamed and ran out into the street in her panties, pursued by her husband shouting: "Stop, bitch!" Carilda begged: "Please, kill me, but don't cause such a scandal in my hometown." But husband and wife continued their outlandish spectacle, disappearing from view in the streets of Matanzas.

The next day I gathered my profits from the sale of clothes that Valero had made among his friends; he himself had purchased a shirt from India that went all the way down to his knees, though he later confessed that the material was too old and rotted. I returned to Havana and, once in my room, locked myself in with a padlock; it was a technique I had developed some time ago to throw any cop or unwelcome visitor off track. Since the door had a hatch that led to the loft, I could close the door with three or four padlocks at once, and also post a note saying that I was not home; I would then climb through the hatch into the loft. No one could possibly suspect that I was in the room.

At dawn I heard somebody trying to force the door open. I looked out cautiously through the hatch and saw a huge black man (he had been one of my lovers during the last six months) who, confident there was no one home, was trying to pry the door open. I quietly took out a club stored under the bed for emergency self-defense, opened the hatch, and hit him over the head so hard it knocked him down. The blow had caught him off guard; he did not know where it came from because, immediately afterward, I had closed the hatch again.

The black man got up, and I opened the hatch and whacked him once more. This time he did not stay to find out where the mysterious blows were coming from, but ran away. He never returned; perhaps he thought the blows were the result of some diabolic or invisible power I possessed.

Only Lázaro knew when I was in my room, and he sometimes brought me food he had stolen from Marta. When the Festival was over, I removed the locks; the general situation became more difficult then because the Festival had totally ruined the country and there was nothing to eat. My own circumstances were worse because I could not get a job. In that crisis my only company were the two turtles that Marta Carriles had given me. For some time I had been feeling sorry for those starving animals; in a way they symbolized my own life. One afternoon I put them in a bag and went to the zoo to release them in the turtle pond, but then I realized that if the guards at the zoo saw me with the turtles, they would think I was stealing them and I would go to jail. There was so much hunger that people frequently stole animals from the zoo to eat them; that was true for the people who killed the lion. Finally, I placed the turtles on the ground; those turtles ran, almost flew over the sand; I never saw two animals so happy and full of energy. They ran until they sank into the water and disappeared in the pond with the other turtles. I felt a great sense of relief. When a few minutes later a heavy downpour flooded the streets of Havana, I ran happily in the rain.

At the Episcopal church there was another scandal similar to the one with Marisol Lagunos. The occasion was a church ceremony in which all the novices and those wanting to be priests could wear their fanciest robes. On that day Toca dressed in white and wore a green cap, which was evidently not his own; he looked like an apparition from a Scandinavian nightmare. Samuel had begged all his friends to come and see him in his full regalia. He had always been an exhibitionist.

The ceremony started, Samuel showed off his splendid attire, the bishop gave his sermon, and then organ music began to flow through the temple. All of a sudden, while the nun kept playing the instrument proficiently, the expected tones were not coming out of that organ; there were only some weird sounds. The choir stopped and although the nun persisted in trying to play her melody, the instrument produced only an infernal noise.

Most of us, including the bishop, went up to the organ pipes and found out what had happened: Hiram Prado, buck naked, was being fucked by the black gardener, and while they were at it, Hiram was hitting and kicking the organ pipes. I do not know if it was due to his state of ecstasy or because the black man's penis was so big that it made Hiram bang the pipes in that manner; the fact is that in the entire history of the Episcopal church nothing like that had ever happened. Hiram and his black paramour fled naked through the gardens.

But the bishop, who knew that Samuel had invited Hiram, asked him the same afternoon to vacate his cell. Samuel said he needed a month to move out and threatened to resort to the offices of Urban Reform. I do not know how he managed it, but he was able to extend his stay at the church for three more months.

It was then 1979 and, as fate decreed, Fidel Castro had decided to get rid of some former political prisoners, many of whom were unimportant. Samuel Toca was one of those former prisoners who received an exit permit. Samuel immediately put on the airs of a great personage; it was he who was going to the free world. Even the bishop gave him a small good-bye party and we again paid Samuel a visit at the church to bid him farewell.

I managed to speak with him in private, and asked him to send a message to my friends Jorge and Margarita to please do all they could to get me out of the country secretly; I asked him to warn them to be very discreet in whatever they did.

As soon as Samuel arrived in Europe he immediately published in the press everything I had asked him to keep secret. A week after Samuel's departure, Víctor came to my room with a copy of *Cambio 16* from Spain. There it was, in large headlines: REINALDO ARENAS THREATENS SUICIDE IF NOT HELPED OUT OF CUBA. This is the way that Samuel kept the secret I had confided to him; he had simply used my name and friendship to gain access to the Spanish and French press.

Margarita and Jorge Camacho put him up for over a month. In October, after they realized that he had no plans to move, they asked him, very diplomatically, when was he intending to leave. Samuel replied, perhaps by the end of the year. I wrote to Margarita and Jorge telling them everything Samuel had done, and they, already aware of what kind of person he was, put him out on the street, but not without first giving him money so that he could move to a hotel.

From the moment he arrived in Europe, Samuel began writing us startling letters; he knew that all our mail was censored by State Security; he even wrote to some people at their place of work or at the university. Everything he wrote was meant to harm us. In one letter he told me that he had done everything possible to get me out of Cuba, that he had talked with Olga, my French friend, to see if it would be possible to get me out as a stowaway on a merchant vessel.

In a letter to Valero he wrote: "I trust you are still meeting at the Episcopal church or at some other place for the counterrevolutionary gatherings that we used to hold every night." He wrote a similar letter to Juan Peñate which cost him his job and, in the end, led to his confinement in an insane asylum.

Valero was then expelled from the university, and as a result, he was sent to prison. There was no place I could be expelled from, and to put me in jail again would have caused further scandal, but I was being watched closer than ever and Víctor told me that if anything similar happened again, they would have no pity whatsoever for me. Of course, I told him that I knew nothing of the matter, that Samuel had done all that to harm me.

Around the same time, Virgilio Piñera received a visit from State Security. They insulted and abused him, and took all his manuscripts, forbidding him to hold any kind of public reading. From then on, he sank into silent, anguished terror.

It was Rafael Arnés who had been reporting that Virgilio's

readings were counterrevolutionary; I was able to verify this later when his friend René Cifuentes, now in exile, confirmed it to me.

G O O D - B Y E   T O
V I R G I L I O   Virgilio also realized that the only salvation possible was to leave the Island. One day, while we were taking a walk in Old Havana, he said to me: "Have you heard that Padilla will be allowed to leave? Listen, if they let Padilla out, they'll let all of us out." Unfortunately, this was not to be the case; Virgilio was never able to leave.

A week later Pepe Malas knocked on my door; for some time he had again been on speaking terms with me, probably on orders from State Security. I opened the door and Pepe said: "Virgilio Piñera is dead; his body is at the Rivero Funeral Home." Víctor came half an hour later to give me the news, and told me it would be better if I did not go. This was too much: I could not even attend the funeral of my dead friend.

As soon as Víctor left my room, I got dressed and went to the funeral home. María Luisa, Lezama's widow, was there, as well as some other friends, but many did not dare to go. The funeral, however, lacked what was most essential: the body of the deceased. Virgilio Piñera's body had been removed from the funeral home by State Security on the pretext that an autopsy had to be performed. This did not make much sense, since autopsies are performed before the body is taken to the funeral home.

Cuban authorities reported that Virgilio had died of a heart attack, but I have my doubts about that. Recently Víctor had asked me if I saw Virgilio often and who did his housecleaning. State Security obviously wanted to know when Virgilio was home alone, and when accompanied by the person who cleaned his house once a week. A person as sinister as Víctor did not ask questions like these out of mere curiosity.

When I arrived at the funeral home and did not find Virgilio's body there, I suspected that his sudden death could very well have been murder.

Fidel Castro has always hated writers, including those favoring the government, such as Guillén and Retamar. But in the case of Virgilio, this hate was even fiercer, perhaps because he was a homosexual and perhaps because his irony was corrosive, anti-Catholic, and anticommunist. He represented the eternal dissident, the inveterate nonconformist, the incessant rebel.

His novel *Presiones y diamantes*, in which a famous diamond is found to be fake and thrown into the toilet, caused Virgilio's fall from grace as far as Fidel Castro was concerned; it was too symbolic. The name of the diamond was Delfi, an anagram of Fidel's name.

Virgilio's body was finally brought back just a few hours before the burial, and taken to the cemetery. At the very moment the body was being removed from the funeral home, I saw Víctor looking radiant and totally satisfied. I realized Security was pleased; it was a job well done.

Virgilio's hearse went at full speed, and was practically impossible to follow. State Security was trying by all means to avoid a crowd at the funeral, but many people, even young boys on skates or bicycles, followed the body. The smarter ones had gone to the cemetery much earlier and were waiting there.

Before the body was lowered into the grave, Pablo Armando read a little speech stating that Virgilio was a Cuban writer who was born in Cuba and had died in Cuba. Of course! He died in Cuba because he had not been allowed to leave.

Silently, his friends and also his enemies stood by: Marcia

Leiseca, one of the most important agents of State Security, all dressed in black like a huge spider, making sure the body was buried properly. Until the last moment, they seemed to be afraid that Virgilio would escape or perhaps hurl one last sardonic guffaw at the regime.

When I returned to my room, my own corpse was there, looking at me from the mirror.

I think that my attitude during Virgilio's funeral placed State Security on guard. In the first place, I had disobeyed Víctor's instructions and gone to the funeral. Second, I had been the only person who had made rebellious remarks in Virgilio's favor; I had said that the whole affair was indeed deplorable. Nobody could now believe the lie that I was rehabilitated. The surveillance around my home increased.

Carlos Olivares was the nephew of the Cuban ambassador to the Soviet Union; he was a gay mulatto who pretended to be a man among other gays so that he could charm them into giving him information; apparently he had also been blackmailed by the Cuban police. One day he was the center of a tremendous disturbance at the Havana Woods. Olivares had invited a great-looking recruit for a walk in the woods. His insinuations were met with diplomatic excuses, but Olivares asked the recruit to fuck him anyway as a favor, arguing that nobody would ever know. Since the recruit insisted that he had to leave, Olivares stood in front of him and said: "You fuck me or I'll scream." The recruit became nervous and walked faster. Soon Olivares's piercing screams could be heard all across the woods, and in response several cops from nearby military units came, at which point the recruit explained what had happened. Perhaps it was then that Olivares became an informer, or perhaps he did so out of pure malice. He was one of the many informers who now visited me on orders from State Security.

That was my life in early 1980; surrounded by spies and seeing my youth vanish without ever having been a free person. I had lived my childhood and adolescence under Batista's dictatorship, and the rest of my life under the even harsher dictatorship of Fidel Castro. I had never been allowed to be a real human being in the fullest sense of the word.

I must confess that I never recovered from my experiences in Cuban jails; I think no former prisoner can. I lived in terror in my country and with the hope of someday being able to escape. All the young people in Cuba thought of nothing else. Often they tried to force their way into one of the foreign embassies.

Many people still remember the trailer full of young Cubans that, while trying to cross the electric fence into the Guantánamo Bay Naval Base, was machine-gunned by the Cuban troops.

It was said there were Cuban exiles who had been living at the Mexican embassy for years, because the Mexican government, always evasive and unprincipled, was holding them perhaps on direct orders from Fidel Castro. Sometimes they would be starving; they were on Mexican territory but subject to Castro's blackmail. To get into an embassy was practically impossible, although all young people dreamed of it.

M A R I E L Around the beginning of April 1980, a driver on the number 32 bus route drove a bus full of passengers through the doors of the Peruvian embassy asking for political asylum. Strangely enough, all the passengers on the bus also decided to ask for political asylum. Not one of them wanted to leave the embassy.

Fidel Castro demanded that all the people be returned, but the ambassador from Perú stated that they were on Peruvian territory, and according to international law, they had the right to political asylum. Days later, during one of his fits of anger, Fidel Castro decided to withdraw the Cuban guards from the embassy, perhaps trying in this way to pressure the ambassador to give in and force the people out of the embassy.

This time he miscalculated. When it became known that the Peruvian embassy was no longer guarded, thousands upon thousands of people, young and old, entered the grounds asking for political asylum. One of the first to do so was my friend Lázaro. I did not believe in the possibility of asylum because the news was even published in *Granma*; I thought it was a trap, and that once all the people were inside the embassy, Castro would arrest them. As soon as he knew who his enemies were—that is, all those who wanted to leave—he could then easily put them in jail.

Lázaro said good-bye to me before going to the embassy. The following day the embassy doors were closed again, but there were 10,800 people inside and 100,000 more outside, trying to get in. From all over the country, trucks were arriving full of young people who wanted to get in, but at that point Fidel Castro knew he had made a big mistake by withdrawing the guard from the Peruvian embassy. Not only was the embassy closed but only people living in Miramar were allowed near the site.

Electricity and water to the embassy were cut off, and for 10,800 people, 800 food rations were delivered. In addition, State Security smuggled in numerous undercover agents who went as far as to murder former high government officials requesting asylum. The area surrounding the embassy was scattered with Communist Youth Organization and Communist Party IDs, discarded by the people inside.

All the world press agencies were wiring the news, but the Cuban government tried to play down the incident. Even Julio Cortázar and Pablo Armando Fernández, stalwart champions of Castro who were in New York at the time, declared that there were only six or seven hundred people inside the embassy.

One taxi driver drove his car at full speed trying to break into the embassy, and was machine-gunned down by State

Security; wounded, he still tried to get out of his car and into the embassy, but he was carried away in a patrol car.

The events at the Peruvian embassy were the first mass rebellion by the Cuban people against the Castro dictatorship. After that, people tried to enter the U.S. Interest Section office in Havana. Everybody was seeking an embassy to get into, and police persecution reached alarming proportions. In the end, the Soviet Union sent a high official of the KGB to Cuba, to hold a number of meetings with Fidel Castro.

Fidel and Raúl Castro had personally taken a look at the Peruvian embassy. There, for the first time, Castro heard the people insulting him, calling him a coward, a criminal, and demanding freedom.

It was then that Fidel ordered that they be gunned down, and those people—who had gone for fifteen days with almost no food, sleeping on their feet because there was no space to lie down, trying to survive amid the filth of their own excrement—faced up to the bullets by singing the old national anthem. Many were wounded.

To avoid the danger of a popular uprising, Fidel and the Soviet Union decided that a breach must be opened to allow a number of those nonconformists to leave; it was like curing sickness by bleeding.

During a desperate and angry speech, accompanied and applauded by Gabriel García Márquez and Juan Bosch, Castro accused those poor people in the embassy of being antisocial and sexually depraved. I'll never forget that speech—Castro looked like a cornered, furious rat—nor will I forget the hypocritical applause of García Márquez and Juan Bosch, giving their support to such a crime against the unfortunate captives.

The port of Mariel was then opened, and Castro, after stressing that all those people were antisocial, said that precisely what he wanted was to have that riffraff out of Cuba. Posters immediately started to appear with the slogans LET THEM GO, LET THE RIFFRAFF GO. The Party and State Security organized a "voluntary" march against the refugees at the embassy. People had no choice but to take part in the march; many went with the hope of perhaps being able to jump the fence and get inside. But the marchers could not get close, not with three rows of cops between them and the fence.

Thousands of boats full of people started to leave for the United States from the port of Mariel. Of course, not all those at the embassy who wanted to leave were able to do so, but only those whom Fidel Castro wanted to get rid of: common prisoners and criminals from Cuban jails; undercover agents whom he wanted to infiltrate in Miami; the mentally ill. And all this was paid for by the Cuban exiles who sent boats to get their relatives out. The majority of those families in Miami spent all their resources renting boats to rescue their loved ones, and when they arrived at Mariel, Castro would often fill their boats with criminals and insane people, and they could not get their relatives out. But thousands of honest people also managed to escape.

Of course, to be able to depart from the Port of Mariel, people had to leave the Peruvian embassy with a safe-conduct issued by State Security, and had to return to their homes and wait until the Castro government gave them the order to leave. From that moment on, State Security, not the Peruvian embassy, was making the decisions as to who could leave the country and who could not. Many resisted, not wanting to abandon the embassy, especially those most involved with the Castro regime.

The mobs organized by State Security waited outside the embassy for those leaving with safe-conducts and in many instances tore up their permits. Besides losing their right to exile, they were beaten up by the rabble.

Lots of people were physically attacked, not only for being at the Peruvian embassy but merely for sending telegrams asking their relatives in Miami to come for them at the Port of Mariel. I saw a young man beaten unconscious and left on the street just as he was coming out of the post office after sending one of those telegrams. This happened daily, everywhere, during the months of April and May 1980.

Twenty days later, Lázaro returned from the embassy and was hardly recognizable; he weighed less than ninety pounds. He had gone to a lot of trouble to avoid being beaten, but he was starving. Now all he could do was wait for his exit permit. The day it came, I accompanied him in a taxi to where the documents were being issued, and he said to me: "Don't worry, Reinaldo, I am going to get you out of here." When he left the taxi, I saw the mob attack him and hit him on the back with steel bars as he ran under a shower of rocks and rotten fruit; in the midst of all that, I saw him disappear toward freedom, while I remained behind, alone. But in my building almost everyone wanted to leave the country, so it felt like a sort of refuge.

During that civil strife, terrible things were happening. To escape being beaten by the mob, one man got in his car and drove it into some of the people who were attacking him. An agent of State Security immediately shot him in the head, killing him. The incidents were even published in *Granma*; to have killed such an antisocial person was considered a heroic act.

The homes of those waiting for exit permits were surrounded by mobs and stoned; in the Vedado, several people were stoned to death. All the terrors suffered for twenty years were now reaching their peak. Anyone who was not Castro's agent was in danger.

Opposite my room someone had put up various posters reading: HOMOSEXUALS, GET OUT; SCUM OF THE EARTH, GET OUT. To get out was exactly what I wanted, but how? Ironically, the Cuban government hurled insults at us and demanded that we leave, but at the same time prevented us from leaving. At no point did Fidel Castro open the Port of Mariel to all who wanted to leave; his trick was simply to let go the ones who posed no danger to the image of his government. Professionals with university degrees could not leave, nor could writers who had published abroad, such as myself.

However, since the order of the day was to allow all undesirables to go, and in that category homosexuals were in first place, a large number of gays were able to leave the Island in 1980. People who were not even homosexual pretended to be gay in order to obtain permission to leave from the Port of Mariel.

The best way to obtain an exit permit was to provide any documentary proof of being a homosexual. I did not have such a document, but I had my ID, which stated that I had been in jail because of a public disturbance; that was good enough proof, and I went to the police.

At the police station they asked me if I was a homosexual and I said yes; then they asked me if I was active or passive and I took the precaution of saying that I was passive. A friend of mine who said he played the active role was not allowed to leave; he had told the truth, but the Cuban government did not look upon those who took the active male role as real homosexuals. There were also some women psychologists there. They made me walk in front of them to see if I was queer.

I passed the test, and a lieutenant yelled to another officer, "Send this one directly." This meant that I did not have to go through any further police investigation. They made me sign a document stating that I was leaving Cuba for purely personal reasons, because I was unworthy to live within the marvelous Cuban Revolution. They gave me a number and told me not to leave my home. The cop filling out my papers said: "Listen carefully, if you are going to have a 'clotheshanger party' you must have it at home, because if you are not there when the exit permit arrives, you'll miss your chance." I think that cop would have been delighted to go to the imaginary nude party that he said I would have at home.

My exit permit had been negotiated at the neighborhood level, the police station. The mechanisms of persecution in

Cuba were not yet technically sophisticated; for that reason, I could leave without State Security finding out about it; I was leaving as just another queer, not as a writer; in the middle of that pandemonium, none of the cops who authorized my exit knew anything about literature or had any reason to know my books, almost none of which, in any case, had ever been published in Cuba.

When I had finally dozed off one night, after a sleepless week locked up in my unbearably hot room, there was a knock at my door. It was Marta Carriles and Lázaro's father calling out: "Get up, your exit permit is here! We knew Saint Lazarus would help you!" I ran downstairs in my pajamas and right there at the building's entrance, holding a sheet of paper, was a cop who asked me if I was Reinaldo Arenas. I answered affirmatively, in as low a voice as I could, and he told me I had thirty minutes to get ready and show up at a place called Cuatro Ruedas to leave the country.

Rushing up the stairs I ran into Pepe Malas, who was always on the watch, and he said: "There is a cop down there looking for you. What does he want?" With panic in my face I told him that they had come to take me in again, that there was going to be another trial. I was so terrified at the thought that he could discover my real reasons, that he believed me.

In those days it was very difficult to get to Cuatro Ruedas in thirty minutes. When the bus came, I told the driver I had an exit permit, and that I would give him a gold chain if he got there in less than half an hour. The driver stepped on the gas and drove at full speed, without making any stops, and I made it on time. I quickly said good-bye to Fernando, Lázaro's father, and ran to the place where a soldier was waiting. I surrendered my ration booklet and the document I had received from the police officer at home, and was immediately given a passport and a safe-conduct stating that I was one of the exiles from the Peruvian embassy. I left for Mariel on the first bus of the day. To cap it all, the bus broke down on the way and we had to wait about two hours for another bus to pick us up and take us to our destination.

We arrived at El Mosquito, the concentration camp near Mariel; it was aptly named because of the swarms of mosquitoes there. We had to wait two or three days for our turn to leave Mariel. During this time I met some friends, and also many who I knew were undercover agents; I tried to stay out of their way so they would not notice me. We were searched, since we were not allowed to take any letters, not even the telephone number of someone in the United States. I had memorized the number of my aunt in Miami.

Before entering the area for people already authorized to leave the country, we had to wait in a long line and submit our passports to an agent of State Security who checked our names against those listed in a huge book; they were the names of people not authorized to leave the country. I was terrified. I quickly asked someone for a pen and since my passport was handwritten and the *e* of *Arenas* was closed, I changed it to *i* and became Reinaldo Arinas. The officer looked up my new name, and of course never found it.

Before we boarded the buses for the Port of Mariel, another officer told us that we were all leaving "clean," that is, that no passport contained any criminal records, and that, therefore, when we arrived in the United States all we had to say was that we were exiles from the Peruvian embassy. There was, no doubt, a dirty and sinister game behind these procedures; the Revolutionary government purposefully intended to create an enormous confusion so that authorities in the United States would not know who were the actual exiles and who were not.

Before boarding the boats, we were sorted into categories and sent to empty warehouses: one for the insane, one for murderers and hard-core criminals, another for prostitutes and homosexuals, and one for the young men who were undercover agents of State Security to be infiltrated in the United States. The boats were filled with people taken from each of these different groups.

It should be remembered that there were 135,500 people in that exodus; the majority were people like myself; all they wanted was to live in a free world, to work and regain their lost humanity.

Finally, at one in the morning of May 4, my turn came. The name of my boat was *San Lázaro* and I remembered Marta Carriles's words. A soldier took several pictures of us and minutes later we were under way. We were escorted by two Cuban police launches; it was a precaution to prevent people who had not received exit permits from illegally boarding those boats.

Something horrendous happened just then. As we were leaving, a member of the coast guard threw his rifle into the water and quickly started to swim toward us. The other coast guard launches approached the swimmer, and the men killed him, while he was still in the water, with their bayonets.

The *San Lázaro* continued sailing away from the coast. The Island turned into a jumble of blinking lights, and then everything became a deep shadow. We were now on the open sea.

For me, who for so many years had wanted nothing more than to abandon that land of horrors, it was easy not to cry. But there was a youth, perhaps seventeen years old, forced on board in Mariel having to leave all his family behind, who was crying disconsolately. There were some women with children who, like me, had not eaten in five days. There were also several mental patients.

The captain of the boat was an exile who had left Cuba for the United States twenty years ago, and had now returned just to get his family out. Instead, he was carrying a ship full of strangers, with the promise that, on his next trip, he would be allowed to take his family with him. He was the navigator because he had no other choice. He told me he knew nothing about navigation, and had chartered that boat in order to rescue his family. There was, to make the situation even worse, nothing to eat on board.

The trip from Havana to Key West is only seven hours. However, we had been sailing for more than a day without seeing that blessed Key West. Finally the captain confessed that he was completely off course and did not know where we were. He did have a radio and was trying to contact other vessels, but to no avail.

On the second day, the boat ran out of gas, and we began drifting in the powerful current of the Gulf Stream. We had not eaten for so many days that we couldn't even throw up; we only vomited bile. One of the mental patients tried to jump overboard several times and had to be held down while some of the ex-convicts yelled at him to control himself, telling him that he was going to "Yuma." The poor man shouted back, "To hell with Yuma, I want to go home." He had no idea that we were going to the United States of America. Sharks were circling around us, waiting to devour anyone unlucky enough to fall overboard.

At last the captain was able to raise another boat, which then called the U.S. Coast Guard, who in turn ordered a helicopter search. Three days later the U.S. helicopter appeared; it dropped almost to water level, shot some photos, and left. It radioed rescue orders to the coast guard and that very night a coast guard vessel came by. They threw us lines and brought us aboard, tied our boat to their stern, and we were soon on our way. They fed us, and little by little, we recovered our strength and began to feel a great joy. At last we reached Key West.

KEY WEST As I was leaving my building on Monserrate Street, the president of my CDR approached me and said, "Don't worry, I won't inform on you; what I want from you is that if you see my son, you tell him that I am all right." Strangely enough, when I arrived at Key West, her son was one of the first persons I met, so I was able to deliver his mother's message. He then took me to a warehouse where Cuban exiles in Miami had stored all donations for the arrivals from Mariel, and he gave me a new pair of shoes, jeans, and a resplendent new shirt. He also gave me a cake of soap, and a huge amount of food. I took a bath, shaved, and started once again to feel like a human being.

Later I met a dancer from Alicia Alonso's ballet company, who told me that shortly after I left Mariel, my name was being paged over all the loudspeakers; the police were after me. Still later I found out that they were checking all passports at boarding time, and were even stopping all the buses and asking for me. The Cuban State Security and UNEAC had been alerted and, believing I was still at El Mosquito camp, had organized an intensive search to prevent my leaving the country.

We were lodged in Key West, waiting for immigration to decide where to place us. In the midst of that crowd I ran across Juan Abreu; we could finally embrace outside Cuba, at last free.

Upon reaching Miami I tried to contact Lázaro, as well as Margarita and Jorge Camacho, who were then in Spain. I was lucky to meet Lázaro when I arrived at my uncle's house; he was waiting for me, and we found it still hard to believe that the two of us, with only a week's difference, were now in the United States. I wrote Margarita and Jorge Camacho; they knew about my escape from a news cable in the Spanish press. I was now trying to recover my manuscripts, and I knew Jorge and Margarita, who were in their country home, did not have them there. They had delivered them to Severo Sarduy in Paris. I called him, and on that first call Severo told me that he did not have them either. I wrote a desperate letter to my friends the Camachos. They told me not to worry; they had the originals and Severo only had copies. It was fortunate they had taken such precautions, because apparently it seemed that Severo Sarduy had no intention whatsoever of returning those manuscripts to me.

M I A M I The International University of Florida invited me to speak at a conference in June of 1980. I entitled my talk "The Sea Is Our Jungle and Our Hope." This was my first lecture before a free audience. Heberto Padilla was next to me; he spoke first. He was in a really pitiful state; completely drunk and stumbling, he faced the audience and improvised incoherently. The public reacted violently against him. I felt pity for the man, destroyed by the system, unable to come to terms with his own ghost and the fact that he had made a public confession in Cuba. In all truth, Heberto has never recovered from that confession. The system managed to destroy him in the most perfect way, and even now seemed to make use of him for its own benefit.

As soon as I started denouncing the tyranny I had been suffering for twenty years, even my own publishers, who had made enough money from my books, covertly turned against me. Emmanuel Carballo, who had published more than five editions of *El mundo alucinante* [in Mexico] and never paid me a penny, now wrote me an indignant letter saying I should have never left Cuba, while, at the same time, refusing to make any payment to me. There were countless promises, but the money never came: it was a very profitable way of exercising his communist militancy.

The same thing happened with Angel Rama, who had published a collection of my short stories in Uruguay. Instead of at least writing me a letter to congratulate me for having left Cuba (he knew of my situation, having met me there in 1969), he wrote a lengthy newspaper article for *El Universal* of Caracas, which he entitled "Reinaldo Arenas on His Way to Ostracism." In that article Rama stated that my leaving Cuba was a mistake, that all my problems had been only bureaucratic, and that now I would be condemned to ostracism. All this was extremely cynical and, moreover, preposterous, considering that Rama was referring to someone who since 1967 had not been able to publish anything in his own country, and who had suffered repression and imprisonment there and had indeed already been condemned to ostracism. I realized that the war had started all over again, now in a much more underhanded manner; it was less terrible than Fidel's war against the intellectuals in Cuba, albeit no less sinister.

To top it all, after numerous phone calls to Paris, Sarduy not only paid me a mere one thousand dollars for the French editions, but one day called my aunt in Miami and told her I had lots of money. And my aunt, of course, never doubted that I am a millionaire.

None of this surprised me: I already knew that the capitalist system was also sordid and money-hungry. In one of my first statements after leaving Cuba I had declared that "the difference between the communist and capitalist systems is that, although both give you a kick in the ass, in the communist system you have to applaud, while in the capitalist system you can scream. And I came here to scream."

E X I L E I then traveled through several countries: Venezuela, Sweden, Denmark, Spain, France, Portugal. In all of these countries I screamed; it was my treasure, it was all I had.

I now discovered a variety of creature unknown in Cuba: the Communist Deluxe. I remember that at a Harvard University banquet a German professor said to me: "In a way I can understand that you may have suffered in Cuba, but I am a great admirer of Fidel Castro and I am very happy with what he has done in Cuba."

While saying this, the man had a huge, full plate of food in front of him, and I told him: "I think it's fine for you to admire Fidel Castro, but in that case, you should not continue eating that food on your plate; no one in Cuba can eat food like that, with the exception of Cuban officials." I took his plate and threw it against the wall.

My encounters with this festive and fascist left stirred a good amount of controversy. In Puerto Rico these people were rather cunning; they invited me to speak at the university and asked me not to talk about politics. I read a paper on Lezama Lima, following which a front man for Castro by the name of Eduardo Galeano read a long political essay attacking me because I had adopted a nonpolitical attitude.

Evidently, the war against communists, hypocrites, and cowards had not ended just because I was out of Cuba.

But while it is true that in exile I met a whole series of opportunists, hypocrites, and people profiting from the suffering of the Cuban people, I also encountered some honest and extraordinary people, many of whom did help me. Professor Reinaldo Sánchez offered me a job as visiting professor at the International University of Florida, where I prepared and taught a course on Cuban poetry. I met excellent students there; it was a way of getting back to what is Cuban, though in a deeper sense because we were away from our country.

I also had the opportunity to establish a relationship with three writers, in my opinion key figures in our history: Lydia Cabrera, Enrique Labrador Ruiz, and Carlos Montenegro.

Lydia's wisdom made me feel close to Lezama again. She had taken upon herself the job of rebuilding the Island, word by word, from a small apartment in Miami, writing nonstop, going through all kinds of economic hardships, with a huge number of unpublished books, and having to pay herself for the few she published in Miami.

Other writers were living in even more distressing circumstances, such as Labrador Ruiz, one of the greats of the contemporary novel; he lived, and still lives, on welfare. He had written his memoirs but never found a publisher for them.

It was paradoxical that those great writers who had left Cuba in search of freedom were now unable to publish their work here.

Such was the case with Carlos Montenegro, a first-rate novelist and storyteller, also living on welfare in a small room in a poor neighborhood of Miami; this is the price to be paid for keeping one's integrity. The sad fact is that Cuban exiles were not very interested in literature; a writer was looked upon as a strange, abnormal creature.

In Miami I met wealthy people, bankers and business owners, and I proposed to create a publishing house for the best of Cuban writers, most of them living in exile already. The reply of all those men, all multimillionaires, was categorical: Literature is not lucrative. Almost nobody is interested in a book by Labrador Ruiz; Lydia Cabrera can sell in Miami, but not to any great extent; in short, it would not work out as a business.

"We might be interested in publishing one of your books because you just left Cuba and you are news," they told me. "But those other authors, nobody is going to buy their books."

Montenegro died the following year in a public hospital, completely forgotten. Labrador is struggling to survive in a small room in Miami. As for Lydia, she is completely blind but still writing. Her small editions hardly circulate beyond Miami.

I once went to the presentation of one of her books. I saw an old lady sitting at a small table under a mango tree, signing books: it was Lydia Cabrera. She had left behind all of her past, her huge country estate in Havana, her extensive library, and was now trying to make ends meet in a small Miami apartment. When I saw this blind old lady signing her books under a mango tree, I understood that she represented a greatness and a spirit of rebellion that perhaps no longer existed in any of our writers, either in Cuba or in exile. One of the greatest women in our history, she was completely forsaken and forgotten, or else surrounded by people who had never read a single one of her books and were now just looking for a quick news story, taking advantage of the splendor that old lady still radiated. It was a paradox and at the same time a good example of the tragic fate Cuban writers have suffered throughout our history; on our Island we have been condemned to silence, to ostracism, censorship, and prison; in exile, despised and forsaken by our fellow exiles. Cubans have a sort of destructive and envious tendency and, in general, do not tolerate greatness well; they find it hard to bear having a person excel, and want to tear all down to the same level of general mediocrity; this is unforgivable. In Miami, the worst part of it is that everyone wants to be a poet or writer, especially a poet. I was amazed when I saw a bibliographic listing of Miami poets, compiled by another Miami poet, who called herself not a poet but a poetess; more than three thousand names were listed. They published their own books, called themselves poets, and held impressive gatherings you had to go to if you didn't want to be ostracized. Lydia called those poetesses "*poetiesas*" [stiff poetesses] and renamed Miami El Mierdal [the Shithole]. Lydia always urged me not to stay in Miami; she said I had to leave at once, for New York, Paris, Spain. She never found a niche in that flat, envious, mercenary environment, but being eighty years old she had nowhere else to go. Lydia Cabrera belonged to a more refined tradition, one richer in depth and world culture, far removed from those poetesses of boring bad taste and corny inanities, for whom nothing mattered but their current participation in social events, and for whom anyone who managed to publish a book in a foreign country and attain some renown was almost a traitor.

I realized immediately that Miami was not for me. The first thing my uncle told me when I arrived was: "Buy yourself a jacket and a tie, have your hair cut short, and walk properly, tall, firm. Also, have some business cards printed giving your name and saying that you are a writer." Of course, he was trying to tell me that I had to become more of a macho man. The typical Cuban machismo has attained alarming proportions in Miami. I did not want to stay too long in that place, which was like a caricature of Cuba, the worst of Cuba: the eternal gossip, the chicanery, the envy. I also hated the flatness of the scenery, which could not compare with the beauty of an island; it was like the ghost of our Island, a barren and pestiferous peninsula, trying to become, for a million exiles, the dream of a tropical island: aerial, bathed by the ocean waters and the tropical breeze. In Miami the obsession with making things work and being practical, with making lots of money, sometimes out of the fear of starving, has replaced a sense of life and, above all, of pleasure, adventure, and irreverence.

During the few months I lived in Miami, I had no moment of peace. I was surrounded by gossip and difficulties, and by an endless succession of cocktail parties, soirées, and invitations. It was like being on display, a strange creature that had to be invited before it lost its luster or until a new personality arrived to displace it. I had no peace to do anything, much less to write. Moreover, the city—not really a city but rather a number of detached houses peopled by cowboys for whom the horse had been replaced by the car —terrified me. I was used to a city with sidewalks and streets, a deteriorated city but one where a person could walk and appreciate its mystery, even enjoy it at times. Now I was in a plastic world, lacking all mystery, where loneliness was often much more invasive. It did not take long for me to become homesick for Cuba, for Old Havana, but my enraged memory was stronger than any nostalgia.

I knew I could not live in Miami. Now, needless to say, after ten years, I have realized that an exile has no place anywhere, because there is no place, because the place where we started to dream, where we discovered the natural world around us, read our first book, loved for the first time, is always the world of our dreams. In exile one is nothing but a ghost, the shadow of someone who never achieves full reality. I ceased to exist when I went into exile; I started to run away from myself.

In Miami, Lázaro had another crisis of total madness; it was getting worse. Everybody lived in a state of constant paranoia, locked up; even my aunt, whom I had not seen for twenty years, seemed more moonstruck. When I arrived in Miami I think I made some statements that people did not like very much. I said: "If Cuba is Hell, Miami is Purgatory."

In August of 1980 I accepted an invitation to speak at Columbia University, in New York. Without a second thought, I prepared my lecture in less than two hours, and took the plane. I was fleeing from a place that only increased my anxieties and wasn't suited to my way of being; I was also, forever, running away from myself.

The exile is a person who, having lost a loved one, keeps searching for the face he loves in every new face and, forever deceiving himself, thinks he has found it. I thought I had found that face in New York, when I arrived here in 1980. The city took me into its fold. I felt as if I had arrived in a glorified Havana, with great sidewalks, fabulous theaters, a transportation system that worked marvelously, streets that were really lively, and all kinds of people who spoke many different languages; I did not feel like a stranger in New York. That very first night, I started walking around the city; it seemed to me that in another incarnation, in another life, I had lived in this city. That evening, a group of more than thirty friends, including Roberto Valero, Nancy Pérez Crespo, and even Samuel Toca, whom I had forgiven, took cars and drove along Fifth Avenue, which, on the first of September, was beginning to be invaded by the mists of autumn.

WITCHES
Witches have played an important part in my life. First, there are those I could consider peaceful and spiritual, those who reign in the world of fantasy. This kind of sorceress, which came to me through my grandmother's imagination, filled the nights of my childhood with mystery and terror, and summoned me later to write my first novel, *Singing from the Well*. But there is another kind of sorceress, of flesh and blood, who has also played an important part in my life. Maruja Iglesias, for example, whom everybody called "the Library Witch": she was the influence that made possible my job transfer to the National Library, there to meet another sorceress, even wiser and more enchanting, María Teresa Freyre de Andrade, who gave me protection and also imparted her extensive, ancient wisdom. María Teresa had the habit of blinking, just like the great witch in one of Shakespeare's plays. Then I met Elia del Calvo, so perfect a witch that she surrounded herself entirely with cats. Her character and personality were very important to me at one point in my life. A sorceress like her indirectly made it possible for me later to leave the country like a nonperson, like an unknown. In Miami I also met several witches dedicated to the traffic of words. Witchlike, they dressed in long black robes, and were thin, with prominent jaws; some of them wrote poems and, like Elia del Calvo, forced me to read them. The world is

really full of witches, some more benign, some more implacable; but the kingdom of fantasy, as well as patent reality, belongs to witches.

When I arrived in New York I met the perfect witch. This lady dyed her hair violet, wanted her old husband to die quickly, and flirted with everyone who would come close to her. It was a platonic flirtation; no doubt she was only trying to fill the immense loneliness of her life, on the West Side of Manhattan, where she tried to communicate in an English impossible to decipher. This witch, a perfect "fag hag," collected homosexuals and welcomed me as soon as I arrived. Though her son was homosexual as well, she, being a witch, had forced him to have a girlfriend and later to marry and even to have several children. This witch, whose name was Alma Ribera, told me I had to stay in New York. Thus she helped me fulfill my destiny, my always terrible destiny. She managed to find me an empty apartment in the center of Manhattan. "Rent it at once," she said. And suddenly I, who had come to New York for only three days, now had a small apartment on Forty-third Street between Eighth and Ninth Avenues, three blocks from Times Square, the most crowded place in the world. I did rent the apartment at once and I entrusted myself, as always, to the mysterious, evil, and sublime power of witches.

A real witch was my aunt Agata, matchless in her wickedness; for more than fifteen years I had to live with her in terror and under the constant threat of being denounced to the police. But I cannot deny that I felt a strange attraction for her; perhaps the attraction of evil, of danger.

Another unforgettable witch in my life was Blanca Romero, who transformed Old Havana into a clog factory, and who gave up prostitution when her tits collapsed, and became an extraordinary painter while, at the same time, denouncing her admirers to State Security.

Witches have dominated my life: witches who never gave up their brooms, not so they would be able to fly but because all their longings and frustrations, all their desires were exorcised through their sweeping: sweeping the rooms, the passageway, the yards at home, as if in this way they could sweep away their own lives.

The image of one major witch stands out above all the others; that of the noble witch, the suffering witch, the witch full of longing and sadness, the most beloved witch in the world: my mother. Also with her broom, always sweeping as if nothing mattered but the symbolic meaning of the act.

Sometimes witches would assume a half-masculine form, which could make them even more sinister. Among the witches that were for so long part of my life, how could I forget Cortés, a fearsome witch with a perfectly witchlike shape, thanks to whom I had to rewrite my novel *Farewell to the Sea* so many times, and who branded my life with terror during the seventies. How could I forget Pepe Malas, another perfect witch, who seemed to be in a constant state of levitation, twisted and insidious in character, misshapen of body (and thanks to whom I landed in jail, in one of the most Dantesque circles of hell). And how could I forget the classic witch all in black, black gloves and black cape, with bulging eyes and wispy hair, the witch with the huge jaws and sinister smile: Samuel Toca, the frightening witch from whom I learned the real meaning of betrayal and who, witchlike, would materialize wherever I happened to be, even riding in the same car with me through the streets of New York.

Witches, my companions since childhood, will escort me to the very gates of hell.

I moved to New York on December 31, 1980, having had to return to Miami to complete the literature course I was teaching. Lázaro had come earlier and was staying at my apartment. I arrived at midnight, at the moment when the whole city was living the euphoria of New Year's Eve. I had positive feelings about my arrival. The taxi driver—there probably are no more of his kind around—had the patience to load the more than twenty suitcases full of books, clothes, and manuscripts that I had brought from Miami. To cross the city on New Year's Eve was a real odyssey, especially Times Square, where more than a million people had gathered. When I arrived at the apartment, Lázaro was not in and I had to go all the way up five flights of stairs, without an elevator, with all those suitcases and boxes full of books. The taxi driver told me to carry the suitcases up one by one while he stayed below until I was finished. When I was done and asked him how much, he said fifteen dollars. I was about to give him twenty and he said, "That's too much money, too much money." It was a really unusual, generous act, something that will probably never happen to me again, but with that gesture I felt the city was welcoming me. And during the years 1981 and 1982, living in New York was for me a true celebration. Winter and snow were a really new experience; I enjoyed watching the snow fall; it was a pleasure to walk around and feel it coming down; I did not even notice the cold. Snow has forever represented an unremitting longing for Cubans. José Lezama Lima, Eliseo Diego, Julián del Casal, all the poets who had never seen snow were always yearning for it, though those who experienced it came to detest it, like Martí and Heredia. One way or another, snow has played an important part in our literature. Lázaro and I now lived in the euphoria of the snow and of the great city that never sleeps: everything one could possibly want was available, day and night; all the fruit we had longed for in Cuba, much of it from tropical countries, could be purchased in the midst of a snowfall. It was really a dream come true and a constant celebration. I was writing a lot then, but New York was never more vital; it will probably never be again as it was then. I have the comfort of having lived those last years, before the plague came, before the curse fell upon this city, as it always falls on all things truly extraordinary.

MARIEL MAGAZINE

There was a small group of Cubans in New York, all of whom had come via Mariel, and we would get together every now and then and read our work. One of our meeting places was René Cifuentes's apartment on Eighth Avenue; we would talk about anything, criticize, read. Sometimes a costume party was announced, and we would all go so artfully disguised that we would not even recognize ourselves in the mirror.

Juan Abreu and some other friends who had also come in the Mariel exodus, like Carlos Victoria and Luz de la Paz, lived in Miami; Roberto Valero was studying at Georgetown University in Washington; in New York there were Reinaldo Gómez Ramos, whose apprehensiveness I had forgiven, René Cifuentes, and myself. All of us *marielitos* decided to create a magazine and call it *Mariel*. When I went to Miami to visit Juan, we sat in the shade under a pine tree and planned the magazine. We had, of course, no home for it, nor the slightest idea of how to publish a magazine; neither did we have any money. Lydia Cabrera was our literary adviser, however, and she offered us her enthusiastic help. We had to finance the magazine by imposing on ourselves a strict fee and paying it rigorously. We never had any official assistance. The first issue came out in the spring of 1983 and was dedicated to José Lezama Lima; it had been a dream and a hope that Juan and I had nurtured for many years, when we were still in Cuba. It was like the birth of the clandestine magazine we had called *Ah, la marea*, which we had created in Lenin Park. We all lived on the edge of poverty, but to sacrifice some of the little money we earned to create *Mariel* magazine was a great event for us. It would have to cause a stir among the other Cuban exiles and, of course, surprise Fidel Castro. The magazine was irreverent, and at peace with no one; it paid homage to great writers and unmasked the hypocrites; it was against the bourgeois morality so prevalent in Miami. We also dedicated an issue to homosexuality in Cuba, which included interviews with people suffering from prejudice in conservative, reactionary societies such as that of Miami and, to a great extent, of the United States. The magazine was not well received except by a small group of liberal intellectuals. It could not, of course, appeal to the frivolous left of the United States, to the hypocrites of that left, to communists and fellow travelers, to Cuban Castrist agents worldwide, especially those living in the United States; nor to the Miami "poetesses." Everyone who was already established in this country viewed us as strange creatures, but the magazine continued to be published for a few years. I remember writing in an article entitled "In Praise of the Furies" that the Furies were the only goddesses who should ever inspire us, and I backed up my assertion with all kinds of quotes, from the *Iliad* to Virgilio Piñera's *La Isla en peso*.

We did not have to pretend to anybody, nor did we aspire to obtain any position or personal advantage. I never even sought nor do I seek U.S. citizenship. After a time, some of the members of the magazine committee got cold feet or drifted away. For this reason, and also due to financial problems, the magazine folded, but not without leaving some issues that are a real challenge to the literature of exile and to Cuban literature in general.

Another great accomplishment of that time was the film *Improper Conduct* by Néstor Almendros and Orlando Jiménez Leal. This film was the first important document that openly denounced the persecution suffered in Cuba by homosexuals and other unconventional people under Fidel Castro's regime. It even showed the UMAP concentration camps, interviews with people who had been at those camps, and repressive documents. It was, moreover, a defiant movie, made with a great sense of humor; it included queers and queens who had fled Cuba and now performed in New York nightclubs as transvestites. Even Fidel Castro appeared in it, stuffed into his olive-green outfit, looking rather ridiculous. The film attracted international attention, aroused fierce controversy, and won the Human Rights Award as the best documentary shown in Europe that year.

The Cuban government was so concerned about this film that it appointed a group of official gays, most of them from the Ministry of the Interior, to travel worldwide giving speeches and stating that gays were not persecuted in Cuba. Those poor gays had to act really queer before the public, and pretend to be more effeminate than they actually were to demonstrate that, without question, there was no persecution of homosexuals in Cuba. Once back in Cuba, of course, they had to hide their feathers, and we never heard what happened later to that official delegation of Cuban gays. In any case, they should be grateful to us because thanks to that film they were able to make their little trip to Europe.

Néstor Almendros is a Republican Spaniard who fled Spain during Franco's dictatorship; he lived in Cuba and suffered first Batista's and then Castro's dictatorships. He is an example of intellectual and artistic integrity, and his attitude has been decisive and courageous, in spite of the fact that it has hurt him in many ways. Being famous and financially secure, he could have opted not to help us, which would even have been understandable. The great majority of U.S. liberal intellectuals, in order to appear progressive and to channel and profit from the logical resentment of people subjected to other social ills, have generally supported Fidel Castro, or have conveniently pretended to overlook his crimes. Now, with the Super-Stalinization of Castro's regime, criticized even in Soviet magazines, I imagine that some U.S. intellectuals are changing their tune for political or financial expediency. But one cannot forget the tremendous propaganda machine and numerous international connections that the Cuban government has maintained for more than thirty years. These include cultural centers, bookstores, publishing houses, and public-relations agencies spread worldwide but especially concentrated in the West, its target of operations.

I remember that after I arrived in the United States, a Cuban exile who lived in Washington said to me: "Don't ever quarrel with the left." For people like him, to attack Castro's government was to fight against the left. But after twenty years of repression, how could I keep silent about those crimes? On the other hand, I have never considered myself as belonging to the "left" or to the "right," nor do I want to be included under any opportunistic or political label. I tell my truth, as does the Jew who has suffered racism or the Russian who has been in the Gulag, or any human being who has eyes to see the way things really are. I scream, therefore I exist.

This attitude has cost me dearly, both financially and professionally as a writer. When I left Cuba my novels were being used as assigned texts at New York University, and when I adopted a radical position against the Castro dictatorship, Haydée Vitale, professor of literature, started to drop my books from the curriculum until not one of them remained. She did the same with all the other Cuban writers in exile. In the end, the program included only a few of Alejo Carpentier's novels. This has happened to me at many universities in the United States and in other parts of the world. Ironically, while I was in jail and could not leave Cuba, my chances of being published were better because I was not allowed to speak out, and foreign publishing companies with leftist leanings would support a writer living in Havana.

This attitude, of course, was directed not just at me but at all Cuban exiles, because in exile we have no country to represent us; we live as if by special permission, always in danger of being rejected. Instead of having a country, we have an anti-country: Fidel Castro's bureaucracy is always ready to undertake all kinds of intrigues and chicanery to destroy us intellectually and, if possible, physically. The situation has made many Cuban intellectuals very cautious.

This political caution is based, above all, on the fear of starving; some no longer dare to sign a document critical of Castro's dictatorship; others prefer to disappear in apolitical lethargy and write articles about Belgium; cowardice is always pathetic, but injustice and stupidity are much more irritating. A famous Spanish literary agent was recently in Cuba on the arm of Gabriel García Márquez and was received with full fanfare by Castro himself. This woman currently represents four Nobel Prize winners in literature. She returned from Cuba ecstatic because Castro told her that her dress was very elegant.

One of the most notorious examples of intellectual injustice in this century is Jorge Luis Borges, who was systematically denied the Nobel Prize simply because of his political views. Borges is one of the most important Latin American writers of the century, perhaps the most important one; however, the Nobel Prize was given to Gabriel García Márquez, the pastiche of Faulkner, personal friend of Castro's, and born opportunist. His work, although not without merit, is permeated with cheap populism, and is not at the level of some other great writers who have either died in oblivion or been ignored.

T R A V E L S For a long time I had wanted to go to Europe and meet with Jorge and Margarita in Spain, but since I had no passport yet or any other official document that would allow me to travel, I could not leave the United States. I had received several invitations since 1980, but it was not until 1983 that I was able to travel with a document to prove my refugee status, a strange and not very reliable piece of paper that almost no foreign consulate or immigration department, nor even desk clerks at hotels, wanted to accept. A refugee is always a problem, because he might want to stay anywhere and generally does not have a penny. That document, issued by the UN, enrages even porters, who do not expect tips from refugees.

Anyway, after a lot of hassles, I was able to go to Madrid in 1983; it was my first trip to Europe. I started my tour in Sweden and, with Humberto López, traveled throughout the country; in freezing trains, we almost made it to the North Pole. I also carried with me a number of documents, including a verdict in which a poet in Cuba had been sentenced to jail because he had written a book about a special variety of insects, which someone had later identified as Raúl and Fidel Castro. With those documents, with that verdict, we traveled through the countryside in winter. I remember that once we stayed in a very desolate place, at the home of a Swedish farmer deeply depressed because his wife had left him. I do not know why the committee that invited us decided on that farm as the place for us to spend the night; perhaps there were no other accommodations available. With the help of those documents I tried to convince the man of the loneliness and desperation the people of Cuba were suffering; his only concern at the moment was the wife who had abandoned him. When I looked at his dilapidated house in the snow, I was surprised that she had not left him much sooner.

At the University of Stockholm I gave a lecture in which all I wanted to do was read excerpts from the Cuban newspaper *Granma*; it was an irrefutable way of demonstrating what was happening in Cuba. Most of the audience was made up of Chileans exiled by the Pinochet dictatorship; they heckled me constantly and almost did not let me speak. They were on their feet insulting me, telling me that everything I was saying was absolutely false. At some point I read several of the laws that the Cuban government itself had published in Cuba. I also read reports from other Cuban newspapers, but there was no way to convince them. They were living very well in Sweden, taking their vacation trips to Chile every year, and then returning to their comfortable apartments in Sweden, where they even had social security benefits. I was wrapped in a big, ill-fitting coat purchased in New York for eighty dollars. But I enjoyed seeing Stockholm, and especially the Swedish king's Royal Guard, a great-looking group of adolescents.

Carlos Franqui and Margot, his wife, had preceded me at that university, and they also had a very hard time there. Some people had even placed something on the floor that could cause Margot to fall, which she did.

I must admit that many Swedish intellectuals received me in a different manner; their views concerning Fidel Castro's dictatorship were more perceptive. They knew about Armando Valladares and many other intellectuals who were in prison; with them I could talk. They even published several of my interviews and I was able to make contact with some publishers, although the fact is I never heard from them again.

To arrive in Spain was, for me, an immensely sentimental event; Jorge and Margarita Camacho were there, waiting for me after so many years. It was now 1983 and we had not seen each other since 1967. During all those years they had never stopped writing, not for a single week, nor had they given up on their efforts to get me out of the country, in any way possible. Now, suddenly, we were together, strolling on Paseo del Prado in Madrid; it was like a dream. We then took the train to Paris. With them I spent some of the most memorable moments of my life, discovering one of the most beautiful cities in the world. To discover a city is in itself a unique event, but when we have the privilege of sharing it with friends most dear to us, it becomes a once-in-a-lifetime experience.

I always thought that with writers it is best to read them without getting to know them personally; we risk terrible disappointments. My friendships with Lezama, Virgilio Piñera, and Lydia Cabrera, who were in fact extraordinary human beings, were marked, because of the Cuban situation, by a sense of doom and despair, ostracism and separation. I later met many other well-known writers, some superfamous whom I would rather not mention; I felt much closer to them when reading their books. Luckily I think I have forgotten their personal conceits. I also do not want these memoirs to become a treatise on literature or a log of my public relations with supposedly important people, because, in the final analysis, what is important really?

Through a prank of destiny, I was visiting with the rector of a prestigious U.S. university. One evening a number of internationally famous writers were present. There was one whose image most daunted me: Carlos Fuentes. He did not behave like a writer but like a computer; he had a precise and apparently lucid answer to any problem or question put to him; all you had to do was press a button. There were a great many American college professors in attendance, and all of them were wearing, like nurses in a hospital, large badges indicating their names and titles.

Carlos Fuentes lectured in perfect English, and seemed to be a man without any doubts whatsoever, not even of a metaphysical nature; he was the extreme opposite of what I would consider to be a real writer. That man, so fashionably attired, was an encyclopedia, perhaps even a little thicker. There are many writers who receive important literary prizes, including the Cervantes and the Nobel, for delivering such impeccable lectures.

I left that meeting terrified. Luckily I was able to catch a local train and return to New York. But among the fauna at that gathering was one outstanding person: Emir Rodríguez Monegal, a lover of great literature, with an intuition far beyond his academic merits, which were countless. This man was not a professor in the conventional sense of the word; he was a great reader, and possessed the magical ability to instill the love of beauty in his students. He was the only Spanish-American professor in the United States who inspired a school of critical thought.

In the three years I had been out of Cuba I had taken part in three international films: *In His Own Words* [1980] by Jorge Ulla; *The Other Cuba* [for Italian television, 1983] by Carlos Franqui and Valerio Rivas; and *Improper Conduct* [1983] by Néstor Almendros and Orlando Jiménez Leal.* I had also traveled through much of Europe, written or rewritten six of my books, founded a literary magazine, and managed, after considerable paperwork, to get my mother all the way from Holguín to New York so that she could spend three months with me in this city, and take home a huge load of clothes for almost everyone in Vista Alegre, the neighborhood in Holguín where her family and friends live. And by then I had been invited to more than forty universities and had enjoyed memorable adventures with the most fabulous black men in Harlem, in Central Park, and on populous Forty-second Street. And I had heard Jorge Luis Borges himself reading his own poems.

In the evenings I would go to the most unbelievable places in Manhattan, with René Cifuentes, Jorge Ronet, or Miguel Contreras. As if my time were unlimited, I had also signed up at a gym and spent part of the day jogging. On weekends I would go to the New York beaches.

Some of those beaches were surrounded by areas of tall grasses, somewhat similar to the Cuban guinea grass, and they were full of queers in the nude, aroused and always ready for a good time. It was as if the good old days were back, the days when I would roam from beach to beach in Havana. I was now making up for lost time, almost recovering the past, the wonderful days of my underwater adventures and the euphoria of my literary creativeness. But now

* After completing his autobiography, R.A. also took part in another documentary, *Havana*, by Jana Bokova, BBC, 1990.—D.M.K.

I had absolute freedom to do and write whatever I wanted, to disappear for a whole month without having to explain to anyone; to take a car and travel anywhere. One of my great adventures, shared with my friend Roberto Valero and his wife, María Badías, and Lázaro, was to drive all over the United States, where for the first time we were able to enjoy the sense of freedom and the thrill of adventure without feeling persecuted; in short, the pleasure of being alive.

M A D N E S S In 1983 a call came from an out-of-state hospital. Lázaro had been in an automobile accident and was in serious condition: his car had skidded and hit a tree. A day after the accident, he was transferred to a private hospital in Manhattan, but when they found out that he had no money and no insurance, they threw him out. After considerable hassle, an ambulance finally picked him up and took him to another hospital, where he stayed for over a month. One of his legs had been pretty much shattered; we feared that it would have to be amputated. He had also banged his head in several places. At about the same time he was discharged from the hospital, his mother came from Cuba. Lázaro was not the same person, no longer the nimble young man who used to run after me in Central Park. He limped and had a brace on his leg; he had gained weight during his stay at the hospital and he was out of shape. When he left the hospital he came to my room, slowly climbing the stairs with a feeling of defeat. It is hard to forget the image of that boy, who had been so good-looking, now slowly dragging himself up the stairs. His mother, instead of helping him, aggravated his mental state. Lázaro finally had to enter the psychiatric ward of a city public hospital, where he stayed several months. I went to see him every week during visiting hours. The ward atmosphere was Dantesque in the worse sense; all possible types of insane people were screaming all the time, day and night. When I entered that building I had an overpowering feeling of bewilderment and anxiety.

One day, when leaving the hospital, I saw a skinny youth, shaved to the scalp, watering an enormous tree with a huge hose; I imagined that he was Lázaro, fatherless since childhood, and now alone in an insane asylum.

Lázaro was not yet well when he left the hospital, but they had to let him go. His mental state made staying with me difficult. I found him a room on Thirty-first Street that was even smaller than mine, with a large tree next to his window. I helped him in spite of my financial situation in exile, which has never been great. Little by little, he recovered. He started working for an airline and was very happy there, when the company went bankrupt and left him jobless again. He was unemployed for a while and then landed a job as a doorman. We were no longer the same; we had witnessed the horror of a New York mental hospital, the craziness, the misery, the mistreatment, the discrimination. But we had to go on and face whatever new calamities came our way.

Our friendship persisted. He always had plans and a great imagination, but he could not channel them into any permanent art form. In exile Lázaro has been the only link to my past, the only witness to my past life in Cuba; with him I have always had the feeling of being able to return to that irretrievable world. It is hard to communicate, in this country or in any other, if you come from the future.

And for Cubans who, like us, have suffered persecution for twenty years in that terrible world, there is really no solace anywhere. Suffering has marked us forever, and only with people who have gone through a similar experience can we perhaps find some level of understanding.

Most people are unable to understand us nor should we expect them to: they have their own terrors and, even if they wanted to, cannot really fathom ours, much less share them.

Working as a doorman, Lázaro met an American woman who lived in the same building, and married her. He then invited me to spend a vacation in Puerto Rico. While we were there, I encouraged him to write his memoirs as one of the ten thousand exiles at the Peruvian embassy. He wrote a book entitled *Desertores del Paraíso* [Deserters from Paradise], edited by Néstor Almendros and Jorge Ulla, and well received by the critics. He then took a course in photography, and today is an excellent photographer, although he continues to work as a doorman, one of the best jobs in the world. Visiting Lázaro at the lobby of his building, I picked up most of the ideas for my novel *The Doorman*, which, of course, is dedicated to Lázaro. Many years ago, rather than friends we had become more like brothers. If at times I feel sorry about abandoning this world, it is because I know the loneliness in which I will leave this brother who, between insanity and genius, has never stopped being a boy, though he is thirty-two years old. I also feel sorry for Jorge and Margarita, and for my mother, lost in one of the neighborhoods in Holguín. In short, I cannot even die in peace.

THE EVICTION It was also in 1983 that the owner of the building in which I lived attempted to evict all the tenants; he wanted to empty the building in order to remodel it and raise the rents. During the war between the landlord and the tenants, the landlord managed to damage the roof of the building. Rain and snow were coming into my room. It is difficult to wage war against the powerful, especially for someone who is not living in his own country, does not know the language, and is not familiar with legal terms. I finally had to give up my one-room apartment. I was then transferred to an old building, not far from my previous one. In this country it is perfectly normal for people to move frequently, but a major problem I had to suffer in Cuba was having nowhere to live: having to be on the move all the time, having to live with the fear of being forced out at whim, never having a place I could call my own. Now in New York it was the same story. I had no choice but to take my belongings and move to the new hovel. I was later told that the people who had stuck it out in the building were paid by the owner up to twenty thousand dollars to move out. My new world was ruled not by political power but by another power, also sinister: the power of money. After having lived in this country for some years, I realize that it is a country without a soul: everything revolves around money.

New York has no tradition, no history; there can be no history where there are no memories to hold on to. The city is in constant flux, constant construction, constant tearing down and building up again; a supermarket yesterday is a produce store today, a movie house tomorrow, and a bank the day after. The city is a huge, soulless factory with no place for the pedestrian to rest, no place where one can simply be without dishing out dollars for a breath of air or a chair on which to sit down and relax.

THE ANNOUNCEMENT

In 1985 two of my great friends died: Emir Rodríguez Monegal, the person who had best understood my books, and Jorge Renut, with whom I had enjoyed wonderful nocturnal adventures. Emir died of a sudden cancer; Jorge died of AIDS, the plague that, until then, had been for me nothing but a distant though persistent rumor; now it had become something real, palpable, obvious: the body of my friend was proof that, very soon, I could be in the same condition.

D R E A M S Dreams and nightmares have been

an important part of my life. I always went to bed like someone getting ready for a long trip: books, pills, glasses of water,
clocks, a light, pencils, notebooks. To go to bed and switch
off the light has been for me to submit to a totally unknown
world, full of delicious as well as sinister promises. Dreams
have always had a great influence on me; the first image I
remember from my childhood is a dream, a terrible dream.
I was on a reddish esplanade and huge teeth were approaching from both sides; it was an enormous mouth that made
a strange sound. The closer the teeth came, the more high-
pitched their sound would become; at the point they were
ready to devour me, I would wake up. In other dreams I
would find myself playing on the eaves of our house in the
country and all of a sudden, due to a wrong move, I would
feel the most extraordinary shivers, my hands would sweat,
and I would start to slide, falling into an immense dark void;
the fall would become an endless agony and I would wake
up right before smashing into the ground.

At other times my dreams were in full color and extraordinary people would approach me offering me their friendship, which I accepted gladly; they were gigantic creatures
with smiling faces.

Later I often dreamed of Lezama, who was at a gathering
in an enormous hall; music could be heard in the distance
and Lezama pulled out a large pocket watch; facing him was
his wife, María Luisa. I was a boy, and when I went up to
him, he would open his legs and receive me smiling, while
saying to María Luisa: "Look how well he is doing." But by
then Lezama was already dead.

Occasionally I dreamed that although I had been in the
United States, I was back in Cuba, I do not know why,
perhaps because my plane was hijacked or because someone
had deceived me by telling me I could return without any
problem. I was in my hot room again, but now I could never

leave; I was condemned to stay there forever. I needed to receive a special notification to go to the airport, someone had to pick me up in a car that never came; I knew I could never leave that place, and that the police would come any moment and arrest me. I had already traveled around the world and learned what freedom was, but due to some strange circumstance I was back in Cuba and could not escape. I would wake up and, seeing the deteriorating walls of my room in New York, feel an indescribable joy.

I had another dream. I want to get into my mother's house and there is a chicken-wire fence in front of the door. I repeatedly call for someone to open the door; my mother and my aunt are on the other side of the fence and I signal them. I move my hand toward my chest and birds start coming out, parrots of all colors, bigger and bigger insects and birds; I start yelling for them to open the gate, and they stare at me through the chicken wire; I continue to scream and all kinds of animals keep coming out of me, but I cannot get through the door.

In some dreams I am a painter; I have a huge loft, and create enormous paintings; I think the paintings I produce have to do with people dear to me; the color blue is predominant and people dissolve in it. Suddenly, Lázaro enters, young, slender; he greets me dejectedly, walks toward the large window facing the street, and jumps out. I scream and run down the stairs of my New York apartment, but as I am going down, I am back in Holguín; my grandmother is there, as well as several of my aunts. I tell them Lázaro has jumped out the window and they all run into the street; it is Tenth of October Street, where my mother lives. There, facedown in the mud, lies Lázaro, dead. I lift his head and look at his beautiful, muddy face; my grandmother comes, looks first at his face and then up at the heavens, saying: "My God, why?" I later tried to interpret this dream in various ways: it was not Lázaro who died but me; he is my double; the person I love most is the symbol of my destruction. For that reason it made sense that those rushing to see the body were my relatives, not Lázaro's.

I have dreamed that when I was a kid the sea came right up to my house; it came rushing over dozens of miles, and the whole yard would be flooded. It was great to let myself float on the water; I swam for a long time in my flooded house, looking at the ceiling, taking in the briny smell of the sea that continued rushing in a torrent.

In New York I once dreamed I could fly, a privilege not granted to humans, even though we gays are called *pájaros* [birds]. But I was in Cuba, flying over the palm trees; it was easy, you only had to believe you could do it. Soon I was flying over Fifth Avenue in Miramar, over the royal palms that line the street; the scenery was beautiful to behold while I, joyful and radiant, flew above it, over the crowns of the palm trees. I woke up here in New York still feeling that I was high in the air.

Once while I was on vacation at Miami Beach, I had a terrible dream. I was in a very large bathroom full of excrement and had to sleep there. Surrounding me were hundreds of rare birds that moved about with great difficulty. More and more of those awful birds kept coming, gradually closing all possibility of escape; the entire horizon was full of birds; they had something metallic about them, and made a dull noise; they sounded like buzzing alarms. Suddenly I realized that all those birds had managed to get into my head, and that my brain was swelling to accommodate them. As they entered my head, I grew old. This same nightmare occurred for several nights in a row while I was in Miami and I would wake up drenched in sweat. When I flew back to New York, I was getting ready as usual for my dream, taking with me all my things and a big glass of water. I always read for at least an hour or two before going to sleep, and I was finishing *A Thousand and One Nights*. This was already in 1986. I had been talking with Lázaro for a while and he had just left; he was still in the building when I heard a tremendous blast in the room; it sounded like a real explosion. I thought one of my jealous lovers or a burglar had broken the window facing the street; the sound was so loud that it seemed someone must have taken an iron bar and thrown it against the window. But the windowpane was undamaged. Something very strange had occurred in the room: the glass of water on my nightstand had exploded without my touching it; it was shattered. I ran to call Lázaro back before he left the building, and we carefully searched the whole apartment. I thought that someone had taken a shot at me and had hit the glass instead. On several occasions I had received death threats from the Cuban State Security; once in a while a person had broken into my apartment and gone through my papers; at times the window that I had left closed was open but nothing had been taken, so it could not have been a burglar. What really happened that night is still shrouded in mystery for me. How could a glass of water explode with such an infernal sound? A week later I understood that this was an omen, a premonition, a message from the gods of the underworld, a new and terrible message announcing that something truly different was about to happen to me, or was already happening. The glass full of water was perhaps a sort of guardian angel, a talisman; something had penetrated the glass that for years had protected me and shielded me from all dangers: terrible illnesses, falls from trees, persecutions, prison, shots in the middle of the night, being lost at sea, or attacked by gangs of armed delinquents in New York City on various occasions. Once I was attacked in the middle of Central Park; some young men searched my pockets, pointing a gun at my head, but they found only five dollars. They fondled me so much while they searched me that we ended up making love. Afterward I asked them for a dollar to get back home and they gave it to me.

Now, the state of grace that had saved me from so many misfortunes had come to an end. On another occasion, I had found an enormous black man inside my apartment in New

York when I returned home. After breaking my window and stealing all my clothes, he was approaching me, threatening me with a gun. I was able to escape and yell that there was a thief in the building; several people came out into the hallway, among them a Puerto Rican neighbor with a double-barreled shotgun, which made the black man run away leaving all my belongings behind, and me unharmed.

One day I had asked a hoodlum who was carrying an umbrella what time it was and he gave me a rude reply. I think I said a few stupid things to him and finally gave him a shove. Clearly enraged, he removed a sort of ice pick or metallic tip from his umbrella and lunged at me with its sharp point. He cut my forehead several times, aiming his attacks at my eyes; evidently he wanted to blind me and failed. I returned to my apartment all bloody, and a week later I was completely healed. My guardian angel had again protected me.

But now, something much more powerful, more mysterious, more sinister than anything I had ever experienced seemed to be controlling my fate; I had fallen out of grace. The bursting of the glass was a symbol of my final destruction. Destruction: that was my interpretation a few weeks later and it seems that, unfortunately, I was right.

Lázaro and I were once in Puerto Rico at a secluded beach where I had taken him because it reminded me of our Cuban beaches. He had opened a book, and was starting to read when a gang of muggers came, more than six of them. One pointed a gun at us that he had hidden under a handkerchief. Another one said, "Lie down on the ground and give us all you have or we will kill you right now." I was ready to grab a stick and go after one of them, but Lázaro warned me not to; they were dangerous. We lay down on the ground while they searched us and took what little we had: swim fins, a diving mask. As the muggers were leaving I asked them to return the diving mask; one did not want to, but another decided they really had no use for it. They could have killed us, but my guardian angel had protected us: the same one who helped me survive El Morro, the one who warned me of the land mines as I was getting close to the Guantánamo naval base. Once again I had been saved.

But now the glass had burst, nothing could save me.

What was that glass that burst? It was the deity that protected me; it was the goddess that had always accompanied me, it was the Moon herself, my mother had turned into the Moon.

O Moon! You have always been at my side, offering your light in my most dreadful moments; since I was a child you were the mystery that watched over my terrors, you were the comfort of my most desperate nights, you were my very own mother, bathing me in a warmth that perhaps she never knew how to give me. In the midst of the forest, in the darkest places, in the sea, you were there with me, you were my comfort, you have always guided me in my most difficult moments. My great goddess, my true goddess, you who have protected me through so many calamities; I used to look up toward you and behold you; up to you rising above the sea, toward you at the shore, toward you among the rocks of my desolate Island, I would lift my gaze and behold you, always the same; in your face I saw an expression of pain, of suffering, of compassion for me, your son. And now, Moon, you suddenly burst into pieces right next to my bed. I am alone. It is night.

FAREWELL

Some time after completing his autobiography, months before his death, R.A. gave several handwritten, sealed copies of the letter below, addressed to friends and newspapers, to D.M.K. for mailing at the appropriate time. It appeared in major U.S. papers and abroad.

Dear friends:

Due to my delicate state of health and to the terrible emotional depression it causes me not to be able to continue writing and struggling for the freedom of Cuba, I am ending my life. During the past few years, even though I felt very ill, I have been able to finish my literary work, to which I have devoted almost thirty years. You are the heirs of all my terrors, but also of my hope that Cuba will soon be free. I am satisfied to have contributed, though in a very small way, to the triumph of this freedom. I end my life voluntarily because I cannot continue working. Persons near me are in no way responsible for my decision. There is only one person I hold accountable: Fidel Castro. The sufferings of exile, the pain of being banished from my country, the loneliness, and the diseases contracted in exile would probably never have happened if I had been able to enjoy freedom in my country.

I want to encourage the Cuban people out of the country as well as on the Island to continue fighting for freedom. I do not want to convey to you a message of defeat but of continued struggle and of hope.

Cuba will be free. I already am.

(signed)

Reinaldo Arenas

TO BE PUBLISHED